John Rodwell,
Peter Manley Scott (Eds.)

At Home in the Future

Studies in Religion and the Environment
Studien zur Religion und Umwelt

published on behalf of the
European Forum for the Study
of Religion and the Environment
by

Sigurd Bergmann

Volume 11

LIT

At Home in the Future

Place & Belonging in a Changing Europe

edited by

John Rodwell and Peter Manley Scott

LIT

Cover image:
Melissa Martin, *Dining Room*, 2006. The Wanås Foundation, Sweden.
Courtesy of the artist. Photo: Anders Norrsell.

This book is printed on acid-free paper.

Bibliographic information published by the Deutsche Nationalbibliothek
The Deutsche Nationalbibliothek lists this publication in the Deutsche
Nationalbibliografie; detailed bibliographic data are available in the Internet at
http://dnb.d-nb.de.

ISBN 978-3-643-90638-0

A catalogue record for this book is available from the British Library

© LIT VERLAG GmbH & Co. KG Wien,
Zweigniederlassung Zürich 2015
Klosbachstr. 107
CH-8032 Zürich
Tel. +41 (0) 44-251 75 05   Fax +41 (0) 44-251 75 06
E-Mail: zuerich@lit-verlag.ch   http://www.lit-verlag.ch
Distribution:
In the UK: Global Book Marketing, e-mail: mo@centralbooks.com
In North America: International Specialized Book Services, e-mail: orders@isbs.com
In Germany: LIT Verlag Fresnostr. 2, D-48159 Münster
Tel. +49 (0) 2 51-620 32 22, Fax +49 (0) 2 51-922 60 99, E-mail: vertrieb@lit-verlag.de
In Austria: Medienlogistik Pichler-ÖBZ, e-mail: mlo@medien-logistik.at
e-books are available at www.litwebshop.de

Contents

DIALOGUES OF PLACE AND BELONGING 1
John Rodwell and Peter Manley Scott

At home or ill-at-ease?

Heimat AND INDIVIDUALITY 15
Stefan Körner

Heimat ON LOCATION: AN ETHNOGRAPHIC AND SOCIAL HISTORICAL
APPROACH TO THE *Heimat* MOVEMENT 33
John R. Eidson

TRANSPORTS OF DELIGHT AND THE MIGRATION OF THE GENIUS LOCI 51
Ian Thompson

Beheimatung: MAKING-ONESELF-AT-HOME WITH THE SPIRIT 65
Sigurd Bergmann

Forgetting and remembering

"TURF WARS": GRASS, GREENERY AND THE SPATIALITY OF
COMMEMORATION 83
Recurring debates and disputes in the uses of horticultural
iconography by the Commonwealth War Graves Commission in
northern Europe
Paul Gough

THE EUCHARIST: LANDSCAPE OF MEMORY, NARRATIVE OF
RECONCILIATION 101
Philip Sheldrake

REMEMBERING THE FUTURE 113
John Rodwell

Separation and connectedness

RECONNECTING COMMUNITIES AND NATURAL SYSTEMS IN THE
LANDSCAPE 127
Paul Selman

BELONGING IN THE PERI-URBAN LANDSCAPE: DO NEW LANDSCAPES
REQUIRE NEW CONCEPTIONS OF "HOME"? 141
Vera Vicenzotti

PLACES AS UNGIVEN, MEMORIES AS COMPETITIVE? 155
Ambiguities of belonging in theological perspective
Peter Manley Scott

THE REFORMATION OF PLACE: RELIGION, SPACE AND POWER 169
Bronislaw Szerszynski

POSTSCRIPT 185
John Rodwell and Peter Manley Scott

CONTRIBUTORS 193

INDEX OF NAMES 201

INDEX OF SUBJECTS 207

DIALOGUES OF PLACE AND BELONGING

John Rodwell and Peter Manley Scott

That there is a shift in our understanding of place and our sense of belonging has been evident for some time among diverse disciplines and can be seen as symptomatic of reactions against modernity with its optimistic emphasis on reason's ability to grasp the infinite and the power of progress. To stimulate a dialogue between thinkers who are exploring new ways of conceiving what it is to be at home in the world, but who would not generally encounter one another, seemed very timely and we offer the fruits of our exchanges here as a way of understanding how we might together belong and have a place in the future.

Our own interest in this dialogue sprang from research carried out for the M.B. Reckitt Trust, a charity which promotes activities that evaluate and develop social structures, processes and attitudes in order to release energies for change, working from the perspective of Christian and other principal faith traditions.[1] The work was focused on the Dearne Valley in South Yorkshire, a region where the loss of the coal-mining and steel-making has left a post-industrial landscape now subject to intensive regeneration. The research was concerned to ask what it meant to "secure the future" as the UK government then called the quest for sustainability; whether there was a spiritual dimension to this vision; and whether some notion of "belonging to place" was considered a part of a sustainable future. It involved listening to development and planning agencies, statutory and voluntary environmental bodies and Christian faith communities, through semi-structured interviews with senior management and leaders, local staff and "customers".[2]

During the research, there was a gathering sense of some serious deficiencies in the assumptions lying behind the sustainability process and the whole notion of securing the future. First, there were some very partial and impoverished understandings of "community" in the Dearne Valley and how (indeed whether) this related to the meanings of "place" – and how communities themselves related to places. Second, it became increasingly hard to see how it was possible to secure a future for the Dearne Valley when there was such a deficient comprehension of its inherited past, or pasts. Certainly, the future as conceived by planners and developers often showed an uneasy fit with such memories, of what had previously been, as were voiced. In all this, the faith communities were generally regarded as clients or partners in delivering an unquestioned future, a role they connived in by virtue of their success in offering such what was seen as their own spiritual capital, their networks, buildings and the provision of welfare services. More critical engagement with the sustainability process or with the received ideas about place and belonging were neither encouraged nor much volunteered. Other researchers were finding similar situations elsewhere.[3]

In fact, among Christian thinkers, there has been a belated response to the challenge that shifting landscapes and changing communities present. Oliver O'Donovan made an early plea about theology's absence from debates about place and belonging[4] but it has only been with the writings of Philip Sheldrake,[5] Tim Gorringe[6] and John Inge[7] that thinking has moved much beyond a preoccupation with place understood as "sacred space" or has invoked cultural ideas of our own rather than drawing on those of other distant tribes, potent as these can be.[8] Even where the idea of space has been taken more seriously by religious commitments, there has often been a strong sense (as in White[9] or Rowland[10]) that what makes places distinctive for religious experience is people – the ethical quality of their shared life or the authenticity of celebratory rites of gathered communities. In popular parlance, it has often been said, for example, that "the Church is people, not buildings". In Christian theology, we are used to the idea that, individually and as a people, salvation history or *Heilsgeschichte* is a crucially important narrative that helps us understand who we are and how we stand, but perhaps we are redeemed not only by events but in and for places such that geographies too may have a spiritual resonance of some kind that exceeds a simple designation as sacred. Such a view might also offer salvation to built environments in the way that meets the hope of Bergmann[11] who has been energetic in his perception of a dynamic "spatial turn" in theology.

With a broad theological perspective on place, Walter Brueggemann[12] has urged a return to biblical notions of "land" in understanding our place in the world. For Brueggemann, land means the actual turf where people find themselves at a particular time but also has symbolic significance, being freighted with social meanings derived from shared spiritual experience in this or that place. Such meanings are particular, expressing disillusionment with the power of anonymity and mobility to ensure the future of human communities, so persuasive for some in Harvey Cox's urban vision[13] and so manifest in many regenerated landscapes, in the Dearne Valley and elsewhere. On such a view, land is not the result of prudent planning, nor an anticipated reward for behaviour or achievement, nor a deserved inheritance. In the Judaeo-Christian tradition, it is rather a place of gift, where a divine encounter is to be had among the words that have been spoken there, promises made and disappointments felt. Such an understanding of land also offers the prospect of a dialogue with those environmental practitioners who do not own an anthropocentric ethic where nature is simply as instrumental to human need, but share the kind of collectivist view of the environment espoused by Aldo Leopold.[14] For him, land, including all its creatures, soils, water and weather, was a community whose integrity, stability and beauty are elevated together to moral status. As John Handley[15] conceded, many in the world of planning and landscape design approach this interface between practice and ethics, let alone religious belief, as hazardous territory.

But this is not universally true and, in our conversations, we chose to engage with various thinkers from the realm of landscape design, planning and ecology who, as well as having practical experience have taken a more creative approach to notions of place and belonging within their own discipline. And, alongside theologians, we included experts in philosophy, public policy and social anthropology. Our exchange has not been an exclusively British one either because, in Germany, too, there have been discussions about the inadequacy of interpretations of sustainability,[16] and also a renewed acceptance of the notion of *Heimat* as expressive of belonging in place. The original meaning of this word, which has no exact equivalent in English[17] but which seemed particularly apposite to our own quest, was "home territory" or "home ground" but, over a millennium, it has acquired a rich variety of resonances;[18] and, after its suborning by National Socialist ideology (indeed, partly in reaction to this) the idea has attracted a new and wide interest, not only in the environmental realm,[19] but also in arts like film, theatre and literature.[20]

Heimat has a core spatial reference as the physical location where an individual or community is "at home" or "on familiar ground" but it acquired additional meanings related to birthplace, the locus of precognitive and unreflective childhood experience, feelings of community or lasting domicile.[21] Sometimes there is a distinctly earthy ring to the idea, invoking the notion of *die heimatliche Scholle*, the sod of ground, the turned furrow, upon which there is a lasting sense of dependence, "a shared life with the soil and every natural, spiritual thing that has grown on it".[22] This, of course, echoes in some ways Leopold's notion of land.

Clearly, the sense of ease or security in feeling at home can define itself all too readily against what is beyond the pale, or by contrast with what is seen as *fremd* – strange, other, foreign, those feelings one has when away from home[23] – or *elend*, being homeless, landless, banished or in exile.[24] And with the passage of time and the arrival of the new, which puts distance between us and where we feel we originally belong, something which can stimulate longing even more,[25] there is *Heimweh*, a homesick feeling for a lost land that can be, for some, a pathological nostalgia.

Ernst Bloch[26] famously described *Heimat* as "somewhere everyone knows from their childhood but where no-one has ever been" but more dynamic interpretations of the concept[27] see belonging as always incorporating a contradiction between real memory and idealised hope, a dialectic between "ever thus" and "not yet". And then there can be a reciprocity of relationship to place, where neither appropriation, nor passivity, are adequate to describe how we might belong somewhere, but where there is a sense of both gift and acceptance. Thus, there is the possibility that belonging might be appropriated over and again in a way that could actually articulate social change,[28] something which, on a theological view, echoes Bergmann's plea for our commitment to *Beheimatung*, or "making ourselves at home".[29]

Nor should it be assumed that this kind of multi-facetedness of place is a concern only within an Anglo-German conversation. The issue of "imagined community" that the citizen belongs to is a concern across Europe. At the most general level, the movement of people in North Africa – partly as a result of the impacts of climate change – raises the question of Europe's southern borders: what is their reaslity and significance? Tensions between racial and religious groups has provoked very different responses in Denmark, France and Germany and raises the largest of questions regarding the "secular state" and the meaning of freedom and tolerance. Recent tensions and conflicting loyalties evident in Ukraine highlight the nature of Europe's ethnic and cultural boundaries. Finally, debates about Scottish independence – a real possibility for the first time in 400 years – present meanings of nationhood, belonging and place in a new way.

It was to stimulate a creative conversation between such varied understandings of what it is to belong in a place, with their echoes one in another, that we convened two gatherings at the Lincoln Theological Institute, an international centre of expertise in the theological study of religion and society at Manchester University in the UK. A preliminary meeting in 2010 helped set the agenda for our shared explorations and a research visit to Germany, jointly funded by the LTI and the St James' Trust, expanded our network of possible participants. The subsequent colloquium in 2011 produced a spirited exchange whose revised papers form the basis of this volume. We have grouped these in three sections but their preoccupations overlap and, in a Postscript, we have ourselves identified what we consider to be the cross-cutting themes.

In opening our section "At Home or Ill-at-Ease", *Stefan Körner*, from the School of Architecture, Urban Planning and Landscape Architecture in Kassel University in Germany, shows how concern for *Heimat* can find its origins in the social expression of a Christian humanist individuality exercised within the bounds of creation, where a shared distinctiveness is negotiated in different expressions of *Land und Leute*. In Germany, scenic expressions of person-nature relationships provided a protest against egalitarianism and abstract industrialization, though could incorporate the modern where this was characterful and fitting. The transformation of Christian humanism into a racist ideology and the appealing prospect of *Heimat* conservation without recourse to democratic argument gave the Nazi ideology a sense of cultural supremacy which came to legitimize the elimination of that which was seen as alien and the export of *Lebensraum*. After World War 2 and German reunification, a rehabilitation of the notion of *Heimat* remains contentious, but it can be seen as part of the renegotiation of German identity and the establishment of a new sense of being at home in a more open and mobile society. More distinctively, it represents resistance to a widespread tendency to separate nature conservation from cultural embedding and thus deny our ability to negotiate a meaningful life in place.

John Eidson, of the Max Planck Institute of Social Anthropology in Halle, takes the town of Boppard in the Rhine valley as his departure for asking what the activities said locally to contribute to its promotion mean to the people who perform them there. In an economy dominated by tourism and commuting to work nearby, social and cultural life is shaped partly by voluntary associations. Careful examination of resource management, text production and performance by the Beautification Society and Neighbourhood Associations over the past hundred years reveals the weakness of assumptions that *Heimat* is born of bourgeois ideology or from mediating between local experience and the supposed community of the nation. It emerges rather as a contested symbol in public discourse, a coming to terms among different groups with contradictory claims to the shared home town. Similar situations pertained widely, even where other social distinctions were in play. What is in common are struggles for inclusion, participation and recognition, such that contemporary understandings of *Heimat* as appropriation and reconstruction were, in fact, in play a century ago. What was absent then was a political and legal frame that could protect all potential participants.

Ian Thompson, Landscape Architect and Town Planner at Newcastle University, is concerned to explore how robust is the notion of *genius loci* as a focus for resistance to the effects of globalization on local cultures, landscapes and building traditions. For him, human migration raises questions of whether such a "spirit of the place" is portable, what happens when two *genii* meet and whether a genius is malleable without losing its essential meaning when there is traumatic economic change that rapidly transforms landscapes. He then wishes to test such notions of *genius loci* against ideas of place as the abode of special beings like deities or spirits; in panpsychism and pantheism where universal consciousness or one deity populates entire landscapes; through the inter-connectedness of ecosystems; in ideas of the "authentic"; through a coherent narrative where place tells its story; in local distinctiveness; and in "character" of place sensitive to change. Of these, he considers all but the last to be wanting in their ability to resist subversion by unwelcome ideas of belonging, particularly those which demonise or exclude those who do not share our own sense of place.

Acknowledging the widespread experiences of mobility and homelessness, the xenophobic misuse of notions of *Heimat* and the challenge of climate change to adjust to shifting surroundings, *Sigurd Bergmann* of Trondheim University eschews familiar approaches to *Heimat* by invoking the notion of *Beheimatung*, "making oneself at home". Within such a dynamic perspective, the familiar and strange need not be in opposition but can be reconciled as homes emerge and fade to come again. Or we can conceive homecoming as a creative to-and-fro in turbulent times and rapidly changing places, as a trans-culturation in landscapes that are changing ethnically and culturally, as our welcoming into a place of our own something of the wider world. In theological terms, God's own making himself at home in his Creation in the person of Jesus and the Holy Spirit's indwelling among the faithful, mean that *Beheimatung* is part of the divine life itself, into which we can be incorporated. The believer should show an abandonment, trusting that loving others can help make a just world where everyone may feel at home; and that it is God himself who will carry us through the process of making ourselves at home in the turmoil of a shared life.

Opening our second section on "Forgetting and Remembering", *Paul Gough* a practising artist, art historian and broadcaster at the RMIT University, Melbourne, Australia, shows that the outward appearance of cemeteries and other places of burial matters greatly to those who value the resting place of their loved ones as places of respectful calm and repose. An unkempt appearance denotes disorder, disgrace and forgetfulness, indications of a neglect that reflects poorly on the lives of those buried nearby and even more poorly on those meant to care for their memory. Nowhere is this sentiment more deeply felt than in the military cemeteries designed, created and maintained by the British and Commonwealth War Graves Commission who are tasked with looking after thousands of garden cemeteries in the UK and on former battlefields across the world. Through images and text, he examines the maintenance of these cemeteries and focuses in particular on the issues aroused by the need to maintain pristine, well-manicured lawns irrespective of environmental, topographical and other conditions. Though these features have been long considered an indispensable feature of Western funerary environments, Gough draws attention to points of tension (and even controversy) that resurface from time to time whenever those organisations charged with maintaining national memory are deemed to have failed in their horticultural duties, or seek to review time-honoured practices.

From his research in the Dearne Valley, South Yorkshire, *John Rodwell*, an ecologist now researching in the Lincoln Theological Institute in Manchester shows that post-industrial landscapes that have experiencing the process of "regeneration" often have a degree of forgetfulness of their past which in humans would be considered a pathology. Technology-driven scenarios for the future are developed and much of the landscape and previous infrastructure are heavy-engineered out of existence. Repetitious new sites are created which have little sense of local distinctiveness or signifiers of former times. In other cases, the past is commodified as some sort of heritage. Little real justice is done to the price paid by earlier lives of local people and their communities and the contested histories to which landscapes bear witness remain unspoken about. Thus, the ends of former lives are poorly handled or ignored and memories are not considered part of inter-generational equity. He asks whether "Securing the Future" (the then government's slogan for Sustainable Development) is possible with such an impoverished appreciation of the past and what are the wider consequences of this kind of forgetfulness for individuals, communities and places, and the psychological, social and religious purchase which richer kinds of remembering might have.

Philip Sheldrake, a theologian with specialisms in spirituality and pastoral theology at Cambridge University, sets the dialectical relationship between environments and human narratives within the context of the "ethical sacra-mentality" performed in Christian celebration of the eucharist. A universal Church claims to offer an inclusive, continuing and metaphysical frame, within which the eucharist opens up the challenge of how believers can exist appropriately in a world of particular places, here and now. More especially, participation in the eucharist demands a costly reconciliation, a making equal room for others, both now and in terms of inherited claims on history and memories; a repentance and forgiveness of wrongs; a refusal to participate in structures and behaviours that violate the other; and a restitution of justice. The eucharist celebrates the end of boundaries that mutually exclude and gives voice to unheard narratives within its own recall of God's dealings with his creation. A theology of reconciled place thus depends on our own belief that God himself determines our identities, bringing into our own place things we would rather exclude. Thus the eucharist sets out a future which radically reshapes where we feel we belong.

In our final section on "Separation and Connectedness", *Paul Selman*, then a specialist in environmental impact assessment and landscape planning at Sheffield University, sees damage to landscapes as a disconnection of physical systems, visual continuity and human attachment that manifests itself in a loss of functionality, ecosystem services, resilience and identity. Such disruption of dependencies between people and place may also lead to moral dereliction and have a spiritual dimension, entailing a loss of potential for connecting the ordinary and extraordinary, the secular and the sacred. Landscape restoration should thus aim to reconnect through a commitment to such things as green infrastructure, integrated functionalities and the encouragement of the unique potentials of place. Newly designed landscapes will also gain the capacity to facilitate belonging only if they are so thoughtfully connected as to allow the negotiated and serendipitous emergence of place. Policy makers need a better appreciation of how people experience landscape in ways that are intuitive, visceral or subliminal. Landscape linkages need to be planned and managed in ways that are sufficiently dynamic and synergistic as to ensure a sustainable continuity. Landscapes need to be conceived as arenas for social learning in vivid and imaginative encounters that make abstract ideas a social reality. And moral and spiritual reconnection needs to be explored through landscape narratives and performance. Only thus can landscape incorporate a generous shared well-being, a just basis for living and a wise anticipation of the future.

Peri-urban landscapes are often seen as placeless and anonymous, inimical to any sense of belonging but, for *Vera Vicenzotti*, researching the theory and history of landscape architecture and planning at the Technical University of Municg,

Weihenstephan, the discourse they provoke among landscape architects and urban designers expresses all the familiar rationales concerning loss of identity and reveals different notions of what being at home is about. She explores two conceptions of *Heimat* – a conservative dream of belonging and focus on continuity and a progressive search for an open societal utopia – against the criteria of "origin versus future" and "appropriation versus fitting in". On this analysis, peri-urban places, though presenting a challenge to traditional notions of *Heimat* have been persistently conceptualised in ways that are conservative – conceding, for example, that continuity of occupancy even in such a challenging landscape bestows an inherited sense of identity – or have been so progressive as to dissipate any sense of belonging in a universal landscape that is recognizable but lacking distinctiveness. What persists perhaps is the need for the concept of *Heimat*, without any demonizing of its conservatism yet with a willingness to negotiate what new homes might be, even within the peri-urban.

Peter Scott, Director of the Lincoln Theological Institute at Manchester University, with expertise in political and social theology, questions our loyalty to place in a purgative theological light, asking whether our situatedness on earth can ultimately be established only by reference to others and to God. Our relationships to place are essentially ungiven, our own loyalties negotiated in competition with the memories of others, equally but perhaps differently committed to the same locale. A theological reply to our desire to belong does not subordinate it as a simply natural or fallen state to a graced condition where particular places are of no concern. What matters is that we set our own sense of belonging, and that of others, under the regard of a God to whom all places and all creatures are equally created. Measuring our critical distance from places involves conceding that they do not ultimately depend for significance on our own particular occupation. Place is gift owned by the inhabitation of many loyalties. Such openness guards our memories against nostalgia where relics can trigger partisan pasts and concedes a shared future to which others also may pass through the places we call our own.

Starting from a contrast between Catholic and Protestant performances of territory in sixteenth century Lyon, *Bron Szerszynski*, a specialist in environment, culture and public policy at Lancaster University, sets the role of the Reformation in transforming our experience of space within a longer frame of western religious history, reappraising its claim to effect a shift from absolute to abstract space, from place to space. In an analysis of successive orderings of the sacred, he sees the reshaping of our experience of place as part of a cultural struggle between archaic religion and monotheism, not so much a disenchantment of the world but rather a redefinition of its relationship with the holy, an overcoming of the attachment of spiritual power to specific locales, objects and people. To liberate us from bondage to place without condemning us to placelessness, he draws on Kierkegaard's concept of irony to argue for a (post-)Christian mode of placing.

Such a return gesture, an ironic negation of received meanings, would enable us to reform belonging and find our place with ethical freedom and responsibility.

NOTES

1. http://www.mbreckitttrust.org, 8 April, 2014.
2. Rodwell (2008a, b).
3. For example, Robinson.
4. O'Donovan.
5. Sheldrake.
6. Gorringe.
7. Inge.
8. See, for example, Freeman.
9. White.
10. Rowland.
11. Bergmann (2007, 2008).
12. Brueggemann.
13. Cox.
14. Leopold.
15. Handley.
16. Haber.
17. "Heft" or "heaf" is the closest word we have in English, generally applied rather narrowly to a sheep flock's sense of territory on open grazing land, but the Welsh *cynefin*, originally derived from the same pastoral realm, has been more widely used of human attachment to place. See, for example, Watkins 2004; MacNeillie 2005; Rodwell 2008b.
18. Bausinger; Wickham; Konold.
19. Wurzel & Rottmann.
20. Boa & Palfreyman; von Moltke.
21. Stavenhagen.
22. Spranger.
23. Pott.
24. Heller.
25. Beumelberg.
26. Bloch.
27. Mecklenberg.
28. Vob Bredow; Greverus.
29. Bergmann 2014.

REFERENCES

Beumelberg, W. (1938), *Deutschland: Ein Buch der Heimat*, Berlin: Paul Franke Verlag.
Bausinger, W. (1980), *Heimat und Identitüt*, Neuminster: Wachholtz.
Bergman, S. (2007), "Theology in its Spatial Turn: Space, Place and Built Environments Challenging and Changing the Images of God", *Religious Compass*, Vol. 1, 353–379.
– (2008), "Making Oneself at home in Environments of Urban Amnesia: Religion and Theology in City Space", International Journal of Public theology, Vol. 2(1), 70–97.

– (2014), *Religion, Space & the Environment*, Transaction: New Brunswick and London.
Bloch, E. (1959), *Über Karl Marx*, Frankfurt a.M.: Suhrkamp.
– (1977) *Das Prinzip Hoffnung*, Frankfurt a.M.: Suhrkamp.
Boa, E. & Palfreyman, R. (2000), *Heimat, A German Dream, Regional Loyalties and national identity in German Culture 1890–1990*, Oxford: OUP.
Brueggemann, W. (2002, 2nd edition), *The Land: Place as Gift, Promise and Challenge in Biblical Faith*, Minneapolis: Fortress Press
Cox, H. (1965), *The Secular City*, New York: Macmillan.
Freeman, L. (2006), "Aborigines had been listening to the Word of God sounding at the heart of creation", *The Tablet* (1 July 2006), p. 7.
Gorringe, T.J. (2002), *A Theology of the Built Environment*, Cambridge: Cambridge University Press.
Greverus, I-M. (1987), "The '*Heimat*' problem", in H. Seliger, (ed.). *Der Begriff 'Heimat' in der deutschen Gegewartsliteratur*, Munchen: iudicum Verlag.
Handley, J.F. (2000), *The Spirit and Purpose of Land Restoration*. Birmingham: The Groundwork Federation.
Haber, W. (2002), "Die verschleppte Nachhaltigkeit: frühe Forderungen – aktuelle Akzeptanz" *Schriftenreihe des Deutschen Rates für Landespflege*, Vol. 74, 5–27.
Heller, H. (1984). "Wieviel Heimat hat der Mensch?", *Der Fränkische Tag*, November 10, 1984.
Inge, J. (2003), *A Christian Theology of Place*, Aldershot: Ashgate.
Konold, W. (2005), "Landschaft und Heimat – ein Resümee", *Schriftenreihe des Deutschen Rates für Landespflege*, Vol. 77, 5–16.
Leopold, A. (1949), *A Sand County Almanac*, New York: Oxford University Press.
Mecklenberg, N. (1986), *Erzählte Provinz: Regionalismus und Moderne in Roman*, Konigstein/TS: Athenäum.
O'Donovan, O. (1989), "The Loss of a Sense of Place", *Irish Theological Quarterly*, Vol. 55, 39–58.
Pott, H.-G. (1986), *Literatur und Provinz: Das Konzept 'Heimat' in der neueren Literatur*. Dusseldorf: Eichendorfs-Institut.
Robinson, P. (2005), "Opening the future of the city: masterplanning, culture and a cause for celebration in the East End of Newcastle", *Crucible*, Oct-Dec 2005, 34–42.
Rodwell, J.S. (2008a), "Forgetting the Land", *Studies in Christian Ethics*, Vol. 21(2), 269–286.
– (2008b), "Remembering the Land", *Crucible*, Oct-Dec 2008, 5–16.
Rowland, C. (1998), "Friends of Albion" in S. Platten & C. Lewis (eds.), *Flagships of the Spirit: Cathedrals in Society*, London: Darton, Longman & Todd.
Sheldrake, P. (2001), *Spaces for the Sacred*, London: SCM Press.
White, S. (1995), "The theology of sacred space", in D. Brown & A. Loades (eds.) *The Sense of the Sacramental: Movement and Measure in Art and Music, Place and Tiime*, London: SPCK, 44–58.
Stavenhagen, K. (1939), *Heimat als Grundlage menschlicher Existenz*, reprinted as *Heimat as Meaning of Life* in the British Occupation zone in 1948.
Spranger, E. (1923). *Grundlegende Bildung-Berufsbildung-Allgemeinbildung*, reprinted in J.H. Knoll, ed. (1965), *Grundlagen und Grundfragen der Erziehung*, pp. 24–45.
Von Bredow, W. (1978), "Heimat-Kunde", *Politik und Zeitgeschichte*, 22, 19–30;

Von Moltke, J. (2005), *Locations of Heimat in German Cinema*, Stanford: University of California Press

Wickham, C.J. (1999), *Constructing Heimat in Postwar Germany: Longing and Belonging*, Lewiston: Edwin Mellon Press

Wurzel, A. & Rottmann, R. eds. (2005), "Landschaft und Heimat", *Schriftenreihe des Deutschen Rates für Landespflege*, Vol. 77.

EDITORS' ACKNOWLEDGEMENT

This book emerges out of an extended conversation hosted by the Lincoln Theological Institute at the University of Manchester. The editors would like to thank all those who participated in the meetings for entering into the project's interdisciplinary ethos with enthusiasm, good humour and patience. These meetings and this publication were supported financially by the Manchester Jean Monnet Centre of Excellence and the trustees of the Lincoln Theological Institute, to whom the editors also wish to extend their thanks.

At home or ill-at-ease?

Heimat AND INDIVIDUALITY

Stefan Körner

Image 1 Rural scenery of Middle Germany symbolizing Heimat, homeland of the Brothers Grimm

HUMAN INDIVIDUALITY & THE DISTINCTIVENESS OF PEOPLE AND PLACE

According to Eisel, all the theories of individuality which have developed since the Renaissance seek to explain how personal distinctiveness is possible if, at the same time, we are part of wider groupings such as society, state and nature.[1] For the Christian, what rescues such hierarchies from being simply rational order – the abstract generality of natural principles – is God's desire for the expression of individuality. In each person, individuality is discovered and expressed through an exercise of personal freedom and responsibility within the frame of respect for God's will. And, for Eisel, it is expression of this individuality which enables humankind to explore and fulful its responsibility towards creation, such that the individual collaborates in realizing the universal order of God. Acting only for himself or herself in a selfish fashion, trying to escape the individual responsibilities into which persons are born, these would be blasphemies. Instead everyone has to fulfil a service to the whole in his or her own situation. For liberals, such a conservative concept of bound freedom looks paradoxical but, for Christians, it is a freedom in obligation to the whole which determines our relationships with society, the state and nature.

On Eisel's view, Christian humanism expresses itself not only in the individuality of persons but in the distinctiveness of communities and cultures, where the notion of "bound freedom" is integral to the development of different manifestations of 'Land'. The word *Land* was used by Herder (1784) and others to describe the peculiarities of cultures in their particular settlement areas, the actual places in which people have made the best possible outcome from their natural surroundings – or at least show the potential to do so – registering themselves in geographic terms by putting their particular talents to work in wresting cultural distinctiveness from wild nature.[2] On this view, the emergence of different cultures and customs is more than some sort of materialist and mechanistic adaptation to necessities but comes about through autonomous expression of shared individualities. For Herder, this autonomy is anchored in the diverse peculiarities of the quite different *Volkscharaktere* (national characteristics) and the resulting different lands are the organic stuff of their cultural expression. In this historical-philosophical context, all cultures are in principle of equal value inasmuch as they go their own way in their development and so ultimately realize all their various facets. However, with Herder, there is no doubt that western Christian culture perfected the relationship to nature as one of thoughtful stewardship and realization of the human spirit.

For Eisel, persons already have an individuality created by God, even if this has not been awakened and brought to its full potential through an explicit Christian commitment. And the Christian mission can avoid presumption by an emphasis on kind attention to the individual person within the frame of the universal task. Opposed to this approach stands industrial capitalism, which implements the same principles worldwide and thus, from the point of view of Christian humanism, promotes uniformity, levelling and ultimately loss of quality in all areas of life, the charge currently made against globalization. Rather, on a Christian view, humanity thus becomes a reality in particular in dealing kindly with nature. Cultural progress is not simply a matter of unbounded exploitation of nature in favour of purely economic calculations, which would lead to over-exploitation and ultimately to the decline of the culture, but of remaining moderate and wisely observing the natural conditions present in actual spaces.

This critical perception was the starting point of the German *Heimat* conservation, which began to take shape at the end of the 19th century. At that time, the distinctiveness of *Land und Leute* (land and people) was under threat not merely by egalitarianizing democracy, but by increasing industrialization. A growing uniformity of landscapes and residential areas was taking shape because of the nationwide availability of building materials and goods through modern transport systems and land consolidation which, with agricultural improvements, were beginning to destroy the organic landscape image. The fight against this development was the beginning of *Heimatschutz*.[3] The German middle classes, who understood themselves as the repositories of culture, expressed broad opposition to the utilitarianism and materialism of the new age and nostalgia for wholeness, the symbol for which was the landscape. And in addition to the harsh demands made by the modern age, *Heimat* gained political appeal in the national evocation of the common fatherland.

Heimat CONSERVATION AS A CULTURAL AND POLITICAL MOVEMENT

As a politically-oriented and practically-motivated movement, *Heimat* conservation after Riehl was concerned with the development of landscapes as the spatial expression of a harmonically organic interplay of "land and people" in the service of the German nation.[4] The term *Heimat* is derived from the Old High German *heimöti*, which originally meant settlement. Making a place a *Heimat* has a deep-rooted emotionally significant sense of existential security, which as we have seen can be understood in terms of Christian humanism. In addition, the medieval term *Heimatrecht* (literally, home right) meant having a right to a house and property and thus possession of a place. *Heimat* thus had a material reference. It is also the counter-concept of the "alien" (OHG *eliliente*). This is the origin of the word *Elend* (misery): those deprived of *Heimat*, that is without their own house and property were thus in a state of misery.[5] Beyond this emotionally significant and material meaning, *Heimat* has a dual character because of its political encumbrance of nationalist meanings. It is also always an instrument of popular movements, and we will see, came to express racist politics.

The term *Landschaft* began increasingly to replace *Land* in the German-speaking area of Europe, because the bourgeoisie no longer had any concrete link with rural life and began to construct instead an aesthetic relationship with it. The *schöne Landschaft* (beautiful landscape) or, in the language of *Heimat* conservation, the *malerische* (scenic) landscape was, as man-made landscape, the individual expression of a specific person-nature relationship. The term "scenic" shows that the perceptions of intact landscapes were in fact derived from certain kinds of landscape painting, which had characterized the visual appreciation of actual nature. *Heimat* conservation thus began to concern itself initially with the conservation of the man-made landscape as the model of successful development of culture and nature until, in the Nazi period, a "Germanic" notion of "original landscape" was added.

Stefan Körner

Image 2 Reprint of Heimatschutz from Rudorff (1897)

Because Christian humanism informed understandings of *Heimat* creation in the world, *Heimat* conservation was also, much to the surprise of many German nature conservationsists today, practically conceived from the start as architectural criticism, i.e. as criticism of modern buildings that do not fit the landscape and are not snug. Criticism of abstract industrial progress for Rudorff meant criticism of an exclusively economically motivated landscape development, which he regarded as short-sighted (and which today we would say was not very sustainable).[6] And he was critical too of the associated changes in social conditions that were taking place: that, for example, farm labourers no longer wanted to perform their customary duties, but wanted quick and easy money in factories, so as to be emancipated from the existing conditions instead of taking their place in them. For Rudorff this was an illusory freedom that could be compared with the Christian notion of original sin.[7]

Democracy and industry were thus assigned, and this is central for German thinking, to an abstract concept of technologically rational "civilization". *Kultur* (Culture), on the other hand, was a concrete concept and the empathetic design of landscapes was conceived as comprising units of "land and people". Despite this basic anti-civilizational attitude, the conservative world picture retained that humanist concept of freedom and with it also a certain idea of progress. Progress was the perfection of creation through the diffusion of distinctiveness and its constant differentiation in designing special places. Correspondingly, *Heimat* conservation did not try to prevent the modern, because it could no longer be denied by the turn of the 20th century, but attempted to modify it in accordance with its own ideas. At the landscape design level, this meant that all new buildings and infrastuctures were to be inserted into a frame of landscape distinctiveness. In the process, the new did not necessarily have to be concealed, if it had character itself, as is demonstrated in Lindner's *Ingenieurwerk und Naturschutz (Engineering and Nature Conservation)*.[8] Modern industrial architecture is generally felt to be ugly, but can also be very characteristic. Thus, for example, high voltage power lines might lend a monotonous landscape a *neuartigen Reiz*,[9] and the slag heaps produced by heavy industry in the Ruhrgebiet therefore could have their own *Heimat* qualities: "We do not want to lose the enormous heaps of rubble and slag, and we recognize in them an inseparable complementary feature of mining activity and their atmospheric value for us becomes part of the *Heimat* image".[10] In the 1990s, this perception was incorporated into the programme of the International Construction Exhibition IBA-Emscher Park and helped to design industrial landscapes with the old industrial buildings and slag heaps retained as landmarks,[11] recently celebrated as part of the Ruhrgebiet European City of Culture.

Images 3/4 Auratic old industrial architecture as a part of Natur-Park Schöneberg, Berlin

WHOSE LAND AND *Lebensraum?*

If we think about *Heimat* then, we might tradititionally imagine a rural scene with fields, villages with red roofs and a church at the heart (Image 1). But this scenery is not innocent. What has made the debate about *Heimat* difficult in Germany is that the value placed on our home in the actual locality became associated with a conservative political and nationalist position that was driven by the Nazis to monstrous extremes. The greatest propaganda success of *Heimat* conservation was undoubtedly the Nazi motorway building programme. New modernistic bridges were clad with locally available natural stone and the verges of the motorways were planted with local bushes and trees in order to enhance landscape distinctiveness and diversity. In particular, however, the motorway itself was adapted to the topography with its linearity and thus worked the "body" of the landscape clearly into a unified work of art consisting of nature and technology. So we see expressed Nazi landscape design.

Heimat conservation was phased in unconditionally by the Nazis. Confessing party members, who supported the racism of the new regime, took their place at its head. Two things were decisive in terms of their world view. First, the cultural concept of Christian humanism, which had already been absorbed by a nationalist *Heimat* concept, had to be transformed into a racist ideology. Second, National Socialism opened up new propaganda worlds for *Heimat* and nature conservationists such that *Heimat* conservation assumed it could finally achieve its goals without taking any account of democratic decision-making processes. At least on the legal level, the Nature Conservation Law of the Third Reich was considered to be exemplary in the world and served in Germany as a model for legislation after World War Two.[12]

In the Nazi ideology, the Christian-humanist image of man was transformed into the cultural superiority claim of the "Nordic race". The superiority of that race proved itself in its engagement with adverse nature when it created High Culture and, in particular, the German man-made landscape. Where cultures organize their lives, settle and use and develop their natural bases of living, it is possible to speak of *Lebensraum*. As privileged representatives of this "Nordic race", the Germans had established their position in the creation of their own *Lebensraum*, inasmuch as they had a deep feeling for nature and treated it with the corresponding amount of empathy.[13] An expression of this empathetic treatment of nature was the German hedgerow landscape, in which, for example, the soil was protected from erosion and which, as a man-made scenery marked by hedges and individual trees beloved of Germans, was the embodiment of *Heimat* landscape.[14]

The *Lebensraum* concept was given a strident racist component by the Nazis because the German talent for high culture and especially for landscape culture was seen to result from their genes. The assumption was that cultural traits were inherited and that people could be categorized not just by their national charac-

Image 5 Silberpfeil on the Reichsautobahn

ter, but by race. In fact, of course, if levels of cultural development are tied to the genome, the strategy of Christian humanism of converting other people to the Christian faith and thus realizing their full potential does not make sense any more. Such humanism instead becomes a sentimentality that is to be expunged. The capacity to inherit High Culture should then be much better secured through racial hygiene by ensuring that the hereditary disposition of the "Nordic race" is not mixed with "inferior races". Racism is not a German invention, but the German practice of it was particularly thorough. If there are racial mixtures, they are to be eliminated by breeding selection and extermination. The greatest enemy of the "Nordic race" was the Jews. As a formerly Semitic migrant people, they had become assimilated and begun to play an outstanding role not only in German culture. They exhibited their threat to the racists with their ability to adapt, but were seen by the racists as the offspring of nomads not able to take root in the territory. With their diffusion worldwide in the Diaspora, they became the embodiment of the *Heimatlosen Gesellen* (homeless journeymen) and uncreative mercantilism of international finance. They were, for example, not allowed to cultivate agricultural land.[15]

Compared with nomadism, whose practitioners move on when a space has been used up, National Socialism developed, with its *Lebensraum* principle, an ideology of "correct" *Wandern* (movement). Culture in the racist interpretation of the Christian missionary principle was then promoted if it consisted of the diffusion of landscape culture. Because German landscape culture consists in taking root in one's own ground, the Nazi concept of progress, like the humanist one, is based on a paradox: in the latter, freedom is bound. Being bound for the Nazis meant, being bound to one's own race, one's own settlement territory and to one's own sod (*Heimatliche Scholle*). If culture has to be diffused in order to spread progress, and at the same time it is clear that one's own settlement grounds are overfilled, then Germany had to look elsewhere for expansion of its *Volk ohne Raum* (people without space), preferably in the "empty" spaces of Eastern Europe. Unlike the British or American settlers, the Germans had no colonies or the vast expanse of the West. The East thus came to be seen as the Wild West of the German Reich and their model became the war of extermination waged against the native Americans, which was now being waged with the latest industrial extermination methods in concentration camps.[16] The goal of creating new *Lebensraum* and the embodiment of "correct" movement was a new phase of establishing roots in the conquered Eastern Regions.

To make this possible, a "species-appropriate" environment had to be offered, so the Eastern Regions had to be created after the model of the old *Heimat* landscapes and thus be designed in accordance with the ideal of the German hedge landscape. *Heimat* conservation as landscape design or nature conservation thus became associated by the Nazis with "racial hygiene".[17] Walter Schoenichen, a central and influential German nature conservationist of the time, gave expression to this very clearly after power had been transferred to the Nazis in 1933 in the title of a programmatic essay: "*Das deutsche Volk muss gereinigt werden. – Und die deutsche Landschaft?*" (The German people has to be cleansed – and the German landscape?).[18] This programme was taken very seriously right up to the final days of the war.

Because of its ideological significance, landscape design in the Nazi period and in association with regional planning for the Eastern colonization underwent considerable modernization: for the first time, large-scale landscape design had become conceivable. In 1942 Mäding wrote a text about *Die Gestaltung der Landschaft als Hoheitsrecht und Hoheitspflicht* (Design of the landscape as sovereign right and duty) and demonstrated the – as we would say today – environmentally proper landscape design as the task of public services provided by the State. The concept of the new discipline, which he named, *Landespflege*, includes both landscape architecture and landscape planning and continued to exist as a concept in postwar Germany. With largely the same staffing, it developed so that by the beginning of the 1970s, German landscape planning comprised spatial environment planning together with specialist planning for nature conservation and recreation.[19] This form of landscape planning is thus a specifically German way and does not exist in this form in other European countries. This is what we would understand in Germany as Landscape Architecture.

Heimat TODAY

It is thus not surprising that, after World War Two, the concept of *Heimat* in Germany (in contrast to German-speaking Switzerland) was ideologically deeply contaminated. It was also often stated to have been not simply misused by the Nazis, but also not a concept that expressed a good existential need. In the German Democratic Republic (DDR), there was a firm attachment after the Second World War to the political significance of *Heimat*, only in a somewhat different sense. There, it was a matter of the construction of the Socialist *Heimat* in a new anti-fascist society that had to integrate a large number of displaced persons from the German eastern regions. Unlike in West Germany, it was taboo for the displaced to remember their place of origin. This would have put a strain on the relationship of the DDR to its "socialist brother-countries". The Socialist *Heimat* prescribed a perspective that was to unite the indigenous inhabitants and the so-called new citizens, for example in the wake of land reform and its corollary, the dispossession of the existing farmers for agricultural collectivization.[20]

In the Federal Republic of Germany (BRD), the distinctive German approach came to an end with decisive moves to link with the West and to achieve reconciliation with France in particular as the basis of the present EU. The politically dispossessed quickly became a significant force of the conservative camp, which is still the case today, while intellectual circles regarded the concept of *Heimat*

Heimat and Individuality 25

Image 6 New Heimat Projects in Berlin-Kreuzberg, former West-Berlin

as completely taboo and those who used it, for example in the context of spatial planning or identity, made themselves politically suspect. Only in protest movements did something like *Heimat* play a role: for example, in the early anti-nuclear power movement in South Germany or in squatting as a protest against the clearance of areas in big cities, such as Frankfurt am Main or Berlin in the 70s and 80s where old buildings were re-occupied, refurbished and green areas created in yards and streets. Or, in the wake of the "alternative movements", new *Heimat* creations were sought in the countryside or, for example, in the former West Berlin under the concept of a neighbourhood (*Kiezkultur*). However, these movements were seldom discussed or reflected on under the concept of *Heimat*, except by Greverus.[21] The notion of creating new *Heimat*s, after the *Heimat* in which was one born, a second or even third in which one lived voluntarily, was generally considered to be a sign of a progessive concept of *Heimat*. Associated with it was the emphasis on emancipatory settlement, such that one did not insert oneself into one's place of origin and remain with one's roots, but rather created a new *Heimat*, but this time in a metropolis, like the many squatters in Berlin, who fled from their narrow South German *Heimat* and, incidentally, from military service.

Image 7 New Heimat Projects in Berlin-Kreuzberg, former West-Berlin

With German re-unification the subject of German identity became once again a topic for discussion. It suddenly opened up for West Germans the possibility of travelling to countries that, despite collectivization and large-area regrouping of agricultural land, in some places had not changed much since World War Two and reminded them of the stories told by their own grandparents. At home, the spirit of the age was also changing. In 1990 the *Bundeszentrale für politische Bildung* (Federal Office for Political Education), for example, published a collected volume, the title of which, *Heimat in einer offenen Gesellschaft* (*Heimat* in an open society), itself constituted a programme. The question of what *Heimat* can mean in a democracy became increasingly discussed. People's relationship to their *Heimat* became an increasingly popular topic in the press, for example when fashion designer Joop, who had previously lived in New York and elsewhere, moved back to his *Heimat* town of Potsdam. In 2006 the philosopher of religion Christoph Türcke published an essay "*Heimat – a rehabilitation*". The *Heimat* taboo was beginning to crumble.

Among campaigners to protect the German countryside, the resort to the use of the *Heimat* concept had quite a different background. The starting point was its so-called acceptance deficit, which had arisen when the National Forest in Bavaria and the Wattenmeer were designated as national parks and the interests of the local residents came into conflict with those of state-run and official conservation authorities. The conservationists saw themselves generally speaking as ecologists and thus natural scientists who mostly wanted to provide a narrowly conceived and restrictive protection for species and biotopes, the principle of which was to keep people away from the areas that need protection. The residents refused to accept any regulations imposed on them by nature conservationists and wanted to continue using the areas concerned as they had always done. In other words, they were afraid of losing their *Heimat*. In this situation, on the basis of a reconstruction of the history of German nature conservation,[22] the so-called *Vilmer Thesen zu Heimat und Naturschutz* (Vilmer Theses on *Heimat* and Nature) proposed that *Heimat* should be used as as a concept to reconnect the interests of nature conservation with those of the residents.[23] The precondition is the rediscovery of its cultural and thus also creative tradition as *Naturschutz im weiteren Sinne* (Nature conservation in the widest sense), but at the same reflecting critically on the significance of the *Heimat* concept, particularly as it had been understood and applied under National Socialism.

This proposal was at first broadly welcomed, but there was strong criticism that it was inviting the reactivation of an unfortunate German past. Only a few critics, such as the environmental theorist Konrad Ott, tried to engage with all aspects of the debate. Ott, who had been part of the *Vilmer Thesen* debate, came to the conclusion that he was unable, despite his aversion to the topic of *Heimat* and his unwillingness to subscribe to the theses, to deny that *Heimat*, on condition that it was subjected to a close analysis and process of differentiation, had a certain moral relevance.[24]

Thus it is clear that, for Germans, *Heimat* is associated with a deep-rooted ambivalence. On the one hand, if the basis of our culture is Christian humanism, a personal connection between nature and culture, between place and a meaningful life and thus the making of a *Heimat* for humankind in the world, is a central

Image 8 "Home Sickness": On the search of Heimat– Berlin-Friedrichshain, former East Berlin

idea. On the other hand, the concept cannot be separated from the political implications that were settled in the wake of German nation-forming and which, in the destructive war waged by the Nazis, no longer knew any limits. So all alternative understandings of *Heimat* emphasize that it is dangerous to define the concept "top down" or to see in the tradition of the 70s and 80s a meaningful justification of it in actual projects, yet without talking too much about *Heimat* itself.

Image 9 A New form of Heimat in Urban Gardening in Berlin-Kreuzberg (Prinzessinengärten)

This was the main point of the *Vilmer Thesen zu Heimat und Naturschutz*. It is not that the word *Heimat* should be preserved for its own sake, but that a differentiated argument should be made for the substantial needs it satisfies, acknowledging its relevance for our existence and reflecting on its complex cultural and political tradition. In fact, in official nature conservation everyday life resumed its normal course after the *Heimat* debate but it will be possible to say, albeit with the greatest of circumspection, that one thing has come out of it: *Heimat* arguments and responsiveness to the needs of the people can no longer be completely dismissed.

NOTES

[1] Eisel.
[2] Eisel, 236.

3   Rudorff.
4   Riehl.
5   Cf. Piechocki, 19.
6   Rudorff.
7   Rudorff, 45.
8   Lindner.
9   Linder, 88.
10 Linder, 92.
11 Körner.
12 Radkau & Uekötter.
13 Bensch.
14 Körner.
15 Bensch.
16 Blackbourn.
17 Körner.
18 Schoenichen.
19 Cf. Körner.
20 Cf. Pirschel.
21 Greverus.
22 Körner and Eisel.
23 Piechocki et al.
24 Ott.

REFERENCES

Bausinger, H. (1990), "Heimat in einer offenen Gesellschaft – Begriffsgeschichte als Problemgeschichte", in: Bundeszentrale für Politische Bildung (Hrsg.): Heimat – Analysen, Themen, Perspektiven. Bonn. 76–90.

Bensch, M. (1995), "Die Blut und Boden-Ideologie. Ein dritter Weg der Moderne". *Beiträge zur Kulturgeschichte der Natur*, Bd. 2. Berlin/Freising.

Blackbourn, D. (2007), *Die Eroberung der Natur. Eine Geschichte der deutschen Landschaft*. München.

Eisel, U. (1980), "Die Entwicklung der Anthropogeographie von einer 'Raumwissenschaft' zur Gesellschaftswissenschaft". *Urbs et Regio, Kasseler Schriften zur Geographie und Planung*, Bd. 17. Kassel.

Eisel, U. (2009), "Orte als Individuen", in: Eisel, U. (ed.), *Landschaft und Gesellschaft – Räumliches Denken im Visier*. Münster. 226–279.

Greverus, I.-M. (1979), *Auf der Suche nach Heimat*. München.

Greverus, I.-M.; Haindl, E. (eds), (1983), *Versuche, der Zivilisation zu entkommen*. München.

Jackson J. B. (1952), "Human: All Too Human Geography". *Landscape*. 2/2, 2–7.

Körner, S. (2001), "Theorie und Methodologie der Landschaftsplanung, Landschaftsarchitektur und Sozialwissenschaftlichen Freiraumplanung vom Nationalsozialismus bis zur Gegenwart", *Landschaftsentwicklung und Umweltforschung. Schriftenreihe der Fakultät Architektur, Umwelt Gesellschaft*. TU Berlin. Bd. 118. Berlin.

Körner, S. & Eisel, U. (2003), "Naturschutz als kulturelle Aufgabe – theoretische Rekonstruktion und Anregungen für eine inhaltliche Erweiterung", in: Körner, S., Nagel, A.

& Eisel, u. (eds): Naturschutzbegründungen. Bundesamt für Naturschutz. Bonn/Bad Godesberg, 5–49.
Lindner, W. (1926), *Ingenieurwerk und Naturschutz.* Berlin-Lichterfelde.
Mäding, E. (1942), *Landespflege. Die Gestaltung der Landschaft als Hoheitsrecht und Hoheitspflicht.* Berlin.
Ott, K. (2004), "Der Heimatbegriff in der nachhaltigen Entwicklung", *Vortrag am Institut für Landschaftspflege und Naturschutz*, Universität Hannover. Reprint with the header: "'Heimat' – Argumente als Naturschutzbegründungen in Vergangenheit und Gegenwart", in: R. Piechocki. & N. Wiersbinski, (eds), (2007), *Heimat und Naturschutz. Die Vilmer Thesen und ihre Kritiker.* Naturschutz und Biologische Vielfalt, Bd. 47. Bundesamt für Naturschutz. Bonn/Bad Godesberg. 43–65
Piechocki, R., Eisel, U, Körner, S., Nagel, A. & Wiersbinski, N. (2003), "Vilmer Thesen zu 'Heimat' und Naturschutz", *Naturschutz und Landschaftsplanung.* 78(6): 241–244.
Piechocki, R.; Wiersbinski, N. (eds) (2007), "Heimat und Naturschutz. Die Vilmer Thesen und ihre Kritiker". *Naturschutz und Biologische Vielfalt*, Bd. 47. Bundesamt für Naturschutz. Bonn/Bad Godesberg.
Piechocki, R. (2007), "Heimat – Begriffsentstehung und Begriffswandel", in: R. Piechocki, & N. Wiersbinski (eds), *Heimat und Naturschutz. Die Vilmer Thesen und ihre Kritiker.* Naturschutz und Biologische Vielfalt, Bd. 47. Bundesamt für Naturschutz. Bonn/Bad Godesberg. 19–41.
Pirschel, I. (2007), "Landschaft in den Heimatkonzeptionen der frühen DDR". In: Piechocki, R. Wiersbinski, N. (eds): Heimat und Naturschutz. Die Vilmer Thesen und ihre Kritiker. Naturschutz und Biologische Vielfalt, Bd. 47. Bundesamt für Naturschutz. Bonn/Bad Godesberg. 319–352.
Radkau, J. & Uekötter, F. (eds) (2003), *Naturschutz und Nationalsozialismus.* Frankfurt/New York.
Riehl, W.H. (1854), "Die Naturgeschichte als Grundlage einer deutschen Social-Politik". *Land und Leute*, Bd. 14. Stuttgart.
Rudorff, E. (1897), *Heimatschutz.* Nachdruck, St. Goar.
Schoenichen, W. (1933), "Das deutsche Volk muss gereinigt werden – Und die deutsche Landschaft?", *Naturschutz* 14 (11): 205–209.
Türcke, Ch. (2006), *Heimat – Eine Rehabilitierung.* Springer Verlag.
Vesting, Th. (1998), "Die Ambivalenz idealisierter Natur im Landschaftsgarten. Vom Garten der Freiheit zum republikanischem Garten der Freiheit", *Beiträge zur Kulturgeschichte der Natur*, Bd. 8. Berlin/Freising.

IMAGES

Image 1: Photo Stefan Körner
Image 2: Rudorff, E. 1897, Reprint
Image 3: Photo Stefan Körner
Image 4: Photo Stefan Körner
Image 5: Reuß, E. 2006: Hitlers Rennschlachten. Die Silberpfeile unterm Hakenkreuz. Berlin. Fig. 22
Image 6: Photo Stefan Körner
Image 7: Photo Stefan Körner
Image 8: Photo Stefan Körner
Image 9: Photo Stefan Körner

Heimat ON LOCATION: AN ETHNOGRAPHIC AND SOCIAL HISTORICAL APPROACH TO THE *Heimat* MOVEMENT

John R. Eidson

For the last hundred years or more, the concept of *Heimat* has occupied a central, often controversial place in public discourse in Germany, a discourse dominated by politicians, journalists, cultural critics, planners, artists, pedagogues, theologians, and scholars. In this chapter, however, I approach the topic of *Heimat* from another angle. Rather than beginning with representations of *Heimat* in the arts, pronouncements about *Heimat* in literary journals, or debates about *Heimat* among planners, I take the local home town as my point of departure, asking what the activities that are said locally to contribute to the promotion of the home town mean to the people who perform them. My main purpose is to provide adequate descriptions and interpretations of the things that I witnessed while doing research in a small town in south-western Germany – things that may be viewed within the framework of the historical phenomenon known as the *Heimatbewegung* or *Heimat* movement.

From 1979 to 1981, and for short periods in 1990, 1993, and 2003, I conducted ethnographic fieldwork – long-term research based on direct observation, interviews, conversation, and everyday experience – in Boppard, a town of 7,800 on the western side of the Upper Middle Rhine Valley. Set in a picturesque landscape, Boppard has a local economy that is dominated by tourism, although most members of the local workforce commute to jobs in the nearby city of Koblenz or in other neighbouring towns. Local social and cultural life, which gives an impression of great activity, is shaped not only by the municipality, the churches, schools, and local businesses, but also by many voluntary associations. During my fieldwork, I focused on a particular set of voluntary associations, namely, those that are recognized locally for their contributions to causes that are considered to be eminently worthy: causes such as *Stadtverschönerung* (town beautification), the promotion of *Geschichtsbewußtsein* (historical consciousness), and *Brauchtumspflege* (the cultivation of custom or tradition). Contributions to these causes took many forms, including planting trees, building and maintaining hiking trails, mounting plaques on historically memorable sites, constructing, maintaining, and renovating the home town museum, holding speeches on special occasions, publishing text about local history, hosting festivals, and organizing parades, concerts, or comic theatrical performances. After completing my fieldwork, I discovered that these and similar practices had coalesced in towns, cities, and villages throughout the German Reich in the late nineteenth and early twentieth century in the context of the *Heimat* movement.

In reconstructing the historical context of *Heimat* activities in my field site, I have relied both on local sources and on the secondary literature. The secondary literature is helpful in illuminating the development of the *Heimat* movement and in explaining aspects of institutions that were widely distributed over many local communities, but it is also subject to limitations, as I shall suggest. Restricting our overview to the literature published after World War II and neglecting the remnants of the naively affirmative views of the *Heimat* that were typical of the pre-war era, we can distinguish various schools of thought, which I shall classify, with some oversimplification, as critical, revisionist, and post-critical/post-revisionist. While important differences separate these approaches from one another, they all share assumptions that are problematic from an ethnographic point of view.

The critical view of the *Heimat* movement was developed in the 1970s by scholars who saw it as a manifestation of the German *Sonderweg*, i.e., the "special path" of national development that some historians had attributed to modern German history.[1] In the nineteenth century, it was argued, Germany, while still divided among various kingdoms, principalities, and independent cities, experienced rapid industrialization and commercialization, without, however, the political emancipation of the bourgeoisie, which had accompanied such developments in England, France, and the United States.[2] After the failed revolution of 1848, the weak German bourgeoisie betrayed its liberal principles in celebrating Prussia's victory over France and embracing the authoritarian Bismarckian state of 1871. In the *Heimat* movement, the bourgeoisie resorted to an anti-modern *völkisch* ideology – i.e., nationalist ideology tinged with racism – that served to secure its alliance with reactionary aristocratic and agrarian interests and to suppress further democratization.[3] The idea of *Heimat* was a kind of "internal exoticism," which promoted sentimental local and regional identities, while obscuring underlying social, political, and economic inadequacies and injustices.[4]

In such critical analyses, the *Heimat* and the *Heimat* movement were, evidently, not really the main objects of study; rather, they were treated as symptoms of the main object, namely, of distortions in the political history of the nation – or in the role of the bourgeoisie in the political history of the nation. Ultimately, these critics of all things related to the *Heimat* were seeking an answer to the question of "what went wrong" with Germany in the twentieth century.

Somewhat later, in the 1980s and 1990s, German authors produced new overviews of the *Heimat* movement[5] and several studies devoted to the organization and leadership of the *Heimat* movement in the provinces.[6] These works provided an important empirical basis for research on the topic; but, because they focused on the ideas, organizations, and policies of leading figures, and because they continued to view these leading figures as spokespersons for the bourgeoisie as a whole, they usually confirmed the conclusions of the critical theorists of previous decades.

Also in the 1990s, specialists in German history who were not themselves German rejected or qualified the critical interpretations of the 1970s, offering instead various revisionist arguments; but, while enriching our understanding of the *Heimat* movement in various ways, these authors still shared basic assumptions and concerns with their predecessors, while changing their emphases and evaluations. Some revisionist studies are best understood as reinterpretations less of the *Heimat* movement itself than of the role of the bourgeoisie in modern German history: The *Heimat* movement is still described as being essentially bourgeois in character but the German bourgeoisie is now seen to exhibit liberal or progressive tendencies.[7] In any case, revisionist authors continued to view the *Heimat* movement only in its relation to the larger national project, as in Alon Confino's study of the role of the idea of *Heimat* in mediating, especially for the bourgeoisie, between the heritage of German particularism and the imagined community of the German nation.[8]

Finally, in the latest phase of research on the *Heimat* movement or the broader *Heimat* phenomenon, authors have drawn upon or revised critical or revisionist approaches in empirical studies of regionalism, tourism, consumerism, and related topics.[9]

In attempting to understand 'ordinary' *Heimat* activists at the local level, I have found that social class is an indispensable analytical category but that vague generalizations about the role of the bourgeoisie in national history are not helpful. What is more, studies of leading theorists or organizers are valuable only to a limited degree. Such people *were* influential at the local level, but their influence was often only indirect, being mediated by local contact persons. Their influence was also subject to a kind of metamorphosis, because they exerted it not on a tabula rasa but on attitudes and practices that were born of local circumstances. Therefore, I had to start over with the goal of understanding the meaning of local *Heimat* activism for the activists themselves.

There have been various attempts to characterize the *Heimat* movement in terms of institutional forms,[10] typical activities,[11] or substantive themes.[12] My alternative is to identify three functions of the *Heimat* movement, which, in general terms, may be characterized as (1) resource management, (2) text production, and (3) performance. These general functions correspond to more specific German terms, the appropriateness of which depends on particularities of context: e.g, *Denkmalpflege* (historical preservation), *Heimatschutz* (*Heimat* protection), *Verschönerung* (beautification), *Altertumskunde* (archaeology), *Landesgeschichte* (territorial history), *Heimatforschung* (home town studies), *Brauchtumspflege* (the cultivation of tradition), and so on. Once these functions and their variant forms are identified, the next step is to ask how they have been distributed among social groups or organizations, the members of which serve as active proponents of the cause in question – e.g., offices of provincial or local government, local parishes, schools, philanthropists, or local voluntary associations. The precise social composition of membership in such groups or organizations is a crucial variable in attempts to understand *Heimat* activities at the local level.

Examination of the distribution of the three functions of the *Heimat* movement among active proponents causes one to reject the assumptions underlying much of the secondary literature and to conclude as follows: *Heimat* was not an exclusively bourgeois project; those *Heimat* activists who did belong to the bourgeoisie did not necessarily act in concert; and *Heimat* is best viewed not as an expression of a particular class ideology but as a contested symbol in public discourse, especially with regard to strategies employed in the local politics of inclusion and recognition.

THE SOCIAL AND POLITICAL CONTEXT OF LOCAL *Heimat* ACTIVITIES IN THE LATE NINETEENTH AND EARLY TWENTIETH CENTURIES

In its first thousand years, Boppard – a small town located on the western bank of the Rhine in the rugged, sparsely settled landscape between Koblenz and Bingen – had been a pre-Roman settlement, a fortress on the Roman frontier, and, for a brief period in the High Middle Ages, a free imperial city.[13] Beginning in the fourteenth century, it became a local administrative centre and market place in the Archbishopric of Trier, serving towns and villages on both sides of the Rhine. At the end of the eighteenth century, it had an almost entirely Roman Catholic population, a small patriciate, eleven Jewish households, several monasteries and nunneries, and many tradesman's shops and small vineyards.[14] The arrival of the French in 1794 changed Boppard into a border town but also stimulated growth through the secularization of church properties, the standardization of administrative practices, and the modernization of transportation routes. After much of the Rhineland was awarded to Prussia in the Treaty of Vienna in 1815, the town experienced the rationalization of wine production, the further modernization of the infrastructure (including the building of the railway), the concentration of schools serving the wider vicinity and the development of facilities for the new tourist trade.[15]

In the words of a contemporary commentator, Boppard was, in the mid-nineteenth century, a town "torn by factionalism".[16] The two main camps were, first, the majority of native Roman Catholics, including vintners, gardeners, artisans, shopkeepers, day labourers, and members of a few patrician families; and, second, a small elite of "newcomer" Protestants and liberal Catholics, including especially government officials, members of the free professions, retired officers from the Prussian army, and other well-to-do members of a retirement community that had been promoted by town government since mid-century. The most significant fault-line in local social life was confessional, but it ran right through the Catholic population, dividing the Ultramontanes – Roman Catholics who were loyal to the Pope – from a small group of liberal Catholics, who were allied with the Prussian Protestants.[17]

On the basis of illiberal election laws, the liberal minority gained control of both the mayor's office and the town council in the mid-nineteenth century and held on to power for about four decades.[18] This local elite also set the tone for social and cultural life in the many new clubs and associations typical of that era.[19] Nevertheless, the Ultramontanes had their own leaders, including the parish priest, local business persons, and master artisans; and, by the late 1880s, with increasing rates of participation in local elections and the founding of the *Zentrum*, or the Centre Party, as the chief organizational basis of political Catholicism in the German Reich, it was they who took control of local government.[20] Simultaneously, members of the Roman Catholic faction began playing a more prominent role in local public life. Though tensions between Roman Catholics and liberals remained, the extreme factionalism of the mid-nineteenth century was overcome, as opposed groups began to come to terms with one another, at least to a degree. This partial reconciliation coincided with the advent of the *Heimat* movement.

For the remainder of this chapter, I shall examine two institutional loci of *Heimat* activities in Boppard – the *Verschönerungsverein* (Beautification Society) and the *Nachbarschaften* (neighbourhood associations) – and illustrate their interaction in a description of a remarkable local festival of the year 1921. The Beautification Society – originally an organ of the liberal bourgeoisie and, later, after the Roman Catholic majority's rise to power, of the mixed-confessional local intelligentsia – became one of the chief sites for activities typical of the *Heimat* movement; but Beautification Society members restricted themselves largely to resource management and text production. The neighbourhood associations, on the other hand, were the institutional basis, mainly, though not exclusively, of the local Roman Catholic petit bourgeoisie and working class. They were also active contributors to the celebration of the *Heimat*, though largely through cultural performances, i.e., in ways less visible to post-war critics of the *Heimat* movement. In such local organizations, activists were variously motivated and pursued different goals – all in the name of the *Heimat*.

THE BEAUTIFICATION SOCIETY

The Beautification Society, which is still active today, was founded in 1872 by the town mayor and other leaders of the local liberal faction.[21] Initially, the main concern of Beautification Society members was to dress Boppard up for the role of spa town and pensionopolis by planting trees in the new suburbs inhabited by officials and retirees, building a network of hiking trails in the hills and forests surrounding the town, and transforming the bare river bank into a park where burghers and spa guests could stroll or attend open air concerts.

Towards the turn of the century, the Beautification Society became the local institution through which two new and interrelated programs were introduced into the community: *Denkmalpflege* (historical preservation) and *Heimatschutz* (*Heimat* protection). Both programs were organized at the provincial level, the first in a new state agency and the second in a voluntary association in which the head of the state agency was the driving force.[22] While historical preservation was concerned largely with the architectural monuments of the Roman era, the Middle Ages, and the early modern period, *Heimatschutz* was supposed to protect distinctive landscapes and their fauna and flora, vernacular architecture, and local traditions from the onslaught of modernization and industrialization.[23]

In Boppard, the local contact persons for historical preservation and *Heimatschutz*, respectively, were Eugen Seidel (1862–1930) and Peter Josef Kreuzberg (1875–1839). Both came to this Rhenish town from the outside in order to take leading positions in the local school system; and both became active in the Beautification Society. Although both were Catholic, Seidel's concentration on the town's extensive Roman ruins was consistent with the interests of the liberal bourgeoisie.[24] He did, however, collaborate with local Roman Catholics, who favoured the medieval and baroque periods, in founding the home town museum in 1912.[25] Kreuzberg corresponds more closely to the type known to us from the secondary literature on the *Heimat* movement: in addition to his work as county school inspector and leader of the local Centre Party, he published local *Heimat* literature and launched campaigns for the restoration of half-timber houses and against billboards and speeding.[26] Kreuzberg was the representative of a new generation of *Heimat* enthusiasts, insofar as he espoused a neo-Romantic view of the nation and advocated *völkisch* ideologies, which led him to prefer things Germanic over the classical heritage so cherished by the older bourgeoisie. These differences in orientation also affected activities in support of the *Heimat*, as will be demonstrated in the example given below.

THE NEIGHBOURHOOD ASSOCIATIONS

Originally a liberal haven and later the common ground of educated persons, both liberal and Roman Catholic, the Beautification Society was an institutional centre for activities associated with the *Heimat* movement; but other local institutions lacking the strictly bourgeois character of the Beautification Society were equally important. My example is the neighbourhood associations, the organizational bases of the local petit bourgeoisie and working class.

The territory of the town of Boppard is divided unofficially among a dozen districts, each of which has its own residents' organization, called a *Nachbarschaft* or neighbourhood association. Neighbourhood associations have statutes, voluntary dues-paying members, elected governing bodies, flags and regalia, regular meeting places (in fact, select neighbourhood taverns), annual meetings, and annual festivals. They also provide pallbearers in the event of death within a neighbourhood family – or, more recently, financial assistance on such occasions.

Such neighbourhood associations are typical of many towns and villages of the Middle Rhine Valley.[27] They are generally understood to be traditional institutions that have survived the transition to the modern era, but this view is too simple. While there is documentary evidence of the existence of local organizations referred to as *Nachbarschaften* in the centuries preceding the French Revolution,[28] it is clear that, in the context of the Roman Catholic revival of the mid- to late nineteenth century,[29] the neighbourhood associations were reconstructed on the model of modern voluntary associations and joined the ranks of those groups specializing in the cultivation of local tradition.

In some senses, Boppard's neighbourhood associations, in their revamped form, were (and remain) indigenous equivalents of the Beautification Society, insofar as neighbourhood festivals involved both older and newly elaborated ways of decorating facades, streets, and public places, which, over time, merged with modern attitudes toward historical preservation.[30] Neighbourhood representatives also contribute to local historical studies and to the production of historical documents and texts, especially in the form of neighbourhood chronicles and the *Festschriften* that are produced on special occasions, usually in collaboration with a local historian. But the main contributions of the neighbourhood associations to local cultural life take the form of performances, especially of the type that qualify as the cultivation of tradition.

In Boppard, neighbourhood festivals are generally held to be the very embodiment of tradition. Examination of local documents shows, however, that neighbourhood festivals became more elaborate in the latter nineteenth century, as members of the local Roman Catholic population gained status and became more experienced with modern forms of public expression. In short, neighbourhood festivals became increasingly elaborate ways of making a statement about the presence and importance of Roman Catholic groups within the local community. Still, such statements did not necessarily join together in a harmonious chorus.

As noted, there are about a dozen neighbourhood associations (their numbers have fluctuated with the fission and fusion of existing organizations and the founding of new ones in modern housing developments); and, although the neighbourhoods have been and still are peopled largely by members of the Roman Catholic petit bourgeoisie and working class, they – or especially their elected leaders – have often represented different local factions, which are distinguishable with reference to differences of class (e.g., small business persons versus labourers or employees), political orientation (Centre Party members or Christian Democrats versus Social Democrats), and style of life (characterized by varying degrees of *embourgeoisement*). Therefore, it should come as no surprise that, among these organizations, which supposedly embody local tradition, there is a good deal of rivalry and jockeying for position. For example, representatives of the older neighbourhood associations make conflicting claims regarding the antiquity, historical continuity, and authenticity of their respective organizations – claims that find expression in the ways in which neighbourhood associations celebrate the anniversary of their founding, as in the following case study.

THE FIVE-HUNDREDTH ANNIVERSARY OF THE *Orgelborn-Kirmes*

I close with an example that illustrates the interaction among the various active proponents of the *Heimat* movement in early twentieth-century Boppard, namely, a commemorative event that was held on what was taken to be the five-hundredth anniversary of the founding of a particular neighbourhood festival. The example in question concerns the festival of two closely allied neighbourhood associations (which have recently merged), namely, the Upper and Lower Town Square Neighbourhoods, located in the town centre on the site of the (former) town hall and the Roman Catholic parish church. The Town Square Neighbourhoods, which many consider to be the oldest and most prestigious neighbourhood associations in Boppard, have been led by prominent members of the indigenous Roman Catholic petit bourgeoisie for the last two centuries.[31] Their annual festival, the *Orgelborn-Kirmes*, held on the third Monday after Pentecost, is a colourful event featuring a procession from the centrally located neighbourhoods to a nunnery on the outskirts of town, a picnic with music and children's games in the nunnery's garden, and the performance of a siege parody, which is supposed to recall the festival's early history, on a rocky ledge above the garden.[32]

The Town Square Neighbourhoods' special anniversary celebration, featuring allusions to Germany's grand past, was held in 1921, while this town in the recently defeated German nation was still subject to French occupation;[33] therefore, one might be tempted to view it as an expression of nationalist sentiment. Indeed, it may, by that time, have acquired supplementary nationalist tones; but, since the idea to celebrate this anniversary was first publicized just after the turn of the century,[34] it must also be seen in the context of contemporaneous local political developments, namely, the empowerment of the Roman Catholic majority and the rise to new prominence of local Roman Catholics and their organizations.

The five-hundredth anniversary of the *Orgelborn-Kirmes* was, then, initiated and hosted by the leaders of the local small-business class, who doubled as local political leaders; and it was attended by many prominent guests.[35] Because the history of the festival provided the *raison d'être* for the celebration, both the planning and staging of it were accompanied by representations of that history. Remarkably, however, two contradictory versions of the festival's history were presented publicly, with, it is true, no indication on the part of participants that anybody had contradicted anybody else.

Different versions of the history of the festival were presented, first, by neighbourhood representatives themselves and, second, by the leading amateur local historian of the day – Peter Josef Kreuzberg, the school inspector and local agent of *Heimatschutz*. Neighbourhood representatives gave expression to their version in two different forms: in a text about the origins of the festival, published in the local newspaper in 1905; and in an historical parade, held during the festival in 1921.

The author of the newspaper article was Fritz Stammer, the owner of a family haberdashery, an active member of the Centre Party, the chair of the Catholic lay council, and president and chronicler of the Upper Town Square Neighbourhood. Citing texts written by the Ultramontane local historians of the mid-nineteenth century, Stammer traced the Town Square festival back to privileges granted to the neighbourhood by a local nunnery.[36] On this basis, he concluded that the festival was founded in 1420 and would be five-hundred years old in 1920. The siege parody, he surmised – this time with direct reference to a well-known local chronicle – was a somewhat later addition which originated in the so-called Bopparder War of 1498, an event marking the definitive loss of municipal autonomy and the consolidation of the authority of the Archbishop of Trier. By linking the siege parody to Boppard's loss of autonomy, Stammer (like the earlier local historians on whom he draws) was suggesting that the modern neighbourhood associations are descended from medieval corporations that had shared in the sovereignty of the free city.

Stammer's attempt to link today's neighbourhood associations with privileged medieval corporations – dubious by the standards of historical scholarship – was also a central theme in the historical parade. Planned and organized by several neighbourhood committees, the historical parade featured costumed groups from different periods of Boppard's history, beginning with the tenth-century emperor, Otto II, who is known to have awarded extensive privileges to the town and, by implication, to the neighbourhoods within it. Thus, the rhetoric of the parade reproduced or reinvented the favourite Roman Catholic themes of the mid-nineteenth century, according to which sovereign local institutions that were medieval in origin had been violated by Trier and, subsequently, by France, Prussia, and the Allies.[37]

The second version of the history of the *Orgelborn-Kirmes* was a text by Kreuzberg that was published in a *Festschrift* and distributed to festival guests.[38] Kreuzberg's assignment to write this text is an early example of a dilemma that is typical of local communities throughout Germany even today. Local organizations, celebrating their own traditions, invite members of the local intelligentsia to lend them legitimacy by holding a speech about their history. It is assumed that these amateur local historians will cooperate in presenting an image of the organization that corresponds to its own self-image; but there are at least two difficulties, both of which stem from social obligation that the local historian has vis-à-vis others, inside and outside of the community. First, amateur local historians aspire for recognition in the eyes not only of a single local client but of the community as a whole. Confirming the self-understanding of one group may be offensive to another, for example, when multiple neighbourhood associations claim to be the oldest and most traditional, as is the case in Boppard. Second, amateur local historians are involved not only in local networks but in networks at the provincial level, which link them to historians in state archives or officials in the field of historical preservation. Therefore, they must not only satisfy particular local clients, or reconcile conflicting demands of various local clients; they must also take steps to maintain their credibility with officials at the provincial level.[39]

As it turned out, Kreuzberg was not willing simply to confirm the self-understanding of members of the Town Square Neighbourhoods. Instead, he propagated his own views (which, when judged by today's standards, are no more convincing than the neighbourhoods'); but he did it without openly offending his clients. After reviewing the various locally espoused theories of the medieval and early modern origins of the neighbourhood associations and their festivals, Kreuzberg offered a kind of reinterpretation that was popular among fellow members of provincial *Heimatschutz* organizations but new to local historical studies, namely, one based on the Germanic mythology of the Brothers Grimm, as developed by two of their successors, Wilhelm Mannhardt and Karl Simrock. He noted that none of the dates proposed for the festival's origin could be substantiated conclusively by documentary evidence; but he concluded that this was irrelevant, since the neighbourhoods were really much older than they claimed to be. The tales of medieval origins were, according to Kreuzberg, merely the "historic garb" of customs that had been passed down over the centuries since the very dawn of the Germanic peoples. The story of the fifteenth century Bopparder War between the freedom-loving town dwellers and a nearby usurper, which was supposed to account for the origins of neighbourhood traditions, really symbolized the ancient Germanic notion of the eternal struggle between summer and winter; thus, the neighbourhood festival was originally and remained essentially a celebration of the summer solstice.[40]

Kreuzberg's views of the origins of the *Orgelborn-Kirmes* seem to justify the critical theorist's interpretation of the *Heimat* movement. After all, he drew on what was then a common trope in nationalist rhetoric[41] in order to emphasize national homogeneity (by dismissing historical details as irrelevant) and promote national unity (by reducing social conflict to harmless natural cycles). This, one might argue, served the conservative goal of *Sammlung* – integration in a coalition of classes, supported by all classes but serving the interest of only the most powerful ones.[42] I do not intend to reject this interpretation out of hand; rather, I am suggesting that it is not the whole story. The elements that are missing from the critical interpretation of the *Heimat* movement can be conveyed in one general point and two specific points, neither of which is addressed adequately by the revisionist historians.

The general point is that participants in local *Heimat* activities did not speak with a single voice, and they usually did not make statements that can be grasped solely in terms of national-level politics. Rather, such activities had various meanings, the most important of which – the most important for local participants, that is – must be understood in terms of local social relations.

The first specific point is that the *Orgelborn-Kirmes* was an expression, first and foremost, not of *Sammlung*, an insidious program of manipulative national elites, but of the local politics of inclusion and recognition. In speculating on the origins of the *Orgelborn-Kirmes* in the local newspaper and in staging the five-hundredth anniversary celebration, the leaders of the Town Square Neighbourhoods were saying, to paraphrase their message as simply as possible, "We are here, we have rights, our rights have strong historical precedents, and we have to be taken into account." This message was delivered in a symbolic language that was common to the *Heimat* movement as a whole, but it is inaudible to the critical theorists, because they have not reconstructed the local contexts that must be reconstructed if statements made in this language are to be registered, let alone deciphered.

The second specific point is that, at the local level, not even expressions of nationalist ideology, such as Kreuzberg's text, can be understood solely in terms of *Sammlung*; rather, they must also be seen in terms of local forms of diplomacy serving to ameliorate local conflicts of various kinds, for example, between representatives of different social classes or of rival organizations. Class conflict is writ large in critical interpretations of the *Heimat* movement, as well it should be; but analysis of class relations must be embedded in adequately reconstructed local contexts, if it is to be helpful. In the cultural life of German local communities, class relations often take the form of an opposition between *Akademiker* (the highly educated) and those with only a vocational education. Modifying a concept borrowed from Karl Marx, we might characterize the crucial difference between social classes in Boppard in terms of variable access to the "means of cultural production." Activists in the Town Square Neighbourhoods were and remain free to develop and propagate their own views of the history of their organizations; but as shopkeepers, artisans, and employees, they had or have only limited access to the means of cultural production, i.e., their theories lack an authoritative "stamp of approval." Kreuzberg, on the other hand, was a graduate of a teachers college, a high ranking official in the county school system, and the author of many published works, who thus enjoyed privileged access to the means of cultural production. This is still true of amateur local historians in Boppard today, most of whom have advanced degrees in the humanities or social sciences.

Given this disparity in access to the means of cultural production among neighbourhood activists and members of the local intelligentsia, contradictory representations of local history may potentially cause problems. But they do not, neither in the case of the five-hundredth anniversary of the *Orgelborn-Kirmes* nor in the many similar cases with which I am familiar. Why not? Because local ceremonial life, despite the differences of class, confession, geographical origins, political orientation, or social faction that separate one person or group from another, is based on a particularly opaque etiquette, which critical theorists mistake for sentimental unanimity. Local organizations honour amateur local historians by inviting them to hold speeches at special events and to write texts for *Festschriften*. Amateur local historians then return the favour by living up to the expectations of local organizations or by expressing contradictions diplomatically. Thus, Kreuzberg's history of the *Orgelborn-Kirmes* was not only an expression of nationalist ideology. It also served, first, to soften his contradiction of the neighbours' self-image by affirming the extreme antiquity of their traditions and, second, to help him maintain his neutrality in local disagreements about which neighbourhood was the oldest – for, in his reading, all neighbourhoods were equally old, insofar as they were all derived from a common Germanic heritage. Kreuzberg was able to "pull off" this rhetorical sleight-of-hand on the basis of his acknowledged position as an authoritative local historian.

Nevertheless, Kreuzberg's interpretation of the festival's history did not become hegemonic in local public life; rather, it merely floated freely in local discourse as one alternative among others. Local neighbourhood associations that celebrated the six-hundredth anniversary of their founding in 1928 and in 1930 stuck to their own views of medieval origins;[43] and, during subsequent celebrations of the *Orgelborn-Kirmes*, Town Square neighbours merely repeated their views of 1905 and 1921, ignoring Kreuzberg's contribution.[44]

What *Heimat* Means

I have argued that it is impossible to impose a single political meaning on *Heimat* – specifically, that *Heimat* is not born out of bourgeois ideology or of the need to mediate between the local world of experience and the imagined community of the nation, but out of local processes of coming to terms among various groups with contradictory claims to the shared home town. If, however, understanding the *Heimat* movement depends on paying attention to local circumstances, which are by definition highly particular, can the lessons learned in a case study be generalized beyond the particular locale in question? Certainly, they can.

The conflicts between liberals and Roman Catholics, which were so important in setting the scene for *Heimat* activities in Boppard, were neither universal nor unique in late nineteenth and early twentieth century Germany. Similar conditions pertained in much of the Prussian Rhineland, a largely Roman Catholic region that had been incorporated into a state ruled by a Protestant dynasty. Even in those regions where local life was structured by other social distinctions, however, variable yet comparable dynamics were necessarily in play.

By 1900, German society was divided among opposed camps, in the terminology of some social historians, which were characterized by a combination of socio-economic, confessional, and cultural differences. These grand societal groupings, which included the aristocracy, the liberal bourgeoisie, Roman Catholics, and the working class, may be characterized in terms of distinctive ideologies, social milieus, cultural activities, and political parties.[45] In the case study that I have presented, the main opposition was between the liberal bourgeoisie and Roman Catholics; but in another project, set in an agricultural and industrial region in Saxony, south of Leipzig, the main conflicts of the early twentieth century were those between middle-class family farmers who supported bourgeois political parties and industrial workers (railroaders, coal miners, workers in power plants and in the chemical industry) who were integrated in the labour movement, unions, and the Social Democratic or Communist Party.[46] Each of these groups had its own local organizations and its own ways of expressing its relation to its local surroundings – through resource management, text production, and performances; and investigation along these lines reveals dynamics that are quite different from but still comparable to those in the Prussian Rhine Province.

Whether local conflicts are framed in terms of an opposition between liberals and Roman Catholics or between farmers and industrial workers, in each case, local social relations will, predictably, be characterized by struggles for inclusion, participation, and recognition. In this sense, the critical theorists may have provided us with an important key to understanding the *Heimat* movement, without having realized it. Hermann Bausinger – since the late 1950s, a distinguished scholar in the field of *Volkskunde* (folk cultural studies) or *empirische Kulturwissenschaft* (empirical cultural science), to employ his own neologism – was also a leader in articulating the critical view of the *Heimat* movement. Writing in the 1970s, however, at the culmination of a process of liberalization and democratization that had changed West German society profoundly, Bausinger heralded the arrival of a "new wave" of *Heimat* sentiment, one in which the old contradiction between *Heimat* and democracy seemed to have been overcome:

Heimat and the open society are no longer mutually exclusive. *Heimat* [may now be understood] as appropriation and reconstruction, undertaken cooperatively; ... as an intimate world to which one may make one's own contribution, a world which provides security, ... a humanely constructed environment.[47]

In my analysis, this understanding of the "new wave" of *Heimat* corresponds to the historical reality of early twentieth-century *Heimat* activities in Boppard with one important difference. From the very beginning, *Heimat* activists were intent on appropriating and reconstructing their town. What was missing, or what was almost available and then lost, was a political and legal system that protected the rights of all suppressed groups – not only Roman Catholics but Jews and others as well – to make the town their home. We can argue about who was to blame; but such arguments should not blur our perception of what was actually happening in local communities.

NOTES

1. Cf. Bergmann.
2. Cf. Wehler; Blackbourn and Eley.
3. Kramer (1973, 1981).
4. Bausinger, 20.
5. Klueting.
6. Cf. Christiansen; Steensen; Ditt (1988); Hartung.
7. Cf. Applegate; Rollins.
8. Confino (1993; 1997).
9. Cf. Johler, Nikitsch, and Tschofen; Schramm; Murdock.
10. Bausinger, 17.
11. Ditt (1989).
12. Applegate, 63–103; Confino (1993), 50.
13. Heyen.
14. Klein, 160–172; Burkard and Thill, 34; Maier.
15. Mißling/Korn, 13–70.
16. Schüller, 272.
17. In the mid- to late nineteenth century, there were about fourteen Jewish households in Boppard, made up of 70 to 80 individuals – under two percent of the total local population. Mostly involved in shop keeping and commerce, Jewish families were gradually integrated into local social life, at least to a degree, as a result of political emancipation (made law in 1869) and increasing prosperity (Burkard and Thill, 50–59). Jewish household heads were members of voluntary associations favoured by the liberal bourgeoisie (e.g., the so-called *Casino*) but also belonged to the neighbourhood associations (Kreuzberg and Ledebur, 35; Pauly [1990]; Burkard and Thill, 67–69). Jewish children were disproportionately represented in higher schools for boys and girls, including the Roman Catholic schools (Burkard and Thill, 59–66). From the turn of the century until 1933, when Jews in Boppard suffered the same fate as others throughout Germany, their numbers rose to about 100. Given the small size of their community, Jews did not figure decisively in the kinds of factional struggles described in this chapter.
18. Mißling/Korn, 101–114, 127–141.
19. Dann.
20. Mißling/Korn, 141–144; cf. Blackbourn (1987).
21. Stollenwerk.
22. Clemen; Kreuzberg (1913); cf. Speitkamp; Koshar.
23. Speitkamp; Rollins.
24. Benner, 2.
25. Eidson (2000).
26. Kreuzberg (1913, 1925); Benner, 31.
27. Zender; Ruland.

[28] Maier, 445–448.
[29] Hegel, 378–395; Sperber.
[30] Eidson (1990, 2000).
[31] Pauly, 197–245.
[32] Pauly, 211–223.
[33] Mißling/Korn, 158–162.
[34] Stammer.
[35] M. (1921); Pauly, 232–237.
[36] Stammer.
[37] Eidson (2000).
[38] I mention only briefly a complication in the organization of the five-hundredth anniversary celebration that explains the discrepancy between the date of the published festschrift and the date of the festival. The Upper and Lower Town Square Neighbourhoods alternated, year for year, in hosting the *Orgelborn-Kirmes*; and, as a result, the anniversary celebration was, in some ways, spread over two years. Kreuzberg's festschrift was published under the auspices of the Upper Town Square Neighbourhood in 1920, and the historical parade was hosted by the Lower Town Square Neighbourhood in 1921.
[39] Eidson (2005).
[40] Kreuzberg (1920).
[41] Weber-Kellermann and Bimmer (1985), 34–41.
[42] Cf. Wehler; Blackbourn and Eley (1984).
[43] Eidson (1990), 370.
[44] Cf. Vorstand der Untermärkter Nachbarschaft.
[45] Lepsius; Adam and Bramke.
[46] Eidson (1998); cf. Retallack.
[47] Bausinger, 23.

REFERENCES

Adam, Thomas, and Bramke, Werner (eds.). (1999), *Milieukonzept und empirische Forschung*. Theme issue of *Comparativ: Leipziger Beiträge zur Universalgeschichte und vergleichenden Gesellschaftsforschung* Vol. 9 (2).

Applegate, Celia (1990), *A Nation of Provincials: The German Idea of Heimat*. Berkeley, CA: University of California Press.

Bausinger, Hermann (1984), "Auf dem Wege zu einem neuen, aktiven Heimatverständnis: Begriffsgeschichte als Problemgeschichte", in: Hans-Georg Wehling (ed.), *Heimat Heute*, Stuttgart: W. Kohlhammer, 11–27.

Benner, Ferdinand (1992), *Bopparder Persönlichkeiten*, Boppard: Verkehrs- und Verschönerungsverein (mimeograph).

Bergmann, Klaus (1970), *Agrarromantik und Großstadtfeindschaft*, Meisenheim am Glan: Verlag Anton Hain.

Blackbourn, David (1987), "Catholics and Politics in Imperial Germany: The Centre Party and its Constituency", *Populists and Patricians: Essays in Modern German History*, London; Boston: Allen & Unwin, 188–214.

Blackbourn, David and Eley, Geoff (1984), *The Peculiarities of German History: Bour-*

geois Society and Politics in Nineteenth-Century Germany, Oxford: Oxford University Press.

Burkard, Karl-Josef and Thill, Hildburg-Helene (1996), *Unter den Juden: achthundert Jahre Juden in Boppard*, Boppard: Dausner Verlag.

Christiansen, Jörn (1980), *"Die Heimat": Analyse einer regionalen Zeitschrift und ihres Umfeldes*, Neumünster: Karl Wachholtz Verlag.

Clemen, Paul (1896), *Die Denkmalspflege in der Rheinprovinz*, Düsseldorf: L. Schwann.

Confino, Alon (1993), "The Nation as a Local Metaphor: Heimat, National Memory und the German Empire 1871–1918", *History und Memory* Vol. 5, 1, 42–86.

– (1997), *The Nation as a Local Metaphor*, Chapel Hill, NC: University of North Carolina Press.

Dann, Otto (ed.) (1984), *Vereinswesen und bürgerliche Gesellschaft in Deutschland*, Munich: R. Oldenbourg.

Ditt, Karl (1988), *Raum und Volkstum: Die Kulturpolitik des Provinzialverbandes Westfalen 1923–1945*, Münster: Aschendorff.

– (1989), "Vom Heimatverein zur Heimatbewegung: Westfalen 1875–1915", *Westfälische Forschungen*, Vol. 39: 232–255.

Eidson, John R. (1990), "German Club Life as a Local Cultural System", *Comparative Studies in Society and History*, Vol. 32, 2, 357–382.

– (1998), "Funde aus dem Archiv: Einblicke in die Geschichte von Breunsdorf auf Basis ausgewählter Schriftquellen der letzten hundertfünfzig Jahre", *Südraum Journal 5: Die Arbeit der Archäologen – Breunsdorf* (theme issue), Rötha and Espenhain: Christliches Umweltseminar Rötha/Kulturbüro Espenhain, 95–104.

– (2000), "Which Past for Whom? Local Memory in a German Community During the Era of Nation Building", *Ethos*, Vol. 28, 4, 575–607. (Theme issue on "Subjectivity in History," edited by Geoffrey White.)

– (2005), "Between Heritage and Countermemory: Varieties of Historical Representation in a West German Community", *American Ethnologist*, Vol. 32, 4, 556–575.

Hartung, Werner (1991), *Konservative Zivilisationskritik und regionale Identität. Am Beispiel der niedersächsischen Heimatbewegung 1895 bis 1919*, Veröffentlichungen der Historischen Kommission für Niedersachsen und Bremen 10, Hannover: Hahn.

Hegel, Eduard (1979), "Die katholische Kirche in den Rheinlanden 1815–1945", in: Franz Petri and Georg Droege (eds.), *Rheinische Geschichte. Vol. III. Wirtschaft und Kultur im 19. und 20. Jahrhundert*, Düsseldorf: Schwann, 329–412.

Heyen, Franz-Josef (1956), *Reichsgut im Rheinland: Die Geschichte des königlichen Fiskus Boppard*, Bonn: L. Röhrscheid.

Johler, Reinhard; Nikitsch, Herbert; and Tschofen, Bernhard (1995), *Schönes Österreich: Heimatschutz zwischen Ästhetik und Ideologie*, Vienna: Österreichisches Museum für Volkskunde.

Klein [Josef] (1909), *Geschichte von Boppard*, Boppard: Dr. Keil's Buchhandlung (Bruno Piwowarski).

Klueting, Edeltraud (ed.) (1991), *Antimodernismus und Reform: Zur Geschichte der deutschen Heimatbewegung*, Darmstadt: Wissenschaftliche Buchgesellschaft.

Koshar, Rudy (1998), *Germany's Transient Pasts: Preservation and National Memory in the Twentieth Century*, Chapel Hill, NC: University of North Carolina Press.

Kramer, Dieter (1973), "Die politische und ökonomische Funktionalisierung von 'Heimat' im deutschen Imperialismus und Faschismus", *Diskurs*, Vol. 6, 7, 3–22.

- (1981), "Die Provokation Heimat", *Zeitschrift für Sozialistische Politik und Wirtschaft*, Vol. 13, 32–40.
Kreuzberg, Bernhard Josef and von Ledebur, Alkmar (eds.) (1989), *Aus dem alten Boppard: Eine fortlaufende Chronik für die Jahre 1855 bis 1876 von Wilhelm Schlad*, Boppard: Rheindruck.
Kreuzberg, Peter Josef (1913), "Denkmalpflege und Heimatschutz in ihrer Beziehung zur Lehrerbildung", *Blätter für preußische Lehrerbildung*, Vol. 6, 151–158, 182–187.
- (1920), *Die Orgelbornskirmes: Ein Gedenkblatt zum fünfhundertjährigen Bestehen im Jahre 1920*, Boppard: H. Conrad.
- (ed) (1925), *Der Kreis St. Goar: Ein Heimatbuch*, Boppard: A. Zimmermann.
Lepsius, M. Rainer (1966), "Parteiensystem und Sozialstruktur: Zum Problem der Demokratisierung der deutschen Gesellschaft", in: Wilhelm Abel (ed.), *Wirtschaft, Geschichte und Wirtschaftsgeschichte. Festschrift zum 65. Geburtstag von Friedrich Lütge*, Stuttgart: G. Fischer., 371–393.
M. [Maisel, Otto] (1921), "500 Jahre Orgelbornkirmes", *Bopparder Zeitung*, June 4, Vol. 55, 66, 1–2.
Maier, Franz (1997), "Boppard in der frühen Neuzeit", in: Heinz E. Mißling (ed.), *Boppard: Geschichte einer Stadt am Mittelrhein. Vol. I. Von der Frühzeit bis zum Ende der kurfürstlichen Herrschaft*, Boppard: Dausner Verlag, 413–511.
Mißling, Heinz E. (ed.) (1994), *Boppard: Geschichte einer Stadt am Mittelrhein. Vol. II. Bruno Korn. Von der französischen Revolution bis zum Ende des Zweiten Weltkrieges (1789–1945)*. Mit einem Beitrag von Karl-Josef Burkhard [sic], Boppard: Dausner Verlag.
Murdock, Caitlin E. (2007), "Tourist Landscapes and Regional Identities in Saxony, 1878–1938", *Central European History*, Vol. 40, 4, 589–621.
Pauly, Ferdinand (1990), *Beiträge zur Geschichte der Stadt Boppard. Vol. II. Die Nachbarschaften*, Boppard: Rheindruck.
Retallack, James (ed.) (2000), *Saxony in German History: Culture, Society, and Politics, 1830–1933*, Ann Arbor, MI: University of Michigan Press.
Rollins, William (1997), *A Greener Vision of Home: Cultural Politics and Environmental Reform in the German Heimatschutz Movement 1904–1918*, Ann Arbor, MI: University of Michigan Press.
Ruland, Josef (1964), *Nachbarschaft und Gemeinschaft in Dorf und Stadt: Ihre Formen auf dem Vorderhunsrück, auf dem Maifeld und in der Stadt Andernach*, Düsseldorf: Rheinland Verlag.
Schramm, Manuel (2002), *Konsum und regionale Identität in Sachsen 1880–2000*, Stuttgart: Franz Steiner.
Schüller, Andreas (1936), "Pfarrer Jean Baptiste Berger (1806–1888)", *Pastor Bonus: Zeitschrift für kirchliche Wissenschaft und Praxis*, Vol. 47, 8/9, 263–273; 10, 310–316; 11/12, 345–353.
Speitkamp, Winfried (1996), *Die Verwaltung der Geschichte: Denkmalpflege und Staat in Deutschland 1871–1933*, Göttingen: Vandenhoeck & Ruprecht.
Sperber, Jonathan (1984), *Popular Catholicism in Nineteenth-Century Germany*, Princeton, NJ: Princeton University Press.
Stammer, Friedrich (1905), "Das Orgelbornsfest", *Bopparder Zeitung*, No. 76, July 1.
Steensen, Thomas (1986), *Die friesische Bewegung in Nordfriesland im 19. und 20. Jahrhundert (1879–1945)*, Neumünster: Karl Wachholtz.

Stollenwerk, Alexander (1972), "Die wechselvolle Geschichte des Bopparder Verkehrs- und Verschönerungsvereins", *Rund um Boppard: Lokale Wochenzeitung und amtliches Bekanntmachungsorgan*, No. 24, 25, 26, 27, 28, 30, 32, 33, 34, 37, and 40.

Vorstand der Untermärkter Nachbarschaft (1956), "536 Jahre Orgelbornkirmes", *Rund um Boppard: Lokale Wochenzeitung und amtliches Bekanntmachungsorgan*, No. 23, June 9.

Weber-Kellermann, Ingeborg, and Bimmer, Andreas C. (1985), *Einführung in die Volkskunde/europäische Ethnologie: eine Wissenschaftsgeschichte.* 2nd rev. ed., Stuttgart: J. B. Metzlersche Verlagsbuchhandlung.

Wehler, Hans-Ulrich (1973), *Das deutsche Kaiserreich 1871–1918*, Göttingen: Vandenhoeck & Ruprecht.

Zender, Matthias (1960), "Gestalt und Wandel der Nachbarschaft im Rheinland", in: Max Braubach, Franz Petri, and Leo Weisgerber (eds.), *Aus Geschichte und Landeskunde: Forschungen und Darstellungen. Franz Steinbach zum 65. Geburtstag gewidmet*, Bonn: Röhrscheid, 502–534

Transports of Delight and the Migration of the Genius Loci

Ian Thompson

The notion of the *genius loci*, often translated as the "spirit of the place" has its origins in antiquity. The Greeks and the Romans practised a form of animism, believing that places, like people, had inner spirits which determined their outer character. In the eighteenth century landscape designers and their patrons latched on to the concept of the *genius loci* and it became central to the philosophy of the English Landscape School. In his *Epistle to Lord Burlington* (1731),[1] Alexander Pope gave the following advice:

> To build, to plant, whatever you intend,
> To rear the Column or the Arch to bend,
> To swell the Terras or to sink the Grot;
> In all, let Nature never be forgot.
> Consult the *Genius of the Place* in all…

The principle here is that to design well the landscape gardener must enter into a conversation with the in-dwelling spirit of the place. Writing for landscape architects, toward the end of the twentieth century, Tom Turner called the injunction to consult the *genius loci* the "Single Agreed Rule of Landscape Architecture".[2] *Genius loci* has also played a prominent role in architectural theory, where it was employed by Christian Norberg-Schulz as the cornerstone of his architectural phenomenology.[3]

In a period of widespread anxiety about globalisation and its corrosive effect upon local cultures, communities and landscapes and upon vernacular traditions of building, concern for the *genius loci* offers a rallying point for resistance, but even its supporters admit that the concept is vague, while those of a positivist persuasion are apt to dismiss it as so much mumbo-jumbo. I do not want to devote this paper to a defence of the *genius loci*— I have attempted this elsewhere[4] – but rather to examine some of the problems inherent in the concept when it is considered in the context of the contemporary consensus whereby the world is seen as a complex, even chaotic, interweaving of flows. However it may be conceived, for *genius loci* to have any use or value, it must represent at least relative stability amid these swirls and eddies.

What I intend to do in the rest of the paper is to take various conceptions of the *genius loci* and to test them in a form of thought experiment against various scenarios involving change. These interpretations will be drawn from a paper entitled "Can Spirit of Place Be a Guide to Ethical Building?" by the environmental philosopher Isis Brook.[5] They range from mystical or quasi-religious notions of indwelling beings, pantheistic manifestations and placeminds, to more commonplace ideas of character, distinctiveness and narrative.

The scenarios of change I wish to consider are as follows:
1. Human migration. What happens to the *genius loci* of a particular place when a large number of people from a different culture settle there? There are really two questions here: what is the effect of the inward migration upon the existing *genius loci*? And, to what extent is *genius loci* portable? Can the migrants, in some sense, bring their *genius loci* with them? And, if so, what happens when the two *genii* meet?
2. Traumatic economic change. What I have in mind here is the sort of rapid change involved in industrialisation or, conversely, de-industrialisation, which can alter the face of a landscape within a generation. The question is not whether *genius loci* is portable, but whether it is malleable? Can it change, and, if so, how much change can be accommodated without the concept becoming meaningless?

It is important to keep in mind that it is conceptual interpretations that are being tested. This is not a piece of empirical sociology, although it may prompt sociological questions. I will not follow the same order that the various interpretations of *genius loci* are presented in Brook's article, but begin by looking at those interpretations which seem to call for more extensive religious or metaphysical commitments, before considering those which make more modest claims. I have also simplified Brook's list, omitting some of the interpretations (Essence, Energy Fields) which seemed obscure or unpromising.

ABODE OF SPECIAL BEINGS

In Western culture the concept of *genius loci* can be traced back to the Greeks and the Romans who believed that certain special places were inhabited by gods, goddesses or nature-spirits such as dryads and naiads. Animistic beliefs are found in many cultures. In Shinto, for instance, there are nature spirits known as *kami* which inhabit (among other things) trees, rocks, rivers and mountains. The places where these being dwell are regarded as sacred. Before approaching a Shinto shrine, for example, believers must first purify themselves by washing. If we hold a belief that the landscape is inhabited by beings with personalities, and moreover, that these beings may have powers to influence the course of our lives, we are likely to treat their dwelling places with reverence. Such beliefs suggest that there may be two categories of landscapes – those which are inhabited by resident deities and the rest which are not. We might even imagine a map of the earth where the realms of the deities glow like little pools of light, but the rest is unenchanted and can thus be treated in any way we like.

In a practical sense, beliefs in such beings may have some conservation value, in a patchy sort of way, at least as long as they remain strong. One of the ironies of contemporary Japan is that a culture with a highly aestheticised attitude towards landscape has nevertheless presided over the catastrophic destruction of aesthetic value in the name of modernisation and progress.[6] Secular values have little room for enchantment. A belief in animistic spirits will be anathema to secularists as well as to many religious believers who might consider it heretical. On the other hand, many of those who invoke the deities of place do so in a poetic or metaphorical way, without believing in the actual existence of such beings.

With regard to the first of the two thought experiments, it is possible to imagine that a goddess or a nymph might decide to change her abode. At first sight, there does not seem to be a conceptual difficulty about a deity migrating and re-settling along with those by whom it is revered, though it would, of course, then become the spirit of a different place, but when we try to think this through problems soon arise. Would the abandoned place be left without a spirit or would a different one take up residence? Would the migrating spirit be welcome anywhere else? Can we assume that she would look for a similar place? If the whole world were truly enchanted, would not all the best places already be taken and might this not lead to conflict in the faery realm?

Research into human migration has shown that migrant populations often have complex ideas of home. Leah Garrett, for example, has shown that for many Diaspora Jews the idea of home as the "here-and-now" is shadowed by the idea of "not-yet-home" and a sideward glance towards Eretz Yisrael, the biblical Land of Israel.[7] From an anthropological perspective, it would be interesting to know what actually happens to the beliefs of animists when they become migrants. Do they leave their native gods behind in what might, in some sense, still be regarded as their true home? Even if we think all this talk of spirits is fanciful, these difficulties do mirror some of the real problems faced by migrant populations. The power of mythology is that it illuminates aspects of the human condition.

When we come to the second thought experiment, there initially does not seem to be any conceptual problem in imagining a deity being driven out of its abode by the encroaching bulldozers, nor of such a being returning to a landscape that has been suitably restored. Once again, however, it requires the imagination of a story-teller to explain where the deity might lodge in the meantime. If the reclamation is done badly will the faery ever return? If it is done well, but the place created is different does a different spirit take up residence, and, if so, where does it come from? Thinking in this way soon deposits us back into the coils of myth.

PANPSYCHISM AND PANTHEISM

Panpsychism is the doctrine that all things, including those which we would usually consider to be inanimate, like rocks or mountains, have their own form of consciousness, from which it might follow, if we extend the same sorts of arguments made by advocates of animal-rights that they have rights and that we owe them duties. Though James Lovelock would probably distance himself from such a view, one of his prominent followers, the ecologist Stephan Harding, advocated just such a worldview in his book *Animate Earth*.[8]

This interpretation of *genius loci* offers us an advantage over the "resident deities" view, in that it offers complete, rather than patchy, coverage of the whole landscape, though this in turn presents another difficulty if we want to distinguish between places that are somehow special and those that have no extraordinary qualities. There are also difficulties, as Brook points out, in imagining how all these individual mind-like qualities – of every rock, plant or paving slab – can come together to form a sort of "placemind", but suggests an analogy based upon the relationship between human individuals and the groups to which they might belong.

Pantheism, on the other hand, predicates a single deity of which the whole of nature is a manifestation. God and the universe are ultimately identical. The *genius loci* must then be considered as a local materialisation of the divine. Again, there is nothing patchy about the coverage, but problems appear when we consider landscapes which appear to be debased or ugly. How can these be aspects of God?

Both panpsychism and pantheism seem to offer rooted versions of the *genius loci*. In the case of the former, it is hard to see how a placemind could migrate. Human migrants would leave the *genius loci* behind (changed, perhaps, because they themselves were no longer part of it). If they settled elsewhere, that place would already have its own placemind, but presumably it could be altered by the settlers, who themselves would become elements within it. In the pantheistic case, an omnipresent God would never need to migrate. The idea of transporting the *genius loci* from one place to another would be meaningless.

Panpsychism places duties of respect upon humans while pantheism adds a duty of reverence. In both cases human beings are constrained in the ways in which they can treat their surroundings, which make these ideas interesting from the viewpoint of environmental ethics. Both views seem to contain a presumption against environmental change brought about by humans. At the very least, before altering anything humans should enter into the sort of dialogue envisaged in Pope's *Epistle*. In the case of pantheism, perhaps this would involve some form of prayer. In the absence of such communion, it is possible to see how a placemind might disintegrate in the event of traumatic disturbance, and how such disturbance might anger a pantheistic God and be regarded as sacrilegious by a pantheist. However, neither set of beliefs is completely closed against all change. We can see how *genius loci* as placemind might maintain its integrity if changes are gradual and not overwhelming. A parallel could be drawn here with a human group, a choir, for example, or a committee, whose overall character depends upon the personalities of its members and the chemistry of their interactions. Such groupings maintain their integrity despite the coming and going of individual members. It would be presumptuous to imagine how a pantheistic God might react to local change. Presumably He might not be angered by minor changes, but this is a matter of interpretation and degree. Many of us might sympathise with Wordsworth, who had strongly pantheistic leanings and was outraged by the prospect of a railway being driven through the heart of the Lake District – but the poet could also be troubled by the moving of a single boulder or the felling of a tree. This form of pantheism leads directly to a very conservative version of landscape conservation.

ECOSYSTEM

Many of the metaphors which originated in ecological science seem to have the potential to illuminate the idea of *genius loci*. There is the word "ecology" itself, which takes the Greek word for "household" or "home" as its root. Then there is the organic metaphor which suggests that species relate to their environments in the way that organs are related to a body. There is also the community metaphor and the notion of the "climax community", a sort of superorganism characterised by stability, unity, balance and health. Through all of these runs the idea that places are more than the sums of their parts – it is the way the parts work together that is the unifying force. While such ideas have made their way into popular culture, the ecologists themselves have abandoned them in favour of a more strictly Darwinian view in which there are no harmonious wholes, but just raw competition between species, and no tendency towards stability, but a chaotically shifting mosaic of species. Peters[9] suggested that the idea that diversity and stability was essentially unscientific and owed much to prescientific ideas of the "balance of nature". It is possible to see how the idea of stable climax communities could have been linked to the notion of *genius loci*, since there would have been an appropriate climax community for each individual place, towards which, through succession, the community would have advanced in a teleological way. But without this idea it becomes difficult to find within ecological theory the element of permanence which seems necessary to the notion of *genius loci*.

However, one of the central ideas in ecological thinking, that of interconnectedness, does survive such critiques. Whether one's view of nature is one of co-operation, competition, or a mixture of the two, there is no doubting that the elements of the system influence one another in profound and complicated ways, and changing one will affect all the others in ways which are often hard to predict. Although stability might not deliver the *genius loci*, perhaps connectedness can. *Genius loci* becomes something relational rather than something constant or absolute.

Turning to the two thought experiments, it can easily be seen that a complex interconnected ecosystem is not something which can be easily transported. It is true that there are now techniques for moving or for recreating particular habitats, so that, for example, a species-rich meadow in the path of some development might be lifted and re-laid on a prepared site away from the threat. Whether a whole place with its manifold connections to a matrix of surrounding places can be moved in this way is very doubtful; indeed, because these very connections are part of what it is to be that place, I would argue that it is a logical impossibility.

Places do however change. Even protected landscapes such as national parks are subject to change in response to alterations in economic or climatic conditions.

Not only may places be altered physically, but our conceptions of them may also change. As cultural geographers would argue, places are socially constructed. So mountains which were once considered useless and barren became places for physical and spiritual refreshment and wetlands which were once condemned as fetid and unhealthy are now prized both for their aesthetics and their species diversity. Ecologists recognise that ecosystems can be disrupted by perturbations and study the factors that might make them resistant or able to recover from such disturbance. If we have a view of *genius loci* which is based upon connections, then we could continue to talk of the spirit of a place for as long as these connections remained intact. It would be a view of *genius loci* that was rooted in the particularities of place, but open to ecological change. However, if the change was sudden and overwhelming, it would be difficult to maintain this sense. As with placeminds, a *genius loci* based upon local ecological conditions could only maintain its integrity if any changes were gradual.

AUTHENTICITY

To call a place 'inauthentic' is generally to criticise it. It is the sort of remark we might make about a theme park, mock-Tudor villa, or a Victorian shooting lodge in the form of a sham castle. All of these things are pretending to be something which they are not. We contrast them with vernacular architecture and cultural landscape practices which have been developed gradually over centuries. Of course, it is possible to perform an aesthetic *volte-face* and find something to admire in theatricality, artificiality and superficiality, indeed one might argue that these values have been in the ascendant in Post-Modern architecture. However, if we promote authenticity in our critical system, we must expect some major and surprising casualties. What could be less authentic than a Greek temple or a Roman villa standing in the English countryside?; yet many of the culturally valorised country houses and landscaped estates protected by English Heritage and the National Trust fall into this category. To deepen the irony, these landscapes were created by the very designers who set greatest store in consulting the genius of the place.

If authenticity were the touchstone for *genius loci*, we would be forced to say that only vernacular building possessed it, and that would be a deeply conservative and troubling prospect. The professions of architecture and landscape architecture would be condemned to perpetual inauthenticity. This *reductio ad absurdum* shows that authenticity cannot play this role, or should not be allowed to play this role.

If authenticity were the touchstone for *genius loci*, the latter would become a very inflexible concept. It would certainly not be portable. Any structure built by a migrant who had settled in a new land would have to follow the vernacular of his new domicile. To reproduce something in the style of his country of origin would have to be condemned for its inauthenticity. Yet surely we can recognise that in towns and cities where migrants have settled, interesting hybrid forms often arise which are a sort of new vernacular and that the places where this hybridisation occurs develop an intriguing *genius loci* of their own.

Turning to the second thought experiment, there are scenarios of significant change where nothing inauthentic is being done. For example, without government subsidy, upland sheep farming would collapse and the open fellsides of places like the Lake District would turn to scrub and eventually woodland. The character of the place would be changed and so would the *genius loci*, yet the new landscape would be as authentic as the old. On the other hand, there are changes which do involve inauthenticity. Building a golf course anywhere other than the sandy coast of Scotland, where the sport began, might qualify – and putting one in the middle of Arizona where the fairways can only be kept green through constant irrigation would certainly count. Whether human industry is always inauthentic is a moot point. Wordsworth, who decried many inappropriate forms of development in the Lake District, was sanguine about small-scale quarrying and craft industries. Perhaps there is indeed an issue of scale: some industries, such as open cast mining, obliterate the pre-existing qualities of a place, destroying the *genius loci* as they do so.

NARRATIVE

Brook suggests that "a place which tells its story, where the layers of past history are evident, and preferably not consciously preserved, is one that expresses a spirit of place".[10] Past and present are connected by a coherent narrative, so that not only does the past explain the present, but the present reveals the past. She goes on to argue that just having a past is not enough (everywhere has a past); that past must have a "working connection" to the present. She condemns the sort of heritage street furniture installed in an attempt to revitalise declining industrial towns (such additions might equally fail the test of authenticity). On this account, places with a coherent narrative retain their genius loci, but in places where the narrative has been broken the *genius loci* is lost.

Such an account of *genius loci* can fairly easily accommodate the realities of migration. After all, migrants have their own narratives which can mesh with the narratives of the places they leave, pass through or settle. The arrival of a group of migrants can form a chapter in the history of a place. Some places, such as the East End of London are celebrated as places where migrants are able to make a new life and it could be argued that this characteristic has become central to their *genius loci*.

Similarly, economic change, industrial exploitation and post-industrial recovery might all be chapters in the stories of some places which have gone through marked changes. The very facts of these transformations become the essential ingredients of their current *genius loci*. Seen in this way, a place does not have to be beautiful, undisturbed or sanctified to have a spirit.

LOCAL DISTINCTIVENESS

The UK charity Common Ground campaigns to preserve what is unique or distinctive in local landscapes, resisting the homogenising tendencies of global flows. A place has its *genius loci* when it has not succumbed to outside forces such as international corporations or centralised bureaucracies, but has preserved its difference. To have a *genius loci* a place must not be bland. The preservation of distinctiveness would seem to depend upon an active and democratically engaged population which can see off external threats. Common Ground promotes local distinctiveness through activities such as tree dressing, parish mapping and the commissioning of place-specific public art. It celebrates local culture and customs and does not intend to exclude. Nevertheless we must recognise that the word 'parochial' is a synonym for the narrow-minded and bigotry, and that there are dark possibilities in the promotion of localism.

If the *genius loci* is tied to what is locally distinctive, does this mean that its name will be invoked against all intrusions, not just the international coffee-shop franchise that wants a place on the High Street, but also the migrant workers who have come to help with the harvest? It is not hard to imagine a xenophobic spirit of the place becoming militant about alien incursions. The recent furore in Switzerland about the building of minarets is an instance. Is the *genius loci*, understood as local distinctiveness, able to change? Sudden change, I would argue, would destroy this sort of *genius*, but perhaps slower adaptive change might not.

If we ask whether migrants could take their *genius loci* with them and establish it in a new place, the answer is likely to be no, because this version is tied to the particularities of a given place. What is more likely is that migrants will seek out places in their new surroundings that remind them of their homeland. Writing in the *Guardian* the journalist Maya Jaggi remembered her family's holidays near Coniston Water. Her father, who had lost land in the Punjab during Partition, would roll up his trouser legs and wade in the Lake District becks. Packed lunches on the fells stood in for lavish picnics at Himalayan hill stations. It is often the similarities, not the local differences, between landscapes which allow them to play this bridging role.

Can local distinctiveness be threatened by economic upheaval? The history of coal-mining suggests that it can. Deep mining alters the landscape by addition and the pre-mining landscape is disfigured. New structures such as winding wheels and pithead baths are built, whole new villages spring up for the miners' families and the spoil from the mines is piled up in heaps. But in time, one might argue, it is this new landscape which becomes locally distinctive and bound closely to the local culture. When the mines close and the tips and surface structures are removed, the *genius loci* is changed again. At least, it might be said, deep mining produces its own distinctive landscape. The landscape produced after the restoration of opencast pits, on the other hand, can often be bland. An industry like mining is, at least, bound to place in a way that other activities like warehousing or retail are not. Perhaps it is the peri-urban shedscape of economic regeneration which is really destructive of the *genius loci*?

CHARACTER

Character, according to Brook, is a notion that combines both depth and surface (she contrasts it with the more problematic notion of "essence"). "The term is not used", she says, "to express a hidden nature behind an uncompromising façade but the place as it both appears and is".[11] She also quotes Norberg-Schulz, for whom "A place is a space which has a distinct character".[12] There is a fairly obvious analogy between human character and the character of a place. Just as human character is something which, in the absence of trauma, develops gradually over time, yet admits of fluctuating moods over shorter periods of time, so too does the character of a place develop gradually while fluctuating in atmosphere according to diurnal or seasonal cycles and patterns of use. Brook cautions against anthropomorphism, but relating to places as if they were people does seem to be necessary if one is to have the sort of conversation with the *genius loci* advocated in Pope's *Epistle*.

This interpretation of *genius loci* is a useful and flexible one. The issue of change produces no great conceptual difficulties. If we consider the first of our problematic scenarios, the existing character of a place could be changed by migrants who settle and this could happen quickly or slowly. To push the analogy with human character a little, it is rather like someone's character being changed by new experiences. It is not so much that the settlers bring the *genius loci* with them, but they bring cultural practices which hybridise with existing ways of doing things and the character of the place – its genius loci – is altered. Of course, in the real world, rather than the realm of concepts, this change may be resisted, even by force, and this brings us to the issue of contested landscapes, around which there is a considerable literature. Place has long been considered a problematical notion insofar as it is associated with strategies of exclusion and domination. For example, it has been noted that "the desire for some simple return to authentic local roots in "place" has been shown to be enmeshed in practices of cultural domination".[13] I will say more about this towards the end of this chapter.

The concept of genius loci as character is also flexible enough to accommodate the idea of dramatic change produced by economic forces. By analogy with human traumas, we might talk of a landscape suffering a catastrophic event, yet gradually recovering, either to something like its old self or to something different, but valuable in its own right. Pushing the analogy a little further, the process of reclamation should be a kind of therapy which allows the new landscape to emerge. All too often it has been another trauma.

Genius Loci, Stabilitas Loci AND MOBILITY

Norberg-Schulz argued that the possibility of living in a settled place, which he referred to as *stabilitas loci*, was a basic human need.[14] It is sometimes argued that increasing mobility and migration, combined with the advent of digital communication technologies, virtual environments and cyberspace have eroded traditional notions of place to the point where they are irrelevant. However, as David Morley has observed, "most people's actual experience of geographical mobility is still very limited".[15], That is to say, "global cultural forms still have to be made sense of within the context of what, for many people, are still very local forms of life".[16]

There is clearly a strong link between *stabilitas loci* and *genius loci* and we might hypothesise that genius loci is strongest when there is a continuous history of occupation. However there is clearly a darker side to such ideas which can be appropriated by virulent nationalisms and linked to ideas of racial purity. In such instances there are no gradual accommodations or gentle hybridizations. During World War II National Socialist landscape architects believed that the land supported native people, just as it supported native plants, and "exotics" were not welcome. As Jan Woudstra has expressed it: "the attitude of avoiding exotics in the German landscape came to be likened with that of avoiding foreigners in German society, in order to retain the purity of the Nordic race, and which ultimately validated the deportation and extermination of Jews and gypsies".[17] One of the Nazi landscape architects' jobs was to devise policies for the Germanisation of occupied lands in Poland.

The Nazi's "Blood and Soil" ideology is an extreme case, but the *genius loci* could be repressive in less dramatic circumstances. Those who live in places which are subject to planning policies driven by considerations of landscape or architectural conservation are less free to do what they would like with their homes than those who live outside such designated areas. To conserve architectural or landscape heritage as a common good, state-backed coercion seems to be necessary. The repressive and exclusionary aspects of parochialism have already been mentioned. When interpreting the writings of Gilles Deleuze and Felix Guattari for architects, Andrew Ballantyne uses the metaphor of the "hefted" sheep. In Cumbria "there are sheep which have lived in the same territory for countless generations. They know their way around. They do not wander away... The hefted sheep can be given complete freedom because they do not think of making use of it".[18] For Deleuze, Guattari and Ballantyne, this is not an admirable condition for human beings to be in. "If ever a sheep with a philosophical sensibility were born," writes Ballantyne, "the others would see it as mad, bad and dangerous to know, and one way or another it would not last long as part of the flock".[19] To be territorialized is to be unaware, to be stifled, to be submerged in the flock. Deterritorialization, on the other hand, opens up all sorts of creative possibilities. It is "a movement from confinement to expansiveness".[20] The troubling thought here is that the *genius loci* could be seen as part of the mechanism of oppression, and that it could be invoked against all sorts of "transgressions". This is what happened, for example, when Oxford city councillors attempted to have the artwork colloquially known as the Headington Shark removed. This work, a fibreglass shark created by the artist John Buckley, was installed in 1986 so that it appeared to crash through the roof of a terraced house in a residential street. Several residents complained and the councillors tried, but failed, to have it removed on the grounds that it had been installed without planning permission. Ironically, though the initial attempt to have it removed was based upon a conception of what was appropriate or in keeping with the area, the Shark has now become iconic and representative of Headington. This seems to be an instance where a transgressor has succeeded in altering the *genius loci*.

What we seem to need, therefore, is a version of the *genius loci* which cannot readily be used for repressive purposes, one which can guide us but not coerce us when we intervene in our environment and one which is flexible enough, conceptually speaking, to be open to change without becoming vacuous. If we consider the various interpretations of *genius loci* which have just been set out, it can be seen that they range from those which are static and allow little or no prospect for change to those which are open and flexible, without becoming meaningless.

Toward the rigid end are pantheism and panpsychism which are both open to deeply conservative interpretations whereby almost all change introduced by humans would be unwelcome and destructive. The original idea of an abode of special beings is more open, but seems to be riddled with conceptual difficulties, even when taken in a purely metaphorical sense. Authenticity is a flawed concept which seems vulnerable to being hijacked by reactionary forces. Local Distinctiveness is not an absolute notion, because what is locally distinctive might gradually change, but it could also be co-opted by a narrow parochialism. There are ideas of change, flow and connectedness in ecology which make it attractive, but it is difficult to develop a graspable notion of *genius loci* from them.

Narrative at first seems like a useful and flexible notion which could avoid the pitfalls associated with some of the versions just considered, but a difficulty appears the moment we ask who is telling the story. A distinction must be made between the narrative of a place, and the narratives of the people or peoples who live or have lived in that place. It is easy to see that in a contested place, such as Northern Ireland or Palestine, for example, there will be competing narratives, depending upon which group is telling the story. As every narrative must be told from a point of view, it becomes clear that there is no privileged, objective account which belongs only to the place.

Brook theorises *genius loci* as an emergent characteristic which would not be included in any inventory of the contents of the place or of our feelings about it. She rejects the suggestion that we should treat it as a merely instrumental construct, arguing that it is something real. I follow the same line, but would also argue that of all the various interpretations of *genius loci* examined, it is that of *genius loci* as character which is the most helpful and robust. In the absence of trauma, the character of a place generally develops gradually, but fluctuates in atmosphere according to diurnal or seasonal cycles or patterns of use. Change in character, whether gradual or sudden, will equate to a change in the *genius loci* and if we need to talk about character being destroyed, this may sometimes be the prelude for the establishment of a new character. Respect for the *genius loci*, understood as character, need not close the door upon innovation, creativity nor even transgression.

NOTES

1. Pope.
2. Turner.
3. Norberg-Schulz.
4. Thompson.
5. Brook.
6. Kerr.
7. Garrett.
8. Harding.
9. Peters.
10. Brook.
11. Brook.
12. Norberg-Schulz, 5.
13. Dovey, 45.
14. Norberg-Schulz.
15. Morley.
16. Morley, 437.
17. Woudstra, 34.

[18] Ballantyne, 9.
[19] Ballantyne, 10.
[20] Ballantyne, 62.

REFERENCES

Ballantyne, A. (2007), *Deleuze and Guattari for Architects*, Abingdon: Routledge.
Brook, I. (2000) "Can Spirit of Place be a Guide to Ethical Building?" in: Warwick Fox (ed.), *Ethics and the Built Environment*, London: Routledge, 139–150.
Dovey, K. (2002), "Dialectics of Place: Authenticity, Identity, Difference" in: Samer Akkach (ed.) *De-Placing Difference: Architecture, Culture and Imaginative Geography*, Centre for Asian and Middle Eastern Architecture: The University of Adelaide, 45–52.
Garrett, L. (2003), "Landscape in the Jewish Imagination" in: Iain Robertson and Penny Richards (eds.), *Studying Cultural Landscapes*, London: Hodder, 108–119.
Harding, S. (2006), *Animate Earth: Science, Intuition and Gaia*, London: Green Books.
Jaggi, M. (2008), "Four writers revisit summer holiday spots in Britain", *The Guardian* Monday, 18 August.
Kerr, A. (2002), *Dogs and Demons: The Fall of Modern Japan*, London: Penguin.
Morley, D. (2003), "What's 'Home' Got to Do with It?: Contradictory Dynamics in the Domestication of Technology and the Dislocation of Domesticity", *European Journal of Cultural Studies* 6, 4, 435–458.
Norberg-Schulz, C. (1980), *Genius Loci: Towards a Phenomenology of Architecture*, New York: Rizzoli International Publications.
Peters, R.H. (1991), *A Critique for Ecology*, Cambridge: Cambridge University Press.
Pope, A. (1731), *An Epistle to Lord Burlington*.
Thompson, I.H. (2003), "What Use is the Genius Loci?" in: Sarah Menin (ed.) *Constructing Place, Mind and Matter*, London, Routledge, 66–76.
Turner, T. (1996), *City as Landscape*, London, Spon.
Woudstra, J. (2004), "The changing nature of ecology: a history of ecological planting" in: Nigel Dunnett and James Hitchmough (eds.), *The Dynamic Landscape*, London: Spon.

Beheimatung: MAKING-ONESELF-AT-HOME WITH THE SPIRIT

Sigurd Bergmann

LONGING FOR BELONGING

> Wo bist du, mein geliebtes Land?
> Gesucht, geahnt, und nie gekannt!
>
> Where are you, land, beloved home?
> Imagined, sought, but never known![1]

North German poet Georg Philipp Schmidt von Lübeck's poem, "The Wanderer", well-known also through Franz Schubert's musical setting, takes us straight into our theme. For him, *Heimat* is not just simply belonging, but rather longing. Feeling like "a stranger everywhere", his beloved home seems far away even if it can be imagined. The land,

> where all my roses grow,
> where friends shall never meet in vain,
> where all my dead shall rise again,
> the land that speaks my language true,

this land, even if never known, it should be sought. *Heimat* is not just a place but a land to long for and to walk towards. Does it exist at all? Or, is it only imagined, a seductive power that one should avoid rather than commit oneself to?

Rather than conducting a self-righteous deconstruction of this and other kinds of *Heimat* literature, which, without doubt offers a rich source for criticisms of seductive, simplifying and ethically dubious views on the connection between place/space and identity, I would like to explore the creative and constructive power that hides in approaches to *Heimat*. Such a self-critical and complex attitude to our theme also characterises much German literature from Goethe until today. And even though the dark days of Germany's Third Reich—and nationalist hubris in Europe, in general—have thrown an unfortunate shadow on the meaning of belonging, I regard the production of locality, to put it in more appropriate analytic culturalist terms,[2] as a deep existential driving force of being human. Well aware of the broad discourse on place and identity, especially in the English speaking world, I will not walk along its main paths, but draw rather selectively from it. The "place of place", as Lawrence Buell circumscribes it in his rich enlightening environmental criticism, is without doubt at the centre also of culture in late modernity, as "there never was an is without a where".[3]

Longing for belonging, being on the move as well as staying home, coming home and leaving home, being at a place but nevertheless feeling homeless, expelled from a beloved place or migrating to a promised land – all these ambiguous experiences of what it means to belong offer the challenge of a multifaceted and transdisciplinary reflection of which we have so far collected only the shards. First, particularly in more recent times, our species has enormously increased its technical, if not its subjective, capacity for mobility at accelerating speeds and in widened geographical circles, so there are many good reasons to revise the theme of *Heimat* in late modernity. The "ethics of mobilities"[4] which speed up processes and systems of transport, movement, transfer and exchange, as well as increasing migration, represent strong incitements. Mobility and migration can either appear as forced by violent economic, environmental or climate related changes or as a free nomadism fuelled by the attractions of a globally (for some) open world or engineered by translocal labour market interests.[5]

Second, the experience of homelessness, which is catalyzed by mobility and migration, seems to be more and more a central characteristic of modern life. Architect Juhani Pallasmaa talks appropriately about "existential homelessness", and elucidates this in the horizon of mobility with Joseph Brodsky's help:

The more one travels, the more complex one's sense of nostalgia becomes.[6]

Home and *Heimat* are in such a sense, as we already learnt from "The Wanderer", an absent home. For Pallasmaa, and for architects in general, the conclusion is not to romanticise this longing for an absent home but to develop an architecture that can assist men and women in their homecoming. The widespread alienation and detachment required for the acknowledgement "of our existential need for a spiritual homecoming", according to Pallasmaa, can be grounded only in "the re-enchantment, remythification and re-eroticisation of our very existential realm".[7] "Spiritual" should here be understood not as opposed to the physical but instead as the inner driving force for spatial design in all its facets. Existential homelessness represents the crucial challenge to build environments that assist the homecoming of man/woman. This challenge is as valid for the rich in the North as it is for the many refugees and migrants who need shelters and protected spaces to survive and flourish anew all over the South. Late modern homelessness has many faces, voices and places, and one of the strong reasons to catalyze our discourse on place and identity is found in the re-enchantment of human skills to build in order to survive. The settlement close to a garbage dump in Indonesia can serve as an illustration for what I have in mind (see Image 9).

A third reason for catalyzing our reflection on *Heimat* and belonging lies in the xenophobic misuse of *Heimat* concepts, which are so common in our recent

Image 9 Slums built on swamp land near a garbage dump in East Cipinang, Jakarta Indonesia, photo: Jonathan McIntosh 2004, Wikimedia Commons

European history. Is it really so accurate to say that you are where you come from, that you belong to where you are born, and that good life only can take place at home? Should home be our castle, and where then should the borders of "fortress Europe" be drawn and defended? Who is in, who is tolerated and who should be out? Antidotes can often also here be found in early *Heimat* literature itself, for example in A. De Nora's (Anton Alfred Noder's) poem "Erfüllung":

> Nicht außen ist die Heimat. Nicht die Stelle
> Ist Heimat schon, wo unsre Wiege stand!
> Nein, wir erschaffen uns das Vaterland
> Erst in der eignen Brust geheimster Zelle.[8]

Home is not our birth place "where our cradle stood", but something that we create ourselves, not outside but inside, in our most inner and hidden cell.

The production of home and locality is in such a perspective a deeply subjective process, and it occurs, almost as if following Rainer Maria Rilke, in direct opposition to the nationalist code. In his poem "In Dubiis", the one who swears allegiance to the national flag appears in contrast to the one who recoils from the particular and now belongs to the whole world. Homecoming here means to find one's home in the world instead of in narrow nationalist particularities where nations fight each other. Homeland can then become a house *in* a person's "Heimatort". To come home and to be at home then means to find one's home in the world, to identify oneself through neither a limited part nor as just the world in general but to create a homeland *amidst* the open, wide and colourful world. What a challenging vision!

> Der erscheint mir als der Größte, der zu keiner Fahne schwört,
> und, weil er vom Teil sich löste, nun der ganzen Welt gehört.
> Ist sein Heim die Welt, es misst ihm doch nicht klein der Heimat Hort
> denn das Vaterland, es ist ihm dann sein Haus im Heimatsort.[9]

Homelessness is in such a light not just an existential state of being, but provokes rather a becoming by walking, a designing and building of places for homecoming. It contrasts narrow local and territorialising identities by fertilizing what I would call processes of making-oneself-at-home: *Beheimatung*. Home as a sense of place then becomes not a single place but a "composite of all the places that have been significant to a person, or a people, over time".[10] Like Rilke's and Pallasmaa's, my own concern about home, *Heimat* and belonging as a continuous coming home emphasizes not the narrow but the wide-open, not a static condition but a dynamic process. This nevertheless preserves the uniqueness of places that inspired this exchange "that we might negotiate shared ways of belonging together in a wider European context". Reformulated in Rilke's imagery this is about how to build one's house in the place of the world, our home. And, of course, the context should be widened even more to a cosmopolitan eco-citizenship of "Earth, our home",[11]

A fourth reason to deepen our theme is found in ongoing dramatic climatic change. Anthropogenic environmental change today dangerously deepens the challenge of making oneself at home even more as we again need to adjust to changing planetary conditions for survival. The tricky, radically new ethical question with regard to climate change is how to adapt to our changing surroundings—changes that our own species has socially produced, oblivious to our actions' consequences. How to make oneself at home on Earth our home, while we ourselves are spoiling the same home?

HOMES, CLOSE AND DISTANT – EMERGING, PERSISTING AND FADING AWAY

In the following, I will use as a heuristic lens the notion of "Beheimatung", which was originally coined for another workshop in Manchester in 2006 on the habitability of urban space.[12] According to several writers I have asked, Beheimatung translates best into English as making-oneself-at-home, and I am so happy that there exists at least one German adverbial construction without any counterpart in the admirably complex landscape of English adverbials. The word, though, is only very seldom used in German and, if at all, mostly narrowly and diffusely referring to some kind of unclear cultural or individual locating in a 'grey somewhere'—preferably rural—place. We can, in fact, neglect its contemporary German semantics and develop the term as a semantically open word with a nicely shaped contour. *Heimat* at its core represents of course a challenge in all its many overloadings–challenges that are not reduced when dissected in an English-German interdisciplinary context like ours. However, following the poets quoted so far, I hope that this rather laborious adverbial Beheimatung can help us focus on other phenomena than *Heimat* as the place of an always-forever-the-same that we too easily call home.

Beheimatung belongs in my view to the crucial skills that humans require to live. Dependant on our vulnerable bodies, the need for shelter as well as the need to socialise was necessary for survival in Stone Age environments as well as in late modern cities. However, the modes of making oneself at home have changed radically in the developments of civilisation, modernisation and globalisation. Houses are not any longer built by their inhabitants; cities are not any longer planned and constructed by communities.

What are the qualities of a place where one feels at home, and how is mobility related to the process of Beheimatung, as we move between places much more than before due to uprooting labour markets and other mobility-accelerating forces? To feel at home does not necessarily mean only to stay at home, it also includes mobility and travelling. Which modes of mobility can resist homelessness and which ones can nurture it? What is the difference between comfortably leaving a place and then returning to it in contrast to being excluded and dislocated? "Heimwelt" (home world) and "Fremdwelt" (strange world) should not only be contrasted to each other, as philosopher Bernhard Waldenfels rightly claims, but it should also be possible to merge them (verschieben).[13] The challenge of modern life in the context of existential homelessness is not just to build one's house in the world our home but also to move and travel in a way that Heimwelt and Fremdwelt can slide into each other. Without doubt, the increasing experiences of the loss of spatial embeddings in a local life world, which are continuously accelerated by global education and employment markets, are fertilizing the desire for belonging and new modes of making-oneself-at-home. Now, globalisation accelerates de-localisation as well as re-localisation, processes which, in my view, belong to the most powerful driving forces of ecological spirituality and a critique of civilisation on our path to an alternative common future. *Heimat* and homes are in such a perspective not something that is just there but something that – in analogy to nature and life itself – emerges, persists and fades away, always in synergy with human beings who long and act, believe and construct, remember old shores and move towards new ones.[14]

Beheimatung as dwelling "in turmoil"

In a poem, loaded with wisdom about the existential conditions of making-oneself-at-home in the modern world, Rilke directs us towards the entanglement of longing and dwelling.

> And this is longing,
> to live in turmoil,
> to have no home in time.
> And these are wishes
> gentle dialogues
> of day's hours with eternity.
>
> And this is life,
> until from a day long past
> the most lonely hour rises,
> and smiling differently than the other sisters,
> silently greets eternity.[15]

Like The Wanderer above, this poem also locates *Heimat* and belonging in the sphere of longing and desire; it resists homelessness by directing the home-seeker on an open course. The poem contrasts home and dwelling, *Heimat* and Wohnen, on the one hand and time and eternity on the other' a contrast that lays a ground for Rilke's lines. Our desire strives to relate them both, to connect them and to let them touch each other. Gently, the day's hours can talk to eternity, even the most lonely hour can encounter and greet eternity, though silently. As far as we can have no home in time, we are nevertheless homeless but can dwell in turmoil.

The English "turmoil" translates "Gewoge" a bit too strongly; it points towards tumult, chaos and turbulence but there seems no better alternative. "Gewoge" is a bit softer, it stems from "wiegen" (cradle) and is used in contexts like a rocking boat, a swaying movement, or cradling a child. In our poem, it definitively refers to the urban situation where changes in time and place are many, and whose accelerating trails cross each other. To live in turmoil describes the modern condition of metropolitan life characterised by turbulences, attractions and distractions but it is also embedded in a specific longing for home and permanence, indeed for eternity.

One should bear in mind that Rilke does not oppose home and turmoil, time and eternity. Instead, he makes us aware about the longing to let them touch each other, talk to each other, keep silent together and encounter each other. To long is to live in turmoil. Dwelling in modern urban turmoil means longing. Belonging and longing are interwoven in each other. Dwelling is, to use Tim Ingold's term, a *knot* of lines[16] rather than a static belonging to a limited place. The challenge, so true for us in an ever more accelerating urbanisation, is not to build homes as fortresses against modern life but to create our living *in the midst* of the turbulences of time, and in the manifold of short-time and permanent places. Longing and touching eternity is not at all impossible; just the opposite, it morphs and takes new shapes in urban space. Urban life can without doubt dislocate, violate and uproot its inhabitants, but it can, no doubt about this either, locate, comfort and fertilise long-term belonging. One can long and live in turmoil. Urban space offers many places where one can make oneself at home. To rephrase it in German: Beheimatung ist Wohnen im Gewoge. Making oneself at home is living in turmoil. It is an entanglement with a place, or better it is place entangling a person, rather than a person belonging to a place. Beheimatung then occurs as turmoils of place entwining men and women and awakening their longing. It is a part of the "trail *along* which life is lived".[17]

The ambiguity of dwelling in turmoil has been best caught by painters in the opening years of the last century when the progress of urbanisation and technification accelerated rapidly. The futurists especially clearly discovered the deep challenges to the embodied mind in growing urban surroundings, and they focussed especially on the dynamics of accelerating movements. Even if their interpretation of modern life in the key of a fascist glorification of modern man and his unresisted progress and power has refuted itself in two world wars, their configuration of Rilke's turmoil remains outstanding.

In his "synchronic visions" (See Image 10), Umberto Boccioni expresses the synchronicity of our seeing when all is in movement and "everything rotates".[18] Boccioni illustrates a central thought in the futurists' Technical Manifesto, where urban life compresses events and experiences, and where place and space are gone.

Time and Space died yesterday. We already live in the absolute, because we have created eternal, omnipresent speed.[19]

The painting's synchronic visions manifested in the two female heads are drawn into the vortex of the metropolitan field of force: nothing can escape its energy. Closeness and distance, surface and depth, colour and shape, all are intertwined in the painting. Everything turns into a movement, a stream that draws the observer into the depth. Boccioni clearly perceives and composes the forces that fragment and cut into pieces our perceptions, experiences, actions and visions. What does it mean to make-oneself-at-home in such a turmoil, in a world that, according to Marinetti, is nurtured by "fire, hatred and speed"?[20]

The cultural change that has been fuelled by the modern city and its impacts on its inhabitants –not only in urban areas by the way but also in rural areas and today in a global "postmetropolis" (as Edward Soja calls it) – has been encompassed with other phenomena in the notion of *hybridization*. As different mobilities increase, cultures are in modernity characterized by hybridization. Migration processes do not any longer require you to belong to a single territory. Neighbourhoods are replaced by translocal ethnoscapes, identified not just ethnically

Image 10 Umberto Boccioni, Gleichzeitige Visionen, 1911, oil on canvas, 70 x 70 cm, Von der Heydt-Museum, Wuppertal

but culturally and professionally. Mobility makes people more or less global or regional. The inner differentiation of culture, its external networking and the hybridization of individual and collective identities make it necessary also to understand processes of Beheimatung in another key. Identities emerge in processes of "transculturation" rather than identification with one single culture and place.[21]

Theologian Christopher Richard Baker has to his credit grasped the challenge of revising theology and our understandings of the church in the modern city. By applying concepts of "third space", even if only in Homi Bhaba's sense and not so much in the sense of the more ambitious Soja, Baker draws a clear picture of how modern life in urban space demands radically new theological thinking.

His conclusion relates theology and urban sociology ontologically; the hybrid city asks for a hybrid church and a hybrid Christ.[22]

Many of the theoretical sources such as bell hooks and others important for Baker stress in my view all too much the dialectics of belonging versus boundlessness. Geographical location is in such a perspective opposed to non-physical space,[23] and negotiation and translation between differences characterise the postcolonial multi-ethnic context. Baker rightly dives deep into what this means for a revised theology and for the church, and I do not at all want to impede his work. Nevertheless, it is also necessary to focus not only on difference but also on the encounter, not only on the dissolving of localities but also on their re-emergence in new maps, which should be included in a more complex picture. It seems to me it is the late modern acceleration of urban processes that even more challenges and fertilizes the skills to make oneself at home anew. Beheimatung, as we could learn from Rilke's poem, is fertilized, catalyzed and accelerated by turmoil. Disbelonging provokes new forms of belonging, and dislocation increases even more the longing and practical design of belonging. Giddens' often quoted observation of decontextualisation as a main characteristic of modernity provokes new modes of recontextualisation, and Appadurai's rightly noted despatialization accelerates the longing for and making of new forms of respatialization.[24] Living in turmoil is, as Baker rightly suggests, living in third space, both in Bhaba and Soja's meaning. Theologically, it cries for a revised reflection about God as a God who inhabits Creation in turmoil. Where does the Son walk and long for a home in time, and where does the Spirit take place in turmoil?

Before we will dive into the theological waters, German philosopher Otto Friedrich Bollnow offers another way of coming to terms with living in turmoil and Beheimatung in a turbulent modernity. In the conclusion of his unique and pioneering work "Mensch und Raum", he formulates four different demands for what he calls "true living" (wahres Wohnen). These are designed to navigate between the two gaps of either "non-living" (Nicht-wohnen) in the sense of a homeless "Geworfenheit" into hostile space, or "wrong living" in the sense of an anxious stagnation in the shell (Versteifung im Gehäuse). The notion of "Wohnen" (living, dwelling) describes for Bollnow the true form of human life in space.[25]

The philosopher explains three demands for true living and underlines that these should not be understood as a series and order in time but rather as layers where the one is entangled with the other.[26] His first demand aims against the homelessness of the refugee and adventurer who wanders disoriented in space. For him/her, it is necessary to settle at a specific place in space to ground him/herself steadily here and to create a safe and comfortable place of its own (Eigenraum).

The following two demands are formulated in order to resist emphasising this first demand in such a way that true living is threatened. Second, therefore, this "Eigenraum" should not be encapsulated and isolated from the surrounding space, but the surrounding space (Aussenraum) should be fully integrated in it, and the tension between inner and outer space is necessary as a substantial condition for the fulfilment of human life.

Third, and finally, Bollnow demands we transcend the tension of the hostile outer and the stable inner space and strive to be carried by a comprehensive confidence to the outer, surrounding, larger space. In this way, the large scale space loses its threatening character and turns itself into a comforting space. To live in a house means for Bollnow to rely on and become confident towards the larger surrounding space. As we already saw in another of Rilke's poems, home and *Heimat* can only emerge in a complex interplay of exchange and confidence where the "Heim als Welt", the home as world, generates a "Haus im Heimatort", a home space in the place of *Heimat*. Beheimatung is in such a view necessarily Beheimatung *at* place *in* and *with* the world. Local belonging takes place necessarily everywhere, and every time also longing for belonging takes place as an interplay between a wider open horizon wherein this and other places and co-creatures dwell and are at home.

COMING HOME WITH THE SPIRIT

What do considerations such as those presented here demand of Christian theology, and what can theology offer back to our theme?

As theologians recently have started to partake in the so-called spatial turn,[27] and as themes like migration, pilgrimage and architecture have also gained greater significance in the, unfortunately still often apologetic, theological agendas, I content myself with a preliminary suggestion for how to interpret Beheimatung as an encounter of man/woman and the Triune God in the light of faith in the Holy Spirit. The central task for a theology of making-oneself-at-home would then be to reflect about how the life-giving Spirit takes place in synergy with our longing for belonging, how to come home with the Spirit, or, in biblical terms, how to offer the Spirit a home in our body[28] so that we might make ourselves at home in Creation.

In truthful accordance with apophatic theology, which reminds us to constantly keep alive the mystery of God's essential elusiveness in conjunction with his/her caring work in and with earth, one should approach Beheimatung in its spiritual dimension as an encounter with the Triune Spirit. The elusiveness of place,[29] of Beheimatung and of the Triune God, can be so imagined in analogy. A presupposition for such a perspective is to locate theologically the work of the Spirit along the paths of a doctrine of the so-called historical Trinity. Salvation history takes place in three different modes and times, where God's incarnation in the time of the Son (in the earthly and historical Christ) is followed by the time of the Spirit. Here *inhabitation* continues the Incarnation of the Son, and should be classically interpreted as God's indwelling in Creation. Gregory of Nazianzen clearly states:

Now the Spirit Himself dwells among us, and supplies it with a clearer demonstration of Himself.[30]

In such a sense, Beheimatung is not only a term for humans coming home but it can also be developed further into a central theological term where the Triune God makes him/herself at home in creation by the incarnation of the Son and the inhabitation of the Spirit. God comes home to him/herself in encountering the creation. Humans, interpreted as being in God's image, mirror in their longing for Beheimatung this deep desire of the Creator in synergy with his/her creation. Artistic skills transcend human homelessness and architecture, as Pallasmaa demanded, and can assist the homecoming of humans. Both reflect, in my view, what drives a Trinitarian pneumatology of space at its heart: the synergy of the skills of Beheimatung in building oneself a home, not a closed home but one open to the world as in Rilke's vision as well as in Bollnow's true living. As God is the creator of all life in the universe and at the same time appears and acts locally, and as God the Redeemer in his/her liberating work glides between all scales of created life in turmoil, so our processes of Beheimatung, which wants to proceed in conjunction with this mystery, cannot be limited to single places or scales. Beheimatung in a true spiritual sense moves in between places and spaces, and it interconnects macro- and micro scales.

From late antiquity and Cappadocian theology we can learn to keep together Christology and pneumatology as well as the Jewish and Christian mystery of God's presence in a Trinitarian frame by intertwining the incarnation of the Son with the inhabitation of the Spirit. The experience of God's indwelling represents a foundational characteristic of Jewish and Christian faith. The spatial dimension moves hereby into focus. Inhabitation does not mean that the world *is* God. God dwells in the world but he/she is not the world. Quite the opposite: God continues to be a God who dwells in the darkness. Inhabitation is an ongoing dynamic process where God goes into and beyond the world and transfigures it from within. The Creator remains a sovereign God who fulfils in love what s/he has begun. If spelled out in an aesth/ethical key, inhabitation demands that theologians give much more emphasis than usual to the perception of urban space and life in which the pneumatological lens is expected to lead to practices with and discourses about the synergy of the Holy Spirit in-habiting and co-habitating built and other environments.

Another theological line can be developed in accordance to what Bollnow taught us about true living. In his view, true living required confidence. Confidence and trust represent, as we know from Luther's Great Catechism, the main criterion for faith. In his theology, this even determines the definition of a god, as the one whom we trust and rely on.[31] Applied to our theme of *Heimat* and belonging, this means that belonging as Beheimatung necessarily includes confidence and trust and the skill to let the Creator through his/her good creation carry us through the sometimes painful, sometimes comforting, adventures of making ourselves at home in turmoil.

Such an approach also fits well with another theological and classical lyric thought: coming home as an encounter of love. Bollnow has summarised this dimension beautifully in his section, "Die raumschaffende Kraft der Liebe" (The space-creating power of love) where he walks along a path which Goethe has trodden and which other poets have followed.[32]

> Immer war mir das Feld und der Wald und der Fels und die Gärten
> nur ein Raum, und du machst sie, Geliebte, zum Ort.[33]

To begin with, landscape appears simply as field, forest, mountain and garden; it is nothing more than a space, unless the beloved You turns it into a place. *Heimat* arises through the encounter of love in place. Love changes space into place. Processes of Beheimatung are then always processes fuelled by inter-subjective encounters. Theologically interpreted, not only the beloved person, as in Goethe's lines, but also the God who loves his/her creation, is at work in such a Beheimatung. The triple command to love oneself as one's neighbour and as God, can consequently also be applied to our theme of Beheimatung. The place-creating power of love is threefold. Making oneself at home means to love God, our neighbour (including the non-human life forms) and ourselves; coming home means to experience loving and being loved. Home is where love takes place. Such a theology can be sharpened even more in the tradition of liberation theology, where the most perfect love, as it is elaborated in both in Eastern patristics and ecological liberation theology,[34] is the love for the poor. Love for God, the neighbour and oneself is fulfilled at its highest in love for the poor, which indeed also works as a criterion to verify true love in general. Applied to Beheimatung this means that making oneself at home only can take place in a true Christian sense where justice reigns and where all inhabitants of earth, our home, can come to a worthy home.

NOTES

1. Schmidt von Lübeck; cf. Franz Schubert, *Der Wanderer: op. 4, 1, D 489*, 1816, Text von Georg Philipp Schmidt "Von Lübeck".
2. Appadurai (2001), 99–123.
3. Buell, 55.
4. Cf. Bergmann and Sager (2008).
5. Cf. Bauman, 85ff.
6. Pallasmaa, 143–156, 143.
7. Pallasmaa, 156.
8. de Nora.
9. Rilke, 42f.
10. Buell, 69.
11. http://www.earthcharter.org/, 18 September 2006.

12 The workshop "God/city/place: interdisciplinary perspectives" was organised by the Lincoln Theological Institute at the University of Manchester in December 2006, some of its contributions were published in the International Journal of Public Theology 2, 2008. Cf. Begmann (2008), 70–97.
13 Waldenfels, 210.
14 Cf. Bergmann (2010).
15 Rilke, 145:

> Das ist die Sehnsucht: Wohnen im Gewoge
> und keine Heimat haben in der Zeit.
> Und das sind Wünsche: Leise Dialoge
> täglicher Stunden mit der Ewigkeit.
>
> Und das ist Leben. Bis aus einem Gestern
> die Einsamste von allen Stunden steigt,
> die, anders lächelnd als die andern Schwestern,
> dem Ewigen entgegenschweigt.

16 Ingold, 147–161.
17 Ingold, 148f.) develops his understanding of the environment as entangled lines, where not the postulated relation between things or between the organism and the surrounding is in focus but where life is imagined as something that is lived along a trail of movement or growth.
18 As it says in the *Technical Manifesto of Futurist Painting*: "Alles spielt sich mit der größten Schnelligkeit ab! ... und durch das stete Vorhandensein der Dinge auf unserer Netzhaut vervielfältigen sie sich, deformieren sich, folgen aufeinander wie Vibrationen im Raum." (Boccioni et al.)
19 Marinetti.
20 Marinetti.
21 Cf. Welsch; Hannerz; Bergmann (2004).
22 Baker, 137ff.
23 Baker, 19.
24 Giddens; Appadurai (1998), 11–40.
25 Bollnow, 309.
26 Bollnow, 309f.
27 Bergmann (2007).
28 Cf. 1 Corinthians 3:16: "Do you not know that you are God's temple and that God's Spirit lives in you?"; 1 Corinthians 6:19: "Do you not know that your body is a temple of the Holy Spirit, who is in you, whom you have received from God, and you are not your own?"; Ephesians 2:22: "... in whom you also are being built together into a dwelling place of God in the Spirit."
29 Buell, 59–63.
30 Gregory of Nazianz, Oratio 31.26; Cf. Bergmann (1995), 211. The word "dwell" (*endemosantos*) means to be at home and to be a citizen in a city. The New Testament uses the verb to mean "be at home in the body" (2 Corinthians 5:6).
31 On trust as a central category in theology and worldview studies see Kurtén (1995).
32 Bollnow, 266.
33 Goethe.
34 Cf. Bergmann (2005 [1995]).

REFERENCES

Appadurai, A. (1998), "Globale ethnische Räume", in: Ulrich Beck (ed.), *Perspektiven der Weltgesellschaft*, Frankfurt am Main: Suhrkamp, 11–40.
– (2001 [1995]), "The Production of Locality", in: Peter Beyer (ed.), *Religion im Prozeß der Globalisierung*, Würzburg: Ergon, 99–123.
Baker, C.R. (2007), *The Hybrid Church in the City: Third Space Thinking*, Aldershot: Ashgate.
Bauman, Z. (1998), *Globalisation: The Human Consequences*, New York: Columbia University Press.
Bergmann, S. (1995), *Geist, der Natur befreit: Die trinitarische Kosmologie Gregors von Nazianz im Horizont einer ökologischen Theolgie der Befreiung*, Mainz: Grünewald. [Russian edition: Arkhangelsk: Arkhangelsk University Press, 1999; revised English edition: *Creation Set Free: The Spirit as Liberator of Nature* (*Sacra Doctrina: Christian Theology for a Postmodern Age*, Vol. 4), Grand Rapids, Michigan: Eerdmans, 2005.]
– (2004), "Transculturality and Tradition – Renewing the Continuous in Late Modernity", *Studia Theologica: Scandinavian Journal of Theology*, Vol. 58, No. 2, 140–156. [Russian edition, in: Evgeny Arinin et al. (eds.), *Candle*, Arkhangelsk University Press, 2001, 13–18.]
– (2007), "Theology in its Spatial Turn: Space, Place and Built Environments Challenging and Changing the Images of God", *Religion Compass*, Vol. 1, 353–379.
Bergmann, S. and Sager, T. (eds.) (2008), *The Ethics of Mobilities: Rethinking Place, Exclusion, Freedom and Environment* (*Transport and Society*), Aldershot: Ashgate.
Bergmann, S. (2008), "Making Oneself at Home in Environments of Urban Amnesia: Religion and Theology in City Space", *International Journal of Public Theology*, Vol. 2, 70–97.
– (2010), *Raum und Geist: Zur Erdung und Beheimatung der Religion: Eine Theologische Ästh/Ethik des Raums* (*Research in Contemporary Religion*, Vol. 7), Göttingen: Vandenhoeck & Ruprecht.
Boccioni, U.; Carrà, C.; Russolo, L.; Balla, G.; and Severini, G., *Manifesto of Futurist Painters*, originally published in Italian as a leaflet by *Poesia* (Milan), February 11, 1910, http://www.italianfuturism.org/manifestos/futuristpaintersmanifesto/ 15 June 2015.
Bollnow, O. (2004 [1963]), *Mensch und Raum*, 10th ed. Stuttgart: Kohlhammer.
Buell, L. (2003 [2001]), *Writing for an Endangered World: Literature, Culture, and Environment in the U.S. and Beyond*, Cambridge, Massachusetts and London: Harvard University Press.
Goethe, J.W.v. (1827), Vier Jahreszeiten, Sommer, in: *Goethe's Gedichte, Volym 1*, Stuttgart: J.G. Cotta'scher Verlag, 1829, 245.
Hannerz, U. (1996), *Transnational Connections: Culture, People, Places*, London and New York: Routledge.
Ingold, T. (2008), "The Wedge and the Knot: Hammering and Stitching the Face of Nature", in: Sigurd Bergmann, Peter Scott, Maria Jansdotter Samuelsson and Heinrich Bedford-Strohm (eds.), *Nature, Space and the Sacred: Transdisciplinary Perspectives*, Aldershot: Ashgate, 147–161.
Kurtén, T. (1995), *Tillit, Verklighet Och Värde: Begreppsliga Reflexioner kring livsåskådningar hos fyrtioen finska författare*, Nora: Nya Doxa.

Marinetti, F.T. (1909), *Futurist Manifesto*, http://en.wikisource.org/wiki/Futurist_Manifesto, 25 March 2010.

de Nora, A. (1916), *Erfüllung*, 1st ed. http://www.gedichte.eu/71/nora/erfuellung/nicht-aussen-ist-die.php, 3 April 2010.

Pallasmaa, J. (2008), "Existential Homelessness – Placelessness and Nostalgia in the Age of Mobility", in: Bergmann and Sager, 143–156.

Rilke, R.M. (1955), "In Dubiis", in: *Sämtliche Werke, Band 1: Gedichte •Erster Teil*, Frankfurt am Main: Insel, 42–43.

– (1955), "Das ist die Sehnsucht" [tr. Michael Northcott], in: Rilke, 145.

Schmidt von Lübeck, G.P. (1816), *Der Wanderer (Des Fremdlings Abendlied)*, http://d-nb.info/357194357, 3 April 2010. [English translation: http://myweb.dal.ca/waue/Trans/Schmidt-Wanderer.html]

Waldenfels, B. (2005), *In den Netzen der Lebenswelt*, 3rd ed. Frankfurt am Main: Suhrkamp.

Welsch, W. (1999), "Transculturality: The Puzzling Form of Cultures Today", in: Mike Featherstone and Scott Lash (eds.), *Spaces of Culture: City – Nation – World*, London: Sage, 194–213.

Forgetting and remembering

"TURF WARS": GRASS, GREENERY AND THE SPATIALITY OF COMMEMORATION

RECURRING DEBATES AND DISPUTES IN THE USES OF HORTICULTURAL ICONOGRAPHY BY THE COMMONWEALTH WAR GRAVES COMMISSION IN NORTHERN EUROPE

Paul Gough

INTRODUCTION – DISCOURSE AND DEBATES

Where once geographers could argue that the ideological issues surrounding the quintessential character of English and Empire military cemeteries had drawn little comment, there is now a considerable literature exploring the space and place of remembrance. Increasing attention has been paid during the past decade to the value of "situation" in the discourse of death, grieving and commemoration. In this respect, "situation" should be understood to be a focus on "place", "space" and the geopolitical (Gillis 1994). The emerging discipline of cultural geography in the late 1990s created the tools necessary to elaborate "space" in the abstract, to regard "place" as a site where an individual might negotiate definitively social relations, and give voice, as Sara Blair argued, to "the effects of dislocation, disembodiment, and localization that constitute contemporary social disorder".[1] In our post-historical era, further argues Blair, temporality has largely been superseded by spatiality, what has been termed the affective and social experience of space. Almost a century after Freud's treatise *Mourning and Melancholia* (1917), our understanding of how memory and mourning function continues to be challenged, revised, and refined. Issues of place have become important to this debate. Once a marginal topic for academic investigation, there is now a body of scholarly work exploring the complex interrelationship between memory, mourning and what might be termed "death-scapes". Indeed, this fascination with places of death and dying has given rise to myriad academic explorations spawning academic disciplines such as dark- or thana-tourism, which is an extreme form of grief-incited travel to distant prisons, castles, and abandoned battlefields where anthropological enquiry can be conducted. Suspicions of a release of "recreational grief" aroused after the death of Princess Diana in 1997 have also provided sociologists with considerable material for scholarly attention (Walter 1999).

However, this chapter will focus on the many ways in which horticulture, architecture and planning have been mobilized (to borrow the military term) to transform traumatized battle landscapes into permanent sites of memory. Mosse (1990), Morris (1997) and McKay (2001) and others have examined the aftermath of war and observed the creation of what some have also described as "memoryscapes", a *portmanteau* term that fuses an appreciation of once- violated landscapes with personal and discursive memories (Basu 2007).

In this chapter I want to focus not only on the torn and traumatized terrain of war, but on its repair, on the intensive attempts to smoothen the surfaces of war and to dress them in ways appropriate to civic and personal commemoration, to create "homely" and familiar plots of memory forever land-locked in the proverbial foreign field. I will do so by examining the project to create garden cemeteries on tracts of former battlefields after the Great War, 1914–1919. It is an impressive story. Yet, what would appear to be a straightforward narrative of reparation, recovery and rejuvenation is tainted by disharmony and argument. After the war, there was much disagreement about the "proper" form of remembrance; there was an intense dispute about the repatriation of bodies; and an extended (at times quite bitter) public argument about the best way to mark the sites of burial. What is additionally surprising is that these disagreements can seem as alive and vivid today as they did ninety years ago. Conducted by families, remembrance groups, ex-servicemen, politicians, and others, these disputes tell us much about the way we remember our dead, how we create protocols of commemoration and, significantly, how we play out discussions about national identity through horticultural proxies such as trees, shrubs, and most importantly, turfed lawn.

Why should this be the case? In his seminal text on cultural histories, David Lowenthal has argued that landscape is "memory's most serviceable reminder". He suggests that certain places can be regarded as key sites in a continuous educational process, where successive generations "revise or expand their cultural memory through interaction with the artifacts and landscapes of its past".[2] Former battlefields are critical places in Lowenthal's taxonomy of significance. This is because they are not a single, sealed terrain isolated in a given moment of time, they are multi-vocal "landscapes of accretion" stratified by overlapping layers of social, economic and occasionally political history. They are also, Barbara Bender reminds us, invariably politicized, dynamic, and open to constant negotiation (Bender 1983). Official sites of mass burial, ornamented with august memorials and strict planting regimes have not only long provided "pegs" upon which national fiction could be hung, but flagposts from which declarations of national identity and purpose can be articulated. Others have argued that the marking of a battlefield with monuments, memorials and markers fulfills a natural human need to understand, possess, classify and control what happened "so that it is manageable, even if not wholly explicable".[3] Explication, however, needs a certain quorum of authentication; and achieving authenticity is rarely straightforward; it requires careful manipulation and even contrivance (Saunders 2000). These issues of "contrivance", "manipulation", and "authenticity" will be the key considerations of this chapter. Nowhere are such terms more contested than on the British and Empire war cemeteries in northern France and Belgium. To understand why, we will have to first sketch out their origins.

"The Silent Cities"

Given the scale of death on the battlefields of the Great War – the total British dead alone was over one million, of which a fifth were from British dominions overseas – the bold decision taken by the British government (on behalf of the entire British Empire) not to repatriate the bodies of the dead created a need for a comprehensive administration to rationalize, routinise, and standardize the recording of the dead, their site of burial and their marker stone. Initial attempts by the British and Allied armies to co-ordinate the burial and recording of the dead were haphazard. In Flanders, it was the zeal of Fabian Ware and his graves registration unit that laid the foundations of a systematic audit of the dead and their place of burial (Longworth 1967). Ware established a method for graves registration and a scheme for permanent burial sites. He also arranged that all graves should be photographed so that relatives might have an image and directions to the place of burial. By August 1915, an initial 2,000 negatives, each showing four grave markers, had been taken. Cards were sent in answer to individual requests, enclosing details that gave "the best available indication as to the situation of the grave and, when it was in a cemetery, directions as to the nearest railway station which might be useful for those wishing to visit the country after the war".[4] Less than nine months later Ware's makeshift organisation had registered over 50,000 graves, answered 5,000 enquiries, and supplied 2,500 photographs. Little over a year later, the work to gather, re-inter and individually mark the fallen had become a state responsibility. The dead, as Heffernan points out, were no longer allowed "to pass unnoticed back into the private world of their families". They were "official property" to be accorded appropriate civic commemoration in "solemn monuments of official remembrance".[5]

Attempts to dress the cemeteries and so alleviate their barren appearance were in hand as soon as the sites had been agreed. Wooden crosses were fashioned, flowers planted and some attempt at caring for the battlefield graveyards was made where it was safe and practical to do so. As Kenneth Helphand observes in his book *Defiant Gardens* (Helphand 2006), the bucolic habit was already well established: soldiers across the Western Front had created their own flower gardens during the course of the war itself. Amidst the squalor and horror of the front, behind the front lines, in reserve and supply trenches and in the rear zones, combatants from all sides had cleared tracts of land, restored it, laid flower beds or planted seeds and vegetables, tended them, and even harvested their fruit. He cites as a typical example the remarkable garden created in the trenches on Hill 59 near Ypres in 1915 by Lothar Dietz, a student from Leipzig:

As one can't possibly feel happy in a place where all nature has been devastated, we have done our best to improve things. First we built a new causeway of logs, without railing to it, along the bottom of the valley. Then from a pinewood close by, which had also been destroyed by shells, we dragged all the best tree tops and stuck them upright in the ground; certainly they have no roots, but we don't expect them to be here more than a month and they are sure to stay green that long. Out of the gardens of the ruined chateaux of Hollebecke and Camp we fetched rhododendrons, box, snowdrops and primroses and made quite nice flower beds.[6]

Not far from where Dietz transformed his melancholy desert into an idyllic grove, British troops were also establishing trench gardens. In May 1915 the *Illustrated London News* published a full-page image of a "villa" garden on a stretch of trench named "Regent Street", the garden and a shelter sitting neatly amidst scorched undergrowth and shell-torn trees. By the end of the war the British had established a Directorate of Agricultural Production, a large-scale initiative to create a system of farms capable of mass-producing vegetables. Decorative and utilitarian schemes survived throughout the war; soldiers planted and nurtured flower gardens with the aim, argues Helphand, of creating an alternative reality, a tonic for morale, and for use as a boost to morale, a soft-edged weapon in the arsenal against the enemy:

A garden, and especially a plant emerging from the ground, is a sign of regeneration and an indication of the continuation of life. War magnifies our awareness of our human connections to these forces of life and death.[7]

These principles persisted in the immediate peace that followed the Armistice.

Arguing soon after the war for the promotion of English gardening principles and ideas in the military cemeteries, the horticulturalist Sir Arthur Hill, Director of the Royal Botanical Gardens at Kew, insisted that "home flowers" should adorn all soldier's graves of the British Empire. Where possible, he argued, native species should be used to lend an impression that each of the Empire's dead lay within a garden setting. Through creative and sensitive planting, this was largely achieved, despite indifferent soils, fragment-strewn earth, and a northern European climate (where the vast majority of cemeteries are located) which discriminated against plants associated with the dead from the far reaches of the Empire. So, whereas "old fashioned double white Pinks, London pride, mozzy Saxifrages, Cerastium and Thrift...Polyantha Roses, Lavender, Rosemary, Iris, perennial Iberis, small heaths",[8] thrived in the northern climate, more exotic strands – such as bougainvillea – intended to commemorate the graves of soldiers from the West Indies – failed. The scale of the task facing the Commission was immense: its achievements equally so. By 1921, its architects and gardeners had established over a thousand permanent cemetery sites in France and Belgium alone – comprising some 200 acres of lawn, seventy-five miles of flower border and over fifteen miles of hedge.[9]

Not everyone, however, agreed that the numerous military cemeteries should be dressed in this way. Rather surprisingly, several noisy factions argued that the appropriation of the military cemetery as the epitome of a certain quality of "Englishness" was not to be undertaken lightly; floral adornment was seen by some as "a mere dress parade of the dead rather than a celebration of heroic sacrifice".[10] Although Brooke may have articulated an idea that such places were unambiguously a "... corner of a foreign field /That is for ever England", this idea brought together a complex intersection, indeed a clash, of gender, race, and class, underlined by Stuart Hall's admonition that the British have a strong tendency "to 'landscape' cultural identities so as to give them an imagined places or home.".[11] As we shall see, others argued that this tendency to homogenize character and experience led to a synthesized falsehood, a leveling of individuality that reduced the largely volunteer civilian-soldiers to mere ciphers.

However to a grieving public, the military cemetery garden – well-tended, bursting with native species, and with a carefully calculated informality – reasserted the principle of historic continuity, promoting it as a powerful declaration of continuity and "rootedness" that linked nation and soil to a pre-industrial past, even though such myths had apparently been torn asunder by the savagery of the Great War.

FROM FRONT LINE TO FRONT LAWN – CONTESTED TURF

If the planting of flowers, shrubs and trees was, at times, a contested issue then surely the matter of the "green coverlet", the lawn that surrounded, connected and contextualized the headstones of the dead ought to be less problematic? Not necessarily so. Once again, there were carefully articulated points of dispute; some historic and others that were to recur over the decades and were closely attuned to issues of national identity, environmental debate, and the cost of maintenance. Such disparate views have deep historical roots. After all, the lawn – argues George McKay – might be regarded as the most pronounced marker of imperial culture, exported by the English even to those countries with climates or landscapes that make the growing of flat expanses of lush green grass difficult, expensive or time-consuming.[12] Regarding it as *the* pivotal, privileged space of certain green sporting Englishnesses – cricket, croquet, lawn tennis, golf – he suggests that the lawn, and especially the front lawn of one's home, has become the primary formal signifier of one's standing and conformity to social norms. Not to mow, or to clip, or to tend fastidiously to the borders of one's rectilinear tract of turf is not only willfully unsocial, but lowers the financial and moral value of the homes around, and threatens the very integrity of the community. An argument nicely visualised on the front cover of Alain de Botton's book *Status Anxiety* (de Botton 2004) which shows a well-heeled female, clippers on gloved hand, standing on the closely clipped turf of an impressively large estate. A lawn, states Michael Pollan[13] is to be regarded as "nature under totalitarian rule", or as radical gardener Lyx Ish[14] puts it, the lawn is little more than "a symbol of white male civilization".

Today's radical responses may not have impressed those in the 1920s, but strong views about the "verdant turf" were declared from the outset of the Commission's work. Looking for horticultural specialists a year after the war, Arthur Hill doubted that the French might actually be capable of growing a "good lawn":

Doubt was expressed by those in authority whether the sowing of grass was worthwhile and the absence of good lawns in France was held up as an object lesson to the Botanical Adviser and the Horticultural Officers. I chanced to be reading Arthur Young's 'Travels in France' at the time and came across the passage in which he refers to French lawns and says he sees no reason why the French should not be able to have lawns as good as those in England, provided they cut them and looked after them properly.[15]

Hill's ideal was based on a visit to Hascombe village, Godalming in Surrey, where the churchyard's smooth green lawn clipped closely to each headstone deeply impressed him as a paradigm of English values. Diligent and thorough, and mindful of the peculiar conditions pertaining in western Belgium, he also visited Holkham Hall on the Norfolk coast to study the planting of Marram grass on the sand dunes. Although aspirational, he was also realistic about his chances of seeding with grass every military cemetery. He recognized that those on the former battlegrounds in Italy, Macedonia, and Gallipoli, while beautifully located on the shores overlooking the Mediterranean, would never hope to emulate the verdant garden-cemeteries of northern France and Belgium, which were largely staffed by British veterans of the Great War.[16] Their love of gardening was regarded as a prerequisite for the task, endorsed by much popular writing during and after the war which valorized gardening as an essential, even "inherent" trait of the English. Writing on "exciting to be English", Raphael Samuel has located this innate talent in his study of the making (and unmaking) of British national identity (Samuel 1989).

Hill's antipathy to foreign practice was not new. A resistance to French (or indeed any non-English) gardening practices had been a characteristic of the British stance towards continental farming practices for centuries. During his extended *Travels in France* written on the eve of the French Revolution, Arthur Young, the greatest of all English writers on agriculture, "did not hesitate to tell his French readers some blunt home-truths" about their farming practices which he regarded as retarded, although he considered their soil superior to the English.

When relocated to the war grave cemeteries of the Great War, the suspicion of foreign habits was magnified. It is brilliantly captured in Julian Barne's short story, *Evermore* (1995),which tells the tale of the redoubtable 'Miss Moss' who, in the decades after the Great War, undertakes an annual pilgrimage to visit her brother's gravestone in *Cabaret Rouge* Military Cemetery in northern France. Her frequent attempts to customize, even "personalize", the graveside environs of her brother's stone are frustrated by the strict protocols that held in the cemeteries:

There had been problems with the planting. The grass at the cemetery was French grass, and it seemed to her of the coarser type, inappropriate for British soldiers to lie beneath. Her campaign over this with the commission led nowhere. So one spring she took out a small spade and a square yard of English turf kept damp in a plastic bag.

After dark she dug out the offending French grass and relaid the softer English turf, patting it into place, then stamping it in. She was pleased with her work, and the next year, as she approached the grave, saw no indication of her mending. But when she knelt, she realised that her work had been undone: the French grass was back again.[17]

While Miss Moss has eventually to resign herself to alien turf and "dusty geraniums", others were less satisfied with the becalmed appearance of the former battlefield. Great War veteran Edmund Blunden harboured a concern that the leveled ground, the even greensward, which characterised each British and Empire cemetery was a mask that concealed dreadful truths:

The beauty, the serenity, the inspiration of the Imperial cemeteries have been frequently acknowledged by more able eulogists; for my part, I venture to speak of these lovely, elegiac closes (which almost cause me to deny my own experiences in the acres they now grace) as being after all the eloquent evidence against war. Their very flowerfulness and calm tell the lingerer that the men beneath the green coverlet should be there to enjoy such influence; the tyranny of war stands all the more terribly revealed.[18]

Others have observed this uneasy tension between the pristine orderliness of the cemetery and the chaotic causes of death and destruction just centimetres under the surface.[19] However, no single consensus holds. Whereas Mosse (1990) has argued that nature has been artificially distorted to reshape, smoothen and ameliorate the horrors of war, others have taken a different view arguing that it is the very specificity of remembrance – the assiduous clip and mow, the attention to every detail – that prevents the Commonwealth War Graves Cemeteries from becoming simply mawkish (Shepheard 1997). By comparison, the sight of unkempt parkland and overgrown lawn evokes painful associations with traumatized bodies, disintegration, administrative lethargy and neglect. In brief, lawns require regular care and maintenance. Closely mown grass soon shows signs of decay if it is neglected for long, and by extension memory requires equivalent levels of attention if it is not to atrophy (Winter 1995).

It is fascinating to discover how polarized views can be. Alan Bennett, in his edited diaries (2005) dwells on a visit made in the late 1980s to an obscure village somewhere between St Omer and Zillebeke, south-east of the Flemish town of

Ypres in Belgium. He is on a quest to locate the burial site of his Uncle Clarence, who died, aged twenty, in 1917. Once located, the cemetery is typical of the one hundred and seventy others in the Salient, neat and regular, more orderly than the surrounding banal suburbs, the bungalows and factory farms. It is, he notes, as if "the dead are here to garrison the living".[20] Uncle Clarence is easily spotted, the stone is in a row backing onto the railway line though his body lies not beneath it, known only to be buried somewhere in the compact plot. For Bennett, it is an unnerving moment, made more so by the unblemished agelessness of the site. The walls, he writes, are sharp, new-looking, unblurred by creeper, the bleached Portland stones free of lichen, the turf manicured. "The dead", he states, "seeming not to have fertilised the ground so much as sterilized it".[21]

Where he saw only a frigid landscape populated by the absent dead, the architect Maya Lin relied on the smooth folds of rolls of turf to help soften the jagged edges of bitter memory. In her design for the Vietnam Veteran's Memorial in Washington DC, she used generously grassed lawns to repair the deep cuts in the social and political fabric of a country traumatised by an embarrassing and unpopular war. "I thought about what death is, what loss is...a sharp pain that lessens with time but can never quite heal over. A scar. The idea occurred to me there on that site. Take a knife and cut open the earth and with time the grass would heal it".[22] Summarising these many tensions, Morris (1997) suggests that the outwardly serene surfaces of lawn, flowerbed and well-tended shrub stand as uneasy interfaces between a sanitized landscape of national grief and the shattered bodies just beneath the pristine greensward, a tense balancing of the official and unofficial, the public and the private, a landscape at peace, as opposed to one with a veneer of decorum that conceals bodies in pieces.

ISSUES OF ENVIRONMENTAL SUSTAINABILITY: THE COMMISSION AND THE "TURF EXPERIMENTS"

As the challenges of climate change have become ever more apparent and with a proliferation in the level and intensity of media coverage on the topic, organizations such as the Commonwealth War Graves Commission have had to consider the possible impact of environmental change on their horticultural work. In 2009, the Commission began to engage on a series of experiments to test out their preparedness for imminent climate change. Arguing, with some justification, that they had already a great deal of experience in gardening under challenging conditions, they set out their purpose with a series of reflective questions:

What pests and diseases might we encounter and what can we do to mitigate those challenges? How can we practically employ in the cemeteries the breadth and wealth of horticultural experience we already have as an organisation and how might the public react to these changes?[23]

So as to test the validity and durability of its existing environmental policy the Commission set up a controlled experiment. On the premise that the bulk of the cemeteries it maintained were in northern Europe, it chose two sites in France and two in Belgium as showpieces where it could demonstrate the adaptations that might be necessary to combat climate change. Through making these horticultural, design and sartorial changes it was hoped to engage with the visiting public and assess their reaction to the work.

The four cemeteries were, in France, Les Moeres Communal (13km east of Dunkerque) and Ove-Plage Communal (14km east of Calais), and in Belgium, Oostduinkerke Communal (midway between Nieuwpoort and Koksijde) and Railway Chateau Cemetery (2km west of Ieper). Two methods were to be tested – at one cemetery in each country – a "dry landscape" scheme was created whereby the turf was completely removed and replaced with other surfaces; at the two other sites the existing greensward was replaced with drought tolerant turf. Floral borders in all four cemeteries were planted in the time-honoured way but with plants selected for their ability to withstand period of drought.

Image 11 Railway Chateau Cemetery: an experiment in geotextile and dolomite limestone surface as an alternative to turf, 2009–2011. ©Jeremy Banning.

As the Commission was keen to point out, in advance of public reaction, such changes were not new or untested elsewhere. In Mediterranean locations – Greece,

Turkey, Egypt, Tunisia and Libya – which had sizeable numbers of military cemeteries and where a lack of water, or irregular supply, grass could often not be grown, other options had been pursued and successfully implemented. On such sites pebbles or gravel had been used instead, with and without border planting. However, it was acknowledged that this was the first time such a programme of work had been conducted in northern Europe.

Public reaction was invited. It was not long in coming. In addition to direct communications with the Commission, web-based bulletin boards carried a great many colourful exchanges. If we take the *ww2Talk* on-line forum as a typical example of the banter shared between regular visitors to Western Front battlefields, we can discern three slightly overlapping responses to the Commission's experiment. Firstly, some saw it as a rejection (indeed betrayal) of first principles, regarding it as an abdication of responsibility by the commission and an abandonment of an essential component of remembering, which might best be summarized as: "I've only ever seen them as grassed places. It's just the tradition I've grown up with".[24] Secondly, other responses (a minority) saw the pilot exercise as an underhand ruse to cut maintenance costs, hidden behind the unproven arguments of global climate change. Suggesting that Belgium was probably one of the wettest places on the planet, one skeptical correspondent stated categorically: "I suspect it is simply a cost saving experiment under the pretext of global warming".[25] A third set of responses congregated around broader frustrations with sluggish official attitudes to preserving memory, regarding the experiment as yet another erosion of British values, under threat by non-specific "foreign" practices: "I thought the idea of these cemeteries in a foreign land", said another, "was to be forever a bit of England".[26] In several cases these sentiments were laced with anxieties about a waning sense of patriotism, and a betrayal of those we ought to hold in the highest regard:

I have always been touched by the commissions way of making its cemeteries fit for heroes, and a little piece of England. Gravel just doesnt (sic) work, in my opinion.[27]

I am always impressed by the lovely lawns between the headstones. A piece of green, immaculately kept in an oasis of peace.[28]

I really don't want to think the world these guys died for is turning into That. *Find a way of giving them grass. Don't they at least deserve that?*[29]

To these passionate respondents the greensward was being threatened not by others but from within; the quintessential English churchyard cemetery was being defiled so that it looked "more like a goods yard" than a garden. To some it echoed a greater loss of national identity; this was "a metaphor for what's happening to England's green and pleasant land." ('Idler', posted 27 November 09) Of course, context is all. The Commission's experiment had taken place against a backdrop of polarizing views around the larger environmental debate. Take for example, the gardening pages of national newspapers, which offer diverging positions on the

"Turf Wars": grass, greenery and the spatiality of commemoration   93

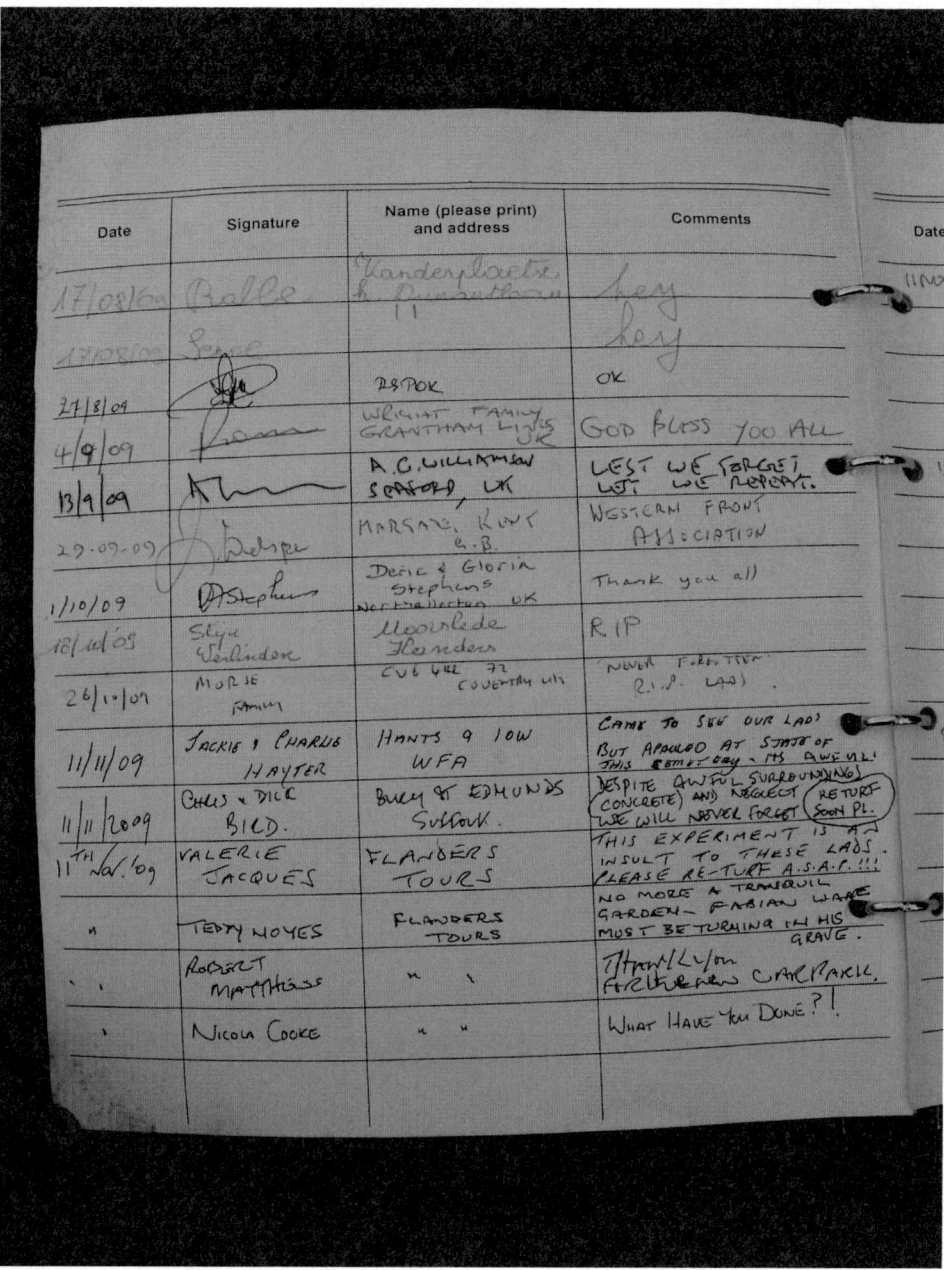

Images 12/13 Railway Chateau Cemetery: Visitors Book 17 August – 8 December 2009. ©Jeremy Banning.

ethical proposition symbolized by the well-maintained grassed lawn. On the one hand there are such expressions as "a lush, well-watered lawn is every Englishman's right", and "if an Englishman's house is his castle then his lawn is most certainly his estate" (Fort, 2001) while on the other hand, there is the environmental lobby which argues that "Clinging to the grassy elegance of English lawns will be signals of social and moral decadence." (Gray, 2009).

Caught in the midst of such debate and faced with a barrage of objection, even ridicule, the Commonwealth War Graves Commission brought an end to this phase of the experiment and drew some conclusions. During the trial period, some 250 members of the public had expressed their views through the on-line survey. 106 of these had actually visited at least one of the four cemeteries, where more comments had been left in the Visitor's Books. The Commission conceded that although many supported their work on climate change and many had recognized the need to consider alternative approaches, there was "little enthusiasm for the hard landscaping approach adopted at Railway Chateau" (CWGC 2009). As a result of the feedback received it would be re-established as a typical lawn cemetery in the spring of 2011. However, the experiment was not to be wholly abandoned: that particular Cemetery would remain part of the climate change demonstrations as the Commission continued to explore the use of drought tolerant plants in the borders and a drought tolerant grass mix, which would continue to be used at Oostduinkerke Communal Cemetery in Belgium.

Image 14 Railway Chateau Cemetery: turf restored after the alternative surface experiment, April 2011. ©Jeremy Banning.

Conceding that it had not won the public relations campaign, the Commission restated its original argument that elsewhere in the world, dry landscaping was commonly and successfully used in other cemeteries where grass cannot be grown or maintained, usually due to a lack of a regular water supply. However, this was the first time it had been demonstrated at one of their cemeteries in northern Europe. Perhaps it had indeed been a step too far and too quickly. To this end the Commission reassured interested parties that the demonstrations would continue to run for another four years and would be closely monitored by their officers and gardeners, and also by the many visitors who maintain their ideological vigilance on these sites of memory.

As a coda to this charged debate we might dwell a little on the fondness, indeed the urgent need, for designed green spaces in times of trauma. In defiance of the grim and challenging conditions of wartime Iraq and Afghanistan we find examples of British and US soldiers creating gardens, growing plants, and even harvesting fruit from small pockets of earth between the tents and temporary huts of their fortified camps.[30] Where the task of managing a plot is too demanding, possibly too dangerous, we can find evidence of "temporary" lawns or symbolic strips of grass planted as an emblem of "home". Possibly the most idiosyncratic of these is an image of a square of green tarpaulin laid out in the midst of a tent city at U.S. Air base at Al Khary, Saudi Arabia in 1990–91. Held down by sandbags, and giving every impression that is it brushed clear of dust and sand daily, the finishing touch to this temporary lawn is a hand-painted sign urging pedestrians to "Stay Off!" the "lawn".

CONCLUDING OBSERVATIONS

Little should surprise us about the intensity of feeling aroused by these proposed changes to the appearance of the "Silent Cities" in France and Belgium. Even though the last of the Great War veterans has passed away, the moral commitment to preserve the inherited memory of the war has put renewed pressure on those maintaining the state of the cemeteries by assuming the moral high ground over what is grown and nurtured. The disputes, which may seem petty to many on the outside, shed a fascinating light on the attributes of Englishness which I have explored elsewhere (Gough 2004, 2007). They tell us much about the palpable tensions between a public and private agenda of grief and how the individual "rememberer" can contest the dictates of a centralised administration. In an interesting reversal of topographical fortune what were once blighted and scarred landscapes, heavily contested by several sides, have (despite their outward calm) remained contested; wounds that ought to be left to heal, are picked at, even allowed to redden, to remain scabrous. Here there is only partial closure. Although the mines, tunnels and dugouts have been capped and fenced off, memory refuses to be parked. As John Rodwell has so eloquently described elsewhere, "closure" has many readings – political, social, geographical – and the siting of parkland or a memorial ground is as much an act of policy as it is an evocation of particular remembering (Rodwell 2008).

Given the fixity of the stone monuments, the weight of official histories and the great burdens of the grand narratives of the war, many of those who want to mark their own, unique and individualised memory have had to do so through rogue planting, the laying of flowers, the surreptitious marking of the foreign field with seeds and saplings. Plants, shrubs, even trees, and other natural interventions act as metaphors for collaboration and interaction in a way that hewn stone, shaped bronze and architectural scale cannot. Just as hand-picked flowers allow the private voice to be heard with equal status alongside the high diction of official rhetoric, so a carefully manicured lawn speaks of attention to detail, egalitarian values and long-term commitment, of turf wars fought by grass roots communities of interest.

NOTES

[1] Blair, 544.
[2] Lowenthal, 103.
[3] Iles, 171.
[4] Ware, vii.
[5] Heffernan, 302.
[6] Helphand, 38–39.
[7] Helphand, 51.
[8] Hill, 8.
[9] Longworth, 87.
[10] Mosse, 112.
[11] Morris, 411.
[12] McKay, 131.
[13] Pollan, 169.
[14] Ish, 123.
[15] Morris, 426.
[16] Morris, 431–432.
[17] Barnes, 108.
[18] Blunden.
[19] Rowlands, 129–147.
[20] Bennett, 26–28.
[21] Bennett, loc.cit.
[22] Danto, 152.
[23] Commonwealth War Graves Commission, http://www.cwgc.org/content.asp?menuid=2&submenuid=9&id=102&menuname=Climate%20Change%20Update%20-%20February%202011\&menu=subsub/, 25 September 2011.
[24] 'Steve G', Commonwealth War Graves Commission online.
[25] 'Steve G', Commonwealth War Graves Commission online.
[26] 'Geoff 501', Commonwealth War Graves Commission online.

27 'Owen', Commonwealth War Graves Commission online.
28 'Auditman', Commonwealth War Graves Commission online.
29 James Daly, Commonwealth War Graces Commission online.
30 Helphand, 243–244.

REFERENCES

Ashworth, Graham and Graham, Brian (eds.) (2005), *Senses of Place: Senses of Time*, London: Ashgate.
Banning, Jeremy, http://jeremybanning.co.uk (accessed 11 November 2014).
Barnes, Julian (1995), *Cross Channel*, London: Jonathan Cape.
Basu, Paul (2007), 'Palimpsest Memoryscapes: Materializing and Mediating War and Peace in: Sierra Leone' in: Gordon F. de Jong & Michael Rowlands (eds.), *Reclaiming Heritage: Alternative Imaginations in West Africa*, Walnut Creek, CA: Left Coast Press.
Bender, Barbara (ed.), (1983) *Landscape: Politics and Perspectives*, Oxford: Berg.
Bender, Barbara and Winer, Margot (eds.) (2001), *Contested Landscapes: Movement, Exile and Place*, Oxford: Berg.
Bennett, Alan (2004), *Untold Stories* (autobiographical and essays), London: Harper.
Blair, Sarah, "Cultural Geography and the Place of the Literary", *American Literary History*, Vol. 10, 3, Autumn 1998, 544–567.
Commonwealth War Graves Commission, http://www.cwgc.org/content.asp?menuid=2&submenuid=9&id=102&menuname=Climate%20Change%20Update%20-%20February%202011\&menu=subsub/, 25 September 2011.
Coombes, Rose E.B. (1983), *Before Endeavour Fades*, After the Battle Publications: London.
Danto, Arthur (1986), "The Vietnam Veterans Memorial", *The Nation*, 31 August 1986.
de Botton, Alan (2004), *Status Anxiety*, London: Hamish Hamilton.
Fort, Tom (2001), *The Grass is Greener: Our Love Affair with the Lawn*, London: Harper Collins.
Gillis, John. R (1994), *Commemorations*, Princeton: Princeton University Press.
Gough, Paul (2004), "Sites in the imagination: the Beaumont Hamel Newfoundland Memorial on the Somme", *Cultural Geographies*, Vol. 11, 3, 235–258.
Gough, Paul (2007), "Planting peace: the Greater London Council and the Community Gardens of Central London', *International Journal of Heritage Studies*, Vol. 3, 1, 22–41.
Gray, L. "Lawns will become sign of 'moral decadence' because of climate change", *Daily Telegraph*, 1 May 2009.
Heffernan, Michael (1995), "Forever England: the Western Front and the politics of remembrance in Britain", *Ecumene*, Vol. 2, 3, 293–324.
Helphand, Kenneth (2006), *Defiant Gardens: Making Gardens in Wartime*, San Antonio: Trinity University Press.
Hill, Arthur (1919), 'Our Soldier's Graves', *Journal of the Royal Horticultural Society*, Vol. 45, 1.
Hurst, Sidney (1929), *The Silent Cities*, London: Methuen.
Iles, Jennifer (2006), 'Recalling the Ghosts of War: Performing Tourism on the Battle-

fields of the Western Front', *Text and Performance Quarterly*, Vol. 26, No. 2, 162–180.
Ish, Lyx (1999), "Peeing on a lily pad (and other musings on gardens and art)" in: Peter Lamborn Wilson and Bill Weinberg (eds.), *Avant Gardening: Ecological Struggle in the City and the World*, New York: Autonomedia, 117–126.
Longworth, Philip (1967), *The Unending Vigil*, London, Commonwealth War Graves Commission.
Lowenthal, David (1985), *The Past is a Foreign Country*, Cambridge: Cambridge University Press.
McKay, George (2001), *Radical Gardening: Politics, Idealism and Rebellion in the Garden*, London: Frances Lincoln.
Morris, Mandy S. (1997), "'Gardens 'for ever England': Landscape, Identity and the First World War British Cemeteries on the Western Front", *Ecumene*, Vol. 4, 410–434.
Mosse, George L. (1990), *Fallen Soldiers: Reshaping the Memory of the World Wars*, Oxford: Oxford University Press.
Pollan, Michael (1991), *Second Nature: A Gardener's Education*, New York: Atlantic Monthly Press.
Rodwell, John (2008), "Forgetting the land", *Studies in Christian Ethics*, Vol. 21, 2, 269–286.
Rowlands, Michael (1999), "Remembering to Forget: Sublimation as Sacrifice in War Memorials", in: Adrian Forty and Susan Kuchler (eds.) (1999), *The Art of Forgetting*, Oxford: Berg, 129–147.
Samuel, Raphael (1989) "Exciting to be English" in: Raphael Samuel (ed.), *Patriotism: The Making and Unmaking of British National Identity*, Vol. 1. London: Routledge,
Saunders, Nicholas (2001), "Matter and memory in the landscapes of conflict: the Western Front, 1914–1919", in Barbara Bender and Margot Winer (eds.) (2001), *Contested Landscapes: Movement, Exile and Place*, Oxford: Berg,
Shepheard, Paul (1997), *The Cultivated Wilderness: or, what is landscape?*, Cambridge: MIT Press.
Walter, Tony (ed.) (1999), *The Mourning for Diana*, London: Berg.
Ware, Fabian (1929), "The Price of Peace", *The Listener*, II, 636–7.
Winter, Jay (1995), *Sites of Memory, Sites of Mourning*, Cambridge: Cambridge University Press.

THE EUCHARIST: LANDSCAPE OF MEMORY, NARRATIVE OF RECONCILIATION

Philip Sheldrake

There are vital connections between place, memory, and identity because "place" implies a dialectical relationship between environments and human narrative. The human sense of place is a critical theological and spiritual issue. Yet, historically, Christianity has been ambivalent about the subject. This in part reflects a tension between "place" and "placelessness" or journey that dates back to the biblical origins of Christian faith. The unfortunate result, however, is that in debates about the future of "place," the Christian voice has contributed little until relatively recently.

I want first to summarise a few remarks about "place" and "belonging" and then to move to my main theme – the Christian practice of the Eucharist as, metaphorically, a landscape of memory and narrative of reconciliation.

PLACE, CULTURE AND WORLD VIEWS

We exist not only in the world but in an *image* of the world. The "world" that surrounds us is not simply raw data but something we experience as bearing meaning. Indeed, the very notion of "the world" is a human construct. We do not dwell in pure "nature" but in "the realm of mediated meaning".[1] Because a sense of "place" has a determining influence on the way people think and organize their lives, few other cultural categories express a world-view so clearly.[2] Many contributions to contemporary thinking about "place" draw upon phenomenology, especially the work of philosophers such as Martin Heidegger (the concept of "dwelling"), Gaston Bachelard and Edward Casey. In recent years, writers on place have turned their attention to the issue of social identity in relation to roots and rootlessness, and, provoked by the various forms of displacement, to the politics of place, especially to what is referred to as "geographies of struggle and resistance". Heidegger, Bachelard, and Casey have underlined that we "come to know" in terms of our knowledge of specific places – tangible, physical, contextual and relational. In his essay "An Ontological Consideration of Place," Heidegger affirmed that "place is the house of being".[3] To be a person was *Dasein*, or "being-there" – in other words, to be is to exist in a particular place.

The American biblical scholar Walter Brueggemann has underscored the religious importance of "place" suggesting that it is within spatial connections that we most deeply encounter the meaning of existence.

Place is space which has historical meanings, where some things have happened which are now remembered and which provide continuity and identity across generations. Place is space in which important words have been spoken which have established identity, defined vocation and envisioned destiny. Place is space in which vows have been exchanged, promises have been made, and demands have been issued. Place is indeed a protest against an unpromising pursuit of space. It is a declaration that our humanness cannot be found in escape, detachment, absence of commitment, and undefined freedom... whereas pursuit of space may be a flight from history, a yearning for a place is a decision to enter history with an identifiable people in an identifiable pilgrimage.[4]

PLACE AND SOCIAL CRISIS

The contemporary preoccupation with "place" reflects in part what a number of commentators refer to as a cultural crisis in Western societies – a sense of rootlessness. Part of the reason lies in a decline of traditional communities as well as shared systems of religious, ethical, and social values. The resulting fragmentation (often labelled postmodernity) tends, among other things, to inhibit coherent world-views. While it is essential to have "place identity", since the Second World War Western societies have de-emphasized "place" for the sake of values such as mobility, centralization, or economic rationalization. The global relativity of space dissolves a human sense of place. "The skyscrapers, airports, freeways, and other stereotypical components of modern landscapes – are they not the sacred symbols of a civilisation that has deified reach and derided home?"[5] Indeed, mobility is frequently interpreted as a freedom purchased by money and education. Remaining in the same place then symbolizes a lack of choice that is the lot of the poor, the elderly, or people with disabilities. In an increasingly placeless culture we become "standardised, removable, replaceable, easily transported and transferred from one location to another".[6]

PLACE AND BELONGING

A sense of placelessness makes the contemporary Western quest for meaning so concerned with belonging. "Belonging" involves both our connection to specific places and also our existence within networks of known and stable relationships.

"Place" and belonging also have a great deal to do with commitment to human contexts and being accepted within them. In Penelope Lively's novel, *Spiderweb*, Stella Brentwood is a cultural anthropologist who retires to settle in an English village after years of wandering the world with no fixed abode. Coming to terms with "home" and making sense of "place" are central themes of the book.

I hope the new home is up to expectations," Richard had said just now, and for an instant she hadn't understood what on earth he was on about. Whose home?

Ah—her home, of course. This was what she now had, apparently. And must set to and play the part. Nest. Embellish. Fix rogue radiators, fit washers to taps.[7]

Really *being* somewhere means to be committed to a place rather than simply an observer. But this not what Stella is used to. As an anthropologist, "the world is out there, richly stocked and inviting observation".[8] One day, while visiting the village shop, Stella receives a little homily on commitment from Molly the shopkeeper who is still unsure about Stella:

You used to know how a person stood, without having to take soundings, know what I mean? You knew if they were farming or trade, church or chapel, you knew who their father was and which way they'd jump if it came to the push. Nowadays people can walk into the shop and it's anyone's guess, frankly...[9]

The difficult challenge put to Stella is to change from observer to committed participant. She never makes that transition, never quite fits in, and eventually leaves.

PLACE AND CONFLICT

Finally, contemporary treatments of place by social scientists and anthropologists increasingly affirm that "place" is always a contested rather than a simple reality and therefore our engagement with place is also a *political* issue. Place is political because it is regularly constructed to give space to some people's stories but not to others. Theological reflections on place can no longer ignore that the world of concrete places is filled with exiles, displaced peoples, inflamed border disputes, violent struggles by indigenous peoples to achieve liberation and, in our UK context, by arguments over immigration.

PARTICULAR AND UNIVERSAL PLACE

In Christian theology there is a tension between the local and universal dimensions of "place". Within every particular context there is understood to be an impulse towards the universal, or what is termed "catholicity" in Christian theology. Christian discipleship simultaneously demands particular "placements" and also a continual movement beyond any specific context in search of a "more", a "further", an ever-greater. The headline command to Christians is "Go out into the whole world" to proclaim the universal "work" of God. In Christian terms, "place" is both *this, here and now*, and at the same time a pointer to an "elsewhere", a "more than simply here".

When I speak of "catholicity", I am not referring primarily to the structures of the Christian Church. "Catholicity" also expresses a fundamental human value of reaching out towards fullness in the image of an all-inclusive, all-embracing God. The word itself derives from the Greek *katholikos*, which means "general" or "universal". This is not limited to "world-wide" in a geographical sense. It is generally thought that the word has its roots in an adverb *kath' holou* – "on the whole" or "in general". This adverb in turn connects with *kata holos*, meaning "in respect of the whole", or "what is not partial". At its root, therefore, "catholic" is the opposite of sectarian or tribal – that is, what is narrowly confined to a limited and exclusive group of people. Thus, St Augustine in his *Epistle* 49, n 3, contrasts a "catholic" community with any group that wishes to separate itself off from the general mass of people.

An interesting way to think of the characteristics of "catholicity" is by means of a variety of spatial images. Thus catholicity implies breadth. It is broadly inclusive, not bound to a single culture, and is opposed to divisiveness and individualism. Catholicity implies length. It indicates a communion with every generation and cannot be limited to a particular historical period or narrative. Catholicity implies depth. It permeates all dimensions of human nature and culture and is open to truth and values wherever they are to be found. Finally, catholicity implies height. That is to say, its ultimate coherence is not achievable by human striving alone but is brought into being by our participation in the life of God.[10]

THE EUCHARIST AS CATHOLIC PLACE

A "catholicity" of place is, for Christians, powerfully expressed by the community of believers filled with the Spirit of Jesus and shaped by Eucharistic practice. On the one hand, every Eucharist exists in a particular time and place. On the other hand, each Eucharist is a practice of transgression and a *transitus*, a transit point, a passageway between worlds that prefigures the conclusive "passing over" brought about in death. Eucharistic space enables the particularity of local "place" to intersect, in the presence of the risen and ascended Jesus, with all times and all places.

My preferred way of approaching the Eucharist as "catholic place" is in terms of "ethical sacramentality". The word "sacramentality" expresses a sense that all material reality, within the economy of God, manifests the sacred. However, a sacramental approach and an ethical approach to reality are not alternatives let alone competing perspectives. They do not merely complement each other but actually demand each other. A truly sacramental view of reality is necessarily an ethical view and vice versa. Because the Eucharist is an enactment of the identity of the Christian community it has profoundly ethical implications.[11] Eucharistic practice necessarily opens up the believing community to the question of how to exist appropriately in the everyday world of places and people. This is expressed powerfully in the two related themes of reconciliation and solidarity.

As the ground-breaking 1982 document of the World Council of Churches on Baptism, Eucharist and Ministry, made clear, a renewed understanding of the Eucharist provides one of the most substantial groundings for the link between sacramental and ethical viewpoints. The Eucharist expresses and somehow shapes an ethical space at the heart of what is existentially a flawed and ambiguous world.

It is in the eucharist that the community of God's people is fully manifested... The eucharist embraces all aspects of life... The eucharistic celebration demands reconciliation and sharing among all those regarded as brothers and sisters in the one family of God and is a constant challenge in the search for appropriate relationships in social, economic and political life... All kinds of injustice, racism, separation and lack of freedom are radically challenged when we share in the body and blood of Christ... As participants in the eucharist, therefore, we prove inconsistent if we are not actively participating in this ongoing restoration of the world's situation and the human condition. The eucharist shows us that our behaviour is inconsistent in face of the reconciling presence of God in human history: we are placed under continual judgement by the persistence of unjust relationships of all kinds in our society, the manifold divisions on account of human pride, material interest and power politics and, above all, the obstinacy of unjustifiable confessional oppositions within the body of Christ.[12]

To live out the meaning of the Eucharist involves being prepared to set aside a damaged condition in favour of something offered by God's grace for "where we habitually are is not, after all, a neutral place but a place of loss and need" from which we need to be relocated.[13] Part of this damaged reality consists of our flawed identities – whether these appear to enhance us as people of power or diminish us as people of no worth. The transforming context of the Eucharist demands that presuppositions about everyone's identity must be radically reordered. This requires honest recognition, painful dispossession and fearless surrender as a precondition of reconciliation. Such reconciliation clearly does not come cheaply.

A PLACE OF RECONCILIATION

So, at the heart of an ethical theology of the Eucharist is the critical theme of reconciliation. The words are important so what does "reconciliation" imply? In the social and political world, reconciliation is often interchangeable with "conciliation" and "accommodation". However, "conciliation", much used in peace negotiations and industrial arbitration, is associated more with pacifying or placating. "Accommodation" enables pragmatic, negotiated arrangements based on compromise. "Reconciliation" is much more costly because it goes further and deeper. The Oxford Dictionary defines it not only as restoring harmony and concord but also, interestingly, as the reconsecration of desecrated places. All those whose lives are excluded from consideration by what we do or say are "desecrated places" because their unique identity as images of God is denied.

Studies of human reconciliation from social, political, psychological and theological perspectives all emphasise as *the* critical factor that it can only take place *between equals*. It is, therefore, the product of a process of *making equal space for "the other"*. This "making space" also involves history. Our historical narratives are never neutral or true in some simple way. All histories are partial in that their narratives are built upon whom or what is included or excluded. A critical question for every human community, including the Church, is what kind of historical sense we foster or live by. Humans tend to rehearse a particular version of history as the justification for maintaining barriers of separation in the here and now. We therefore need to seek new shared narratives to embrace what is other than ourselves – the pluralism of our world.

The process of reconciliation must also make space for *memory*. The Latin word *memoria* has connotations of mindfulness. This relates both to attentiveness (to people, contexts and my own reality) and to "embracing the whole" (the fundamental meaning of catholicity) as opposed to a comfortable and comforting forgetfulness. Reconciliation does not mean forgetting but remembering *together* rather than trading contesting memories as we trade blows. Space for memory enables communities as a whole to begin to come to terms with the truth of the past. Reconciliation involves the healing of memories particularly of belittlement, rejection and denial. Part of a process of healing is to realise the incompleteness of any one story when isolated from the other stories. So a space for memory also celebrates diversity.

Of course, reconciliation is a process over time rather than a single miraculous moment. With remembering comes recognition, not least the recognition by everyone of the destructive forces around and within them – whether that is unacknowledged guilt or destructive hate. Reconciliation also then demands repentance by everyone of those attitudes and actions that promote the exclusion, the diminishment or the demonising of the "other". Only when there is substantial repentance can there be effective forgiveness. There needs, too, to be a commitment to refusal. What I mean by refusal is that within the process of reconciliation all people need to learn how to refuse to participate in structures or behaviour that violate the other in whatever way. Because reconciliation is an ethical task, there is also a need for restitution after repentance. Restitution need not be economic but includes such things as restoring the value and identity of the other or enabling the empowerment of others. Because restitution involves the establishment of a just situation, this will always entail loss for some people so that others may gain. Restitution is also bound up with reconstruction – the reconstruction of a quite different world of discourse and practice.

EUCHARIST AS RECONCILING SPACE

The Eucharist is a space of reconciliation. To celebrate the Eucharist commits participants to cross the boundaries of fear, of prejudice and of injustice in a prophetic embracing of other people, without exception, in whom we are challenged to discover the Real Presence of a "catholic", all-embracing God.

Reconciled in the Eucharist, the members of the body of Christ are called to be servants of reconciliation among men and women and witnesses of the joy of resurrection. As Jesus went out to publicans and sinners and had table-fellowship with them during his earthly ministry, so Christians are called in the Eucharist to be in solidarity with the outcast and to become signs of the love of Christ who lived and sacrificed himself for all and now gives himself in the Eucharist.[14]

To live the Eucharist, as liberation theologians constantly remind us, necessarily involves existing in a state of tension. We celebrate fullness and feasting in the midst of a world in which the existential location of the Eucharist is often one of acute deprivation.[15] There is a painful paradox in proclaiming spiritual plenty in the midst of material want. The Eucharist also celebrates the destruction of the boundaries of mutual exclusion. "As many of you as were baptized into Christ have clothed yourselves with Christ. There is no longer Jew or Greek, there is no longer slave or free, there is no longer male or female; for all of you are one in Christ Jesus." (Galatians 3: 27–28). Yet, sadly, too many eucharistic celebrations are contexts of social, political or religious exclusions. A vital aspect of the future-oriented dimension of eucharistic "place" is that it points towards the hope of final completion that stands in judgment on all human systems of exclusion.[16]

EUCHARIST AND MEMORY

As I already noted, an important element in reconciliation is the reconstruction of memory. Eucharistic "place" is very much a landscape of memory – including ambiguous memories. Beyond the immediate participants, there are wider and deeper narrative currents in any eucharistic celebration. There is one central narrative, the remembrance of the events of God's redeeming action in the world expressed in the life and death of Jesus Christ. This foundational narrative enables all human narratives to have their proper place and at the same time it reconfigures them. God's "narrative" expressed in eucharistic practices makes space for all those who have been given no place in human, public history and whose voices have been excluded or forgotten. In that sense, the narrative of the Eucharist makes space for a new kind of history that tells a different story about humanity beyond the selectivity of tribalism or sectarianism. The painful and difficult reality is that God's narrative, expressed in the eucharistic "memory" of Jesus's life and death, highlights the ambiguities, injustices and pain in human narratives.

The Eucharist as a "place" of reconciliation makes space for memories that refuse to remain silent. To cultivate forgetfulness is simply to excuse all acts of oppression or exclusion. That is neither reconciliation nor forgiveness. The Eucharist as God's action within the Christian community (despite our various human attempts to regulate and control it) engages a power beyond the ritual acts themselves to make space for alternative narratives that break open "history" to offer an entry point for the oppressed, the marginalised, the excluded. The eucharistic action, according to its own inner logic, is as public and also as catholic a space as can be in the contingent world of space and time. There is a perpetual and uncomfortable tension between our sacramental practice of reconciled place and our many efforts to resist the logic of reconciliation.

At the heart of a theology of reconciled place must be the belief that our deepest human identities are determined by God rather than by social or economic networks or obligations. In the redefinition of personal and collective human identities brought about in the ritual of baptism and continually reinforced in the Eucharist, Christian disciples are bound into solidarity with those they have not chosen or whose presence they have not negotiated. Consequently, the new community, the new world, spoken of in eucharistic "place" is deeply challenging for any humanly constructed social order.

However, the Eucharist does not simply challenge and empower believers to reshape the social, economic and political world "out there". The eucharistic action is founded on the transfiguration, however we understand this, of the ordinary material and action of human feeding. We become what we feed upon. The practice of the Eucharist does involve the repetition of familiar words and rituals. However, the most challenging element is one of *recognition*. Who do we recognise as our co-heirs with Christ, and who are we increasingly able to respond to in the real presence of Jesus Christ?

The core of the affirmation of a "real presence" of Jesus Christ in the Eucharist, however one understands this, is the notion of *God's* critical recognition of us, God's affirming and life-giving gaze. All are incorporated solely because of God's recognition. The demands on those who practice the Eucharist may be, as a result, more powerful than any notion of inclusion or solidarity based solely on social theory, however just it seeks to be.[17] The notion of "real presence" also stands in judgement on all eucharistic performances. This implies not only the generalisation that the Christian Church as an institution is sinful. The statement addresses the fact that neither the Church nor its eucharistic celebrations existentially expresses a perfect society. Any affirmation of "real presence" confronts our exclusions and judgements in real time and space. To put it more sharply, eucharistic celebrations are supposed to be ethical practices but are sometimes practised unethically.

The problem is that the encounter with the risen Jesus that Christians affirm is the heart of the Eucharist may continue to be comfortably limited to what the Bolivian theologian, Victor Codina, refers to as "drawing-room communitarianism" whose attractiveness is not marred by the demands of real solidarity with the poor and unwashed.[18] The commitment to solidarity, however, is inextricably bound up with the other key eucharistic themes of repentance and reconciliation. These imply not simply a transformation of perceptions but a real transformation of the practice of everyday life. It is perfectly possible, as Codina suggests, to limit reconciliation and forgiveness to a magic circle of those people who are already like each other and whose social and cultural worlds overlap. Solidarity is a much more challenging concept. It pushes worshippers beyond the familiar boundaries of social, cultural and economic identities and separations. Fundamentally, solidarity challenges every Christian community to find a relational identity beyond its conventional boundaries. By following Jesus' command to "do this in memory of me", to take bread and wine, to bless, break and share, the community does not merely receive Jesus' gift of himself in its own life. Rather, the community, which calls itself the Body of Christ and is the prolongation of Jesus' mission, is also drawn into Jesus' own dynamic of pouring out his life for the life of all. The Christian community in its vocation of "catholicity" develops most authentically in a process of selfless outpouring, in a transgression of its own boundaries, in leaving itself behind, in breaking itself open for the sake of the world.

The most challenging, but rarely noted, element of a doctrine of "real presence" in the Eucharist is the question of who and what the presence of Jesus brings with him into the eucharistic space. In receiving Jesus Christ the disciple receives at the same time all that makes up his Body. We find ourselves in communion not merely in some romantic way with the whole court of heaven, a communion of saints that somehow safely visits us from elsewhere and represents merely our pasts and our futures. We also find ourselves, if we dare to face it, in communion with all that God in Jesus embraces in the present as well. We know from the gospel narratives of the Last Supper (which we claim to re-enact whatever our tradition) that the "catholicity" of Jesus' act of incorporation included not only disciples like Peter who denied him but Judas who betrayed him. Those we prefer to exclude from communion with us in the world of public place are already uncomfortable ghosts at our eucharistic feastings. The story of the centurion Cornelius in Acts 10 raises an even more difficult question about the nature of the body of Christ. However shocking the fact that God had chosen someone who was Gentile rather than Jew, the even more challenging fact was that the Spirit had come upon people who were not baptized, who were not members of our club. The doctrine of "real presence" is a kind of Trojan horse that outflanks our defences and brings into our space all that, from our limited perspective, we would rather exclude. That is undoubtedly particularly disturbing for those who have a well-developed sense of moral or ecclesiastical order. However it is also ultimately encouraging for it suggests that the boundaries of the Body of Christ, as practised by the Eucharist, do not depend on our human powers of incorporation.[19]

EUCHARIST AS FUTURE SPACE

The reconciliation practised in the Eucharist ultimately has a future-oriented dimension. This future perspective does not empty the here-and-now world of time and space of significance by suggesting that real meaning is to be found only in some indefinable future "elsewhere". Rather, a balanced future perspective opens every "present moment", and indeed history as a whole, to what is beyond it or more than the isolated, present instant.

Christians live proleptically. That is, in and through their practice of everyday life, they should affirm that the all-embracing nature of God is bound eventually to triumph. The Eucharist is a space in which God speaks to human beings and acts upon them out of their future. "The Holy Spirit through the Eucharist gives a foretaste of the Kingdom of God: the Church receives the life of the new creation and the assurance of the Lord's return".[20] The Eucharist is a point of *transitus* – where there is an intersection of here and elsewhere, and of the past, present and future. Eucharistic symbolism is founded on death and rebirth. The breaking and sharing of bread is symbolic of a sharing in the power of Jesus' death that opens the doors to new life. However, practising the Eucharist also, by association, points the members of the community towards their entry *now* into a painful death – the death of their protected and self-enclosed ways of existing and selective ways of being social. To celebrate the Eucharist entails the risk of radically reshaping the place where we stand.

NOTES

1. Geertz, 4–5.
2. Gurevich, 94.
3. Heidegger, 26.
4. Brueggemann, 5.
5. Buttimer, 174.
6. Berleant, 86–87.
7. Lively, 13.
8. Lively, 15.
9. Lively.
10. Dulles.
11. William Spohn, 175–84; Saliers, 175–86.
12. *Baptism, Eucharist and Ministry*, 19–20 & 22. Cited subsequently as WCC.
13. Williams, 209–10.
14. WCC, 24.
15. Ford, 268–70.
16. Rowland, 200–215.
17. Williams, 212–214.
18. Codina, 218–219.
19. Ford, 151–52.
20. WCC, para 18.

REFERENCES

Brueggemann, Walter (1977), *The Land: Place as Gift, Promise and Challenge in Biblical Faith*. Philadelphia: Fortress.

Berleant, Arnold (1992), *The Aesthetics of Environment*, Philadelphia: Temple University Press.

Buttimer, Anne (1980), "Home, Reach and the Sense of Place", in: Anne Buttimer and David Seamon (eds.), *The Human Experience of Space and Place*, London: Croam Helm.
Codina, Victor (1996), "Sacraments", in: Jon Sobrino & Ignacio Ellacuria (eds.), *Systematic Theology: Perspectives from Liberation Theology*, ET London: SCM Press.
Ford, David (1999), *Self and Salvation*, Cambridge: Cambridge University Press
Dulles, Avery (1985), *The Catholicity of the Church*, Oxford: Clarendon Press.
Geertz, Clifford (1973), *The Interpretation of Cultures.* New York: Basic Books.
Gurevich A. J (1985), *Categories of Medieval Culture*, London: Routledge & Kegan Paul.
Heidegger, Martin (1958), *The Question of Being*, New York: Twayne Publishers.
Lively, Penelope (1999), *Spiderweb*, London/New York: Penguin Books.
Rowland, Christopher (1995), "Eucharist as Liberation from The Present" in: David Brown & Ann Loades, (eds.), *The Sense of the Sacramental: Movement and Measure in Art and Music, Place and Time*, London: SPCK.
Spohn, William (1999), *Go and Do Likewise: Jesus and Ethics*, New York: Continuum.
Saliers, Donald E (1989), "Liturgy and Ethics: Some New Beginnings" in: Ronald Hamel and Kenneth Himes, (eds.), *Introduction to Christian Ethics: A Reader*, New York: Paulist Press.
Williams, Rowan (2000), *On Christian Theology*, Oxford: Blackwell.
World Council of Churches (1982), *Baptism, Eucharist and Ministry*, Faith and Order Paper 111, Geneva: World Council of Churches.

Remembering the Future

John Rodwell

The lie of the land

As a child, I heard, smelt, tasted on the air even, the coal mines around my home. From the top of the hill where my father, then a pit wages clerk, launched his model aeroplanes and where I first learned, as a budding naturalist, how to tell the difference between the small copper butterfly and the little skipper, I could look down on Cortonwood pit where my grandfather started work, at the age of ten, in 1887. What I see now from the same spot is the 500-hectare Cortonwood Business and Retail Park with a Next, Argos, Boots, distribution warehouses and call centre, a lakeside residential area, the A6195 Dearne Valley Parkway and behind them the graded slopes of the mine spoil, grassed over and planted with blocks of trees.

"Once an abandoned and disused colliery...." is how the St Paul's Developments website describes the past at Cortonwood and that's all.[1] And on the site now, there is almost nothing to give a clue as to its former life, that could tell, for example, that the first shaft was sunk 200 metres or so down to the Barnsley Thick seam in 1873; that the pit employed over 500 men when my grandfather, then 33, worked there during the First World War; three times that many men when *I* looked down on it; was the start and end of the 1984/5 miners' strike and closed six months later, making 690 men redundant, about 1% of the total job-losses with the demise of the coal industry.[2] When I asked at the National Mining Museum for England about the prospect of reconstructing the work record of employees at this colliery, they told me that generally, when pits were closed, filing cabinets with all their records, furniture, office buildings and other superstructure were bulldozed into the shafts which were then capped. As it said in *Transco Business Week*, one of the journals reporting on the regeneration of the Dearne Valley, Cortonwood colliery "has disappeared as if it had never existed".[3]

"Doing justice to place", making this or that place "a great place" in which people have "pride of place" are some of the phrases and ideas in current use in regeneration programmes,[4] but these aspirations rarely entail any sense of particularity or depth in the regenerated post-industrial landscape of the Dearne Valley. And, many of the future landscapes we see in the making now – retail parks, industrial parks, housing developments – these have lost much of the local distinctiveness that came from the intimate association of particular workplace and associated homes and services that preceded them. The complete obliteration of places such as Cortonwood mean that "there is no trace of the landmarks that once announced you were in South Yorkshire"[5] and indeed, as John Handley has memorably described it, much of the regeneration of post-industrial sites in Britain is essentially "turning landscapes into something very bland and then abandoning them"[6]. What we have then is another "non-place", somewhere that is "curiously everywhere and nowhere".[7] They have become what the 18th century Northamptonshire poet John Clare called "vague unpersonifying things", which we can no longer recognise and where we are ourselves unknown.[8] Protests about the loss of particularity of place in the Dearne Valley seem now a distant nostalgic echo: in the 1880s, for example, successful popular resistance to rationalising the dates of the various feasts (fairs) of the area, a move by the colliery owners to enable more economic shut-downs across a wide area, enabled each town to keep its celebratory moment in the spotlight.[9]

"I'm not nostalgic for the pit days", said an ex-miner who went on to manage a chain of fast-food stores whose Cortonwood drive-in opened in 1999.[10] And, of course, the Oxford English Dictionary admits a definition of "nostalgia" which sees homesickness as disease.[11] But such "pain" (*algia*) associated with the desire to "return home" (*nostos*) may in fact be less pathological than the forgetfulness which is now so obvious in post-industrial landscapes – the forgetfulness of people and place, the forgetfulness of the price paid by former lives there. In the Dearne Valley, as in other one-time mining landscapes, this is felt partly in the almost total loss of the built colliery landscape, pit and ancillary buildings and the associated infrastructure of roads, rail links and pedestrian ways. Such buildings have proved less structurally suitable and less appealing than the substantial stone-built heritage of the wool and cotton industries of Northern England, widely retained and refurbished, often with considerable imagination, as retro-fitted dwellings and business premises. Often now, in the post-mining landscape, the only physical reminder of the existence of a colliery will be a headstock wheel, sawn in half and embedded into the roadside of what was once a mining village.

Within the wider post-mining landscape, there is a further loss of memory in that colliery spoil heaps are generally restructured to ensure safe angles of repose of waste that is generally chemically safe but which presents steep slopes and gullies of loose material after abandonment. Such ground is then usually capped with top-soil and planted with grass and trees, often in single very costly capital projects with no endowment for continuing management. By contrast, the last surviving spoil heap in the Dearne Valley, known locally as the "Hanging Gardens of Grimethorpe" became naturally colonised by durmast oak and silver birch and acquired a carpet of wavy hair-grass over a decade or so, at absolutely no public expense.[12] This has now also been landscaped because, the Chief Planning Officer of Barnsley told me, it was seen as "a disincentive to inward investment" being, in his professional opinion, a reminder of a past best forgotten.

Best forgotten, too, maybe, are the uncommemmorated dead beneath the ground still, in the Dearne valley, without official memorial either on the surface above, or in any official written record. There are some impressive monuments to major disasters, of course, many gravestones in local churches and some mining heritage literature detailing disasters.[13] And there have been a few local community responses to particular losses, as at Huskar Colliery where in 1988, a locally-erected memorial, play and church service remembered the loss of 26 children in an inrush of water 150 years before. But often, to find such memories, you have to search the web-site of the Coal Mining History Research Centre[14] where, Ian Winstanley is making it his personal task to compile a list of the 90,000 or so men, women and children who have lost their lives in mining accidents. "My family have called me morbid....", he says there, yet, it is striking how very little serious attention is given, on the ground or in intellectual reflection, to such passing lives and their own claim on the landscape we inherit from them, compared, say, with battlefield memorials about which someone like Paul Gough[15] has produced such impressive reflections. On July 1, for example, we commemorate the start of the Battle of the Somme in the First World War. Wounded in that first assault, Edward Garton died two days later and is remembered in his regimental records. In fact, his father was killed six months earlier in a roof-fall at Cortonwood colliery but for him there is no memorial there.

As to the industrial conflicts in the coalfields themselves, no commemoration of these remains in place, in the Dearne Valley or elsewhere. At Agecroft in Salford, Manchester, where striking miners from Yorkshire picketed the mine and clashed with police, "there is virtually no sign that the once busy pit existed".[16] With the closure of Harworth Colliery in Nottinghamshire, a key battleground during the last major miners' strike in the 1980s, the local village "Bassetlaw will wave goodbye to 86 years of colour and controversy".[17] At Manvers Colliery in Wath, "the characters and causes behind the unrest slip into the history books".[18] At Orgreave, near Rotherham, Paul Darlow, one of the first pickets in what came to be some of the most violent clashes between strikers and the police, thinks that the miners' strike is in danger of becoming forgotten history, "history written by the victors".[19]

In common with many regenerated landscapes, much then has been lost in the Dearne Valley and, by some, best thought forgotten. The built environment of former workplaces, no longer economically viable, is destroyed; the wider landscape, too full of risk and memory for the future, is transformed; the contested claims to the past are difficult to hear now, often unwelcome. Coming from such times and places, as we do, it is often impossible to find where you are now, and to see where you are going, in the lie of the land.

RUINATION AND FRAILTY IN THE LANDSCAPE

In visions of our future, the ruinous is a risk. Of course, with ruins, the temptation to the Romantic is obvious and their rich possibilities when framed with "a Poet's feeling and a Painter's eye" were well explored by such masters of the Picturesque landscape as Capability Brown. In fact, signs of Brown's work can be seen close to the post-industrial heart of the Dearne Valley at Roche Abbey, a Cistercian monastery destroyed at the Dissolution and whose subsequent ruination was fashionably incorporated into a late 18th century terraced landscape with artificial lake, and a dramatic backdrop of natural limestone cliffs and wooded slopes. Another approach to such ruins is to display them as heritage, as happened subsequently at Roche Abbey, Brown's work being undone by the Office of Works in the 1920s, the buildings' foundations being more extensively excavated, displayed and managed now as a national monument by its successor English Heritage.[20] Effectively (and to considerable effect), this heritage approach is what has prevailed with the few remaining mine buildings in the Dearne Valley. At Elsecar, a Heritage Centre offers history, crafts and antiques among what was one of the first 18th century collieries of the area, and provides space for small businesses within a wider early industrial village. At Caphouse Colliery near Wakefield, there is the National Coal Mining Museum of England, which offers the possibility of underground tours of former mine workings as well as surface interpretation in a complex of conserved buildings.

For Christopher Woodward, however, more ruinous remains may have a deeper reach, prompting "a dialogue between an incomplete reality and the imagination of the spectator".[21] Such a prospect would seem to give the measured pleasure of the Picturesque, with its preoccupation with contrast and surprise, a distinctly uneasy edge; and it threatens the interpreted neatness of those ruins that are part of a commodified heritage. However, taking such a risk might help us explore the capacity of ruination to suggest a moral dimension to reminders of the past and offer some capacity to heal.

Ruins, for example, can provide one kind of consolation against the prospect of being forgotten. When John Clare, the Northamptonshire labourer-poet, was working as a lime-digger in a pit that turned out to be "full of foundations and human bones", he sought solace beneath an arch, the sole surviving ruin of the former village in that place, seeking some assurance that he would not himself be so abandoned: "A few more years and I shall be forgot, And not a vestige of my memory left".[22] His 'Elegy Hastily composed and Written with a Pencil on the Spot in the Ruins of Pickworth, Rutland' gains resonance because of his own exile from his home village of Helpstone and the prospect of his never feeling wanted by the women he fell for. In a similar way, Woodward[23] has suggested, ruins were such a preoccupation for John Soane because they worked out a tension between his melancholic and quarrelsome interior life and his punctilious public persona, his autobiographical museum displaying 'treasures salvaged from a shipwrecked dream' that was partly his own life.

Beyond this, where there is allowed some active, uncontrolled interface between the ruinous built environment and natural processes, there may be the prospect of witnessing signs of hopeful regeneration among what has been considered a sign of loss. The greening of the ruins of Rome that greeted Shelley in 1812 was for him a rapturous epiphany[24] and he saw in the striking fecundity of nature within the city walls a triumph of free and fertile forces over some sort of tyrannical imposition, sentiments celebrated in *Promethius Unbound*, the drafts of which he penned among the "flowery glades... the thickets of odoriferous blossoming trees" in the Baths of Caracalla. Forty years afterwards, a *Flora of the Coliseum*[25] catalogued over 400 plants that "without speech... tell us of the regenerating power which animates the dust of mouldering greatness" though, by 1870, for the sake of conserving the archaeology of the ruin, every scrap of greenery had been removed.

At Stowe in Buckinghamshire, before the restoration of its many follies, Girouard recognised an edge of drama and intensity in the landscape because of the uncomfortable story of pride and aggrandisement that lay behind the eventual ruination of its buildings.[26] This was one of the aspects of the place that, in his early visits so appealed to the painter John Piper, for whom "decrepit glory" became such a potent inspiration.[27] In fact, when Piper later turned to the depiction of wartime ruins, like the bombed-out Coventry Cathedral, his work was criticised because of the incongruity of the desolation of the places and their framing in the paintings, empty, so Sillars[28] thought, of any sense of compassion, outrage or loss. Likewise, though Kenneth Clark was energetic in his campaign to preserve the ruins of conflict in the Second World War as memorials,[29] his vision of them as "more than a collection of debris (but each) a place with its own individuality, charged with its own emotion and atmosphere and drama, of grandeur, of nobility, of charm" sounds like a late fling of the Picturesque.

A different approach to ruins of conflict can be seen at Orford Ness in Suffolk, a coastal spit where a variety of radar and weapons-testing installations, dating from the First World War through to the Cold War, had been left to dereliction and the predations of scrap merchants and vandals.[30] Under the new ownership of the National Trust, the decaying buildings and rusting equipment have been retained with minimum intervention and a light touch of interpretation so that, along a demarcated route and, with the more hazardous structures, viewing from a distance, something of the strange and chilling landscape there can be appreciated. Over the ruins and on the shingle on which these structures were built, itself a habitat of rarity in Britain, plants are re-colonising, blurring the boundaries between nature and the built.[31] Here then there is a more uneasy frame that might prompt a meditation on time and the transience of humanity.

An example of how such an approach might work in post-industrial landscapes can be seen in the Emscher Landschaftspark in Germany.[32] There, at the Zollverein colliery and coking plant and the Duisburg Nord steel works, rusting hulks of stupendous scale, their associated spoil heaps and abandoned railway tracks, remain cherished within the wider landscape of the Ruhrgebiet, a complex of continuing heavy industry, new enterprises, long-established settlements and new housing. Moreover, among the industrial ruins, the dramatic uncontrolled reassertion of natural processes of recolonisation by vegetation, creates what the Germans call *Industrienatur*, a striking alternative to the domesticated greenery of most regenerated landscapes in Britain. In this country the planning process, with its unimaginative categorisation of 'derelict, under-used and neglected land' ensures that the boundaries between the built and the green, between the past and the future, are sharp and static. And the less aesthetically appealing and more threatening, untidy aspects of nature, its awkward less manageable dynamism, these are sacrificed to produce what are essentially low-risk landscapes of social engineering.

In research for the M.B. Reckitt Trust,[33] I drew on the work of Walter Brueggemann to suggest that the Judaeo-Christian tradition offered an alternative narrative to the rhetoric of regeneration which prevails in places like the Dearne Valley, in the notion of Sabbath as 'setting a boundary to our best, most intense efforts to manage life and organise land for our own security'.[34] For people who have such faith in place as comes from this tradition, this kind of perspective recognises that the future is dependent on some gift from the past not on a coercive vision that is forgetful, and that such memories might even survive a cry of dereliction. Thus, living with the ruinous, offers a more risky but creative approach to the past than received ideas of "closure". Might there not be something profoundly therapeutic in the slow disintegration of signs of one-time industrial might among those human communities that remain with their memories of such places and what being there cost them? They stand, in the words of Pope Pius II who first moved to protect the classical inheritance of Rome in 1462, as "signs of exemplary frailty"[35] against which can measure the changes in our own lives.

THE DENIAL OF AMNESIA IN PLACE

At Orford Ness, the fast-disappearing resource of human memories of those who worked there and lived nearby is being used by the National Trust to understand what has taken place. And such oral histories and archives are becoming a more common feature of heritage projects. Yet giving voice to the recent past in post-industrial landscapes seems more problematic and the recall of belonging and sometimes painful memories less welcome.

For those professionals concerned with the pathological loss of human memory, "reminiscence" means the process or practice of thinking or telling about past experiences[36] and it is seen to have a crucial role in continually structuring, maintaining and reconstructing our individual self-identity and self-esteem, processes that are important ultimately for self-preservation.[37] There is evidence that such making vivid of the past, preferably with a sympathetic hearer, can be a key resource for maintaining psychological health in the ageing and this may be especially important in the face of threats to or assaults on self-image, such as critical life transitions.[38] In the work of practitioners such as Chaudury, we can see how empirical studies are demonstrating that "place" can be used as a purposeful theme in reminiscence therapy.[39] In this sense, 'place' is space that has been given meaning through personal, group or cultural processes[40] and attachment to place represents emotional links to environmental settings. Past places are thus not empty spaces nor objective locations, nor a realm of purely subjective perspectives. Rather, they are personal worlds anchored in physical reality through meaningful events, activities and experiences.

Reminiscence of such personally meaningful pasts is more likely than remembering an impersonal past to maintain a sense of self and memories of place may be especially important where they are imbued with emotions and where attributes of place are concerned with choice, ownership and belonging. Place-related information from the personal past, presented in verbal or visual form in therapy, thus provides surrogates of the familiar, stable, social self that can be impaired in ageing and memory loss. This prompts an unknown, creative, potential self to be reflexive, thus re-establishing social meaning. For Chaudury, recollection of the past does not duplicate an historical truth; rather, in remembering the past through places, we come to an intersection of past and present and potentially construct a future in place. Remembering connects "then" and "now", the continuity of which services the very pragmatic concern of venturing into the future.[41]

Interestingly, such insights as these are not brought to bear in the process of securing the future for the people of post-industrial communities. There, forgetfulness is encouraged by the planning process and the political momentum of regeneration such that memory is not cherished as part of inter-generational equity. From within the Judaeo-Christian tradition, we find a way of recall that challenges such shallow understanding of the relationship between past and future. Such telling of former experience takes its meaning from the Hebrew root *zkr* the term *zikkaron* indicating some thing – an object, written record, an act – which signifies for those who see and hear it a prior reality from which it derives.[42] This is not some Platonic evocation, but a recall of the significance and power of things that have happened and the places where people had faith in them. It actualises such meaningful past events by bringing them into the here and now.[43] Shared memory and behaviour thus join past and present together in places that are common to both.[44] In the scriptural record, the recall of stories makes sense of experience and shapes human identity, both of individuals and groups. Shared memories are part of "being there" in the sense of Heidegger, where self is revealed in a reflexive way, through *das andenkende Denken*, "thinking that recalls".[45]

What's more, there is a future perspective to this personal and community behaviour since such remembering is expectant. For people of faith, the narratives of recall not only re-present what we have been in the past and how we have related to where we were, they do not simply enable us to live and move now "in the time taken to articulate a memory" as Rowan Williams puts it,[46] but they illuminate what we might be. His claim that "my future will not be mine without the concrete memories of my past"[47] is a striking echo of a neurologist's statement to me that in the human brain, the capacity to conceive of tomorrow is hard-wired into our ability to remember yesterday.

It is often countered by professionals involved in regeneration projects that retaining signs and symbols of the earlier industrial life of the place is unwelcome among the people who live there. And such sentiments can indeed be heard from those who were part of the past. Faced with the prospect of a memorial to the miners' pickets and battles at Orgreave, for example, Ken Capstick, a spokesman for the National Union of Mineworkers, said "It may be something (local people) don't want. They have moved on and they may say 'Let it go'. Local councillor Fred Wright also commented, 'The miners' strike took a lot of forgetting'".[48] In fact this is not as surprising as it seems, nor entirely convincing. Remembering the past is costly because it is a place of ambiguous and conflicting narratives. The past cannot be changed (even by God, Christians would say) but there are ways of deploying costly memories that can change the present and enrich the options for the future. What such recall proclaims is the possibility of "carrying a forgiven past into a transformed future" as Brown & Loades have put it.[49]

Reconciliation between people now and between their present and their past means making space for telling the truth as we ourselves remember it, being given room to tell our own story and hearing and not denying the stories others wish to tell about the same time and place.[50] It involves confession and the public ownership of complicity by people who still belong to a place and represent it.[51] Where such histories speak of wounding, the process of reconciliation is most powerfully initiated in the place(s) where the hurt began.[52]

For Christian communities which go on gathering as landscapes change around them, remembering takes place in celebrations of the eucharist, mass or Lord's Supper at the heart of which is an *anamnesis*, a denial of forgetfulness of shared history and particular places in which God is seen to have revealed himself.[53] Michel de Certeau drew a contrast between "itineraries" which tell spatial stories, tracing narratives through time and space by events and practices, with 'maps' where space is represented on a grid of abstract places. In mapped space, local communities simply mediate the structural plan or vanish altogether in a globalised world where subsidiary levels of allegiance are redundant.[54] Supposed uniqueness of place is thus detached from particular localities and tailored to attract development, modelled on successful localities elsewhere. What the *anamnesis* of the people of faith does is open what de Certeau calls a "legitimate theater for practical actions" challenging the overcoding of the map, telling a story and allowing something to take place.[55] Making a place for memories, listening to unrecalled, unheard narratives interrupts the linear march of time, prising open elite and institutionalised history so that all those who have no standing can be heard.[56] Repeated over and again, this hermeneutic of place reveals more and more meanings in a kind of conversation between landscape, memory and the presence of people at any given moment. In other words, it re-members the land.

NOTES

1. www.st-pauls.co.uk, 28 March 2014.
2. Taylor.
3. Transco Business Week 6, undated.
4. www.yorkshire-forward.com, 28 March 2014
5. Transco Business Week 6, undated.
6. Handley.
7. Augé.
8. Robinson & Powell.
9. Walker.
10. Barnsley Chronicle, 27 October 1999.
11. Stevenson.
12. Rodwell, Ling & Hey.
13. Elliott.
14. www.cmhrc.pwp.blueyonder.co.uk, 28 March 2014.
15. Gough 1998; 2001; 2003 and this volume, pp. 00–00.
16. http://www.manchestereveningnews.co.uk/news/s/1100423, 28 March 2014.
17. http://www.worksopguardian.co.uk/news/local/harworth-the-end-of-an-era-1-625502, 28 March 2014.
18. http://yorkshirepost.co.uk/businessnews/Publishing-giant-moves-to-old.111841, 28 March 2014.
19. http://news.bbc.co.uk/1/hi/uk/7543530.stm, 28 March 2014.
20. Rodwell & Hey.
21. Woodward, 15.
22. Clare.
23. Woodward, 160.
24. Holmes.
25. Deakin.
26. Girouard.
27. Spalding.
28. Sillars.
29. Clarke.
30. Beamish.
31. Watkins.
32. Schwarze-Rodrian, Bauer, Scheuvens, Cuppers, Luchterhandt.
33. Rodwell (2008a), (2000b).
34. Brueggemann.

35 Woodward, 89.
36 Webster & Height.
37 McMahon & Rhudick.
38 Butler.
39 Chaudury (1999), (2008a), (2008b).
40 Low & Altman.
41 Lawton & Nahemov.
42 Gregg.
43 Grisbrooke.
44 Carruthers.
45 Heidegger.
46 Williams (1994), 144.
47 Williams (2000), 77.
48 http://news.bbc.co.uk/1/hi/uk/7543530.stm, 28 March 2014.
49 Brown & Loades 1995, 000.
50 Sheldrake (2008).
51 Parker.
52 Irvine.
53 Gittoes.
54 de Certeau.
55 see also, Cavanaugh.
56 Sheldrake (1995).

REFERENCES

Augé, M. (1997), *Non-Places: Introduction to the Anthropology of Super-modernity*, Verso: London/New York.
Bate, J. (2003), *John Clare: A Biography*, London: Picador.
Beamish, H. (1999), "Defence review – the modern defence heritage and the National Trust", *National Trust Archaeological Review*, 1998–99, 11–17.
Brown, D. & Loades, A. (1995), *The Sense of the Sacramental*, London: SPCK.
Breytspraak, L. (1984), *The Development of Self in Later Life*, Boston: Little, Brown and Company.
Brueggemann, W. (2002, 2nd Edition), *The Land: Place as Gift, Promise and Challenge in Biblical Faith*, Minneapolis: Fortress Press.
Butler, R.N. (1963), "The Life Review: An Interpretation of Reminiscence in the Aged", *Pyschiatry*, Vol. 26, 65–76.
Carruthers, M.J. (1990), *The Book of Memory*, Cambridge: Cambridge University Press.
Cavanaugh, W. (1999), "The Eucharist as Resistance to Globalisation" in S. Beckwith ed. *Catholicism and Catholicity: Eucharistic Communities in Historical and Contemporary Perspectives*, Oxford: Blackwell.
Chaudury, H. (1999), "Self and Reminicsnece of Place: A Conceptual Study", *Journal of Aging and Identity*, Vol. 4/4, 231–253; (2003). – (2008a), "Quality of Life and Place Therapy", *Journal of Housing for the Elderly*, Vol. 17(1/2), 85–103. – (2008b), *Remembering Home: Rediscovering the Self in Dementia*. Baltimore MD: John Hopkins University Press.

Clare, J. (1818), "Elegy Hastily composed and Written with a Pencil on the Spot in the Ruins of Pickworth Rutland", in E. Robinson (ed.), *Champion for the Poor*, Oxford: Carcanet.
Clarke, K. (1945), *Bombed Churches as War Memorials*, Cheam: The Architectural Press.
de Certeau, M. (1984), *The Practice of Everyday Life*, Berkley, CA: University of California Press.
Deakin, R. (1855), *Flora of the Colosseum*.
Elliott, B. (2008), *South Yorkshire Mining Disasters*, Barnsley: Wharncliffe Press.
Girouard, M. (1983), *John Piper's Stowe*, London: Hurtwood Press in association with the Tate Gallery.
Gittoes, J. (2008), *Anamnesis and the Eucharist: Contemporary Anglican Approaches*, Aldershot: Ashgate.
Gough, P. (1998), "Deadlines: Codified Drawing and Scopic Vision in Hostile Space", *Point 1998*, 34–41. – (2001), "Landscapes of War (and Peace)" in J-M. Teutonico (ed.), *Monuments and the Millenium*, London: James & James/English Heritage, pp. 228–236. – (2003), "Can Peace be Set in Stone?", *Times Higher Educational Supplement*, 4 April 2003, 18–19.
Gregg, D. (1976), *Anamnesis in the Eucharist*, Grove Liturgical Study No 5, Bramcote: Grove Books.
Grisbrooke, W.J. (1986), "Anaphora" in J.G. Davies (ed), *A New Dictionary of Liturgy and Worship*, London: SCM.
Handley, J. (2000), *The Spirit and Purpose of Land Restoration*, Birmingham: The Groundwork Federation.
Heidegger, M. (1971), *Poetry, Language, Thought*, London: Harper & Row.
Holmes, R. (1974), *Shelley: The Pursuit*, New York: New York Review of Books.
Irvine, C. ed (1997), *The Pilgrim Manual*, Glasgow: Wildgoose Press.
Lewis, C. (1971), "Reminiscing and Self-concept in Old Age", *Journal of Gerontology* Vol. 26, 240–243.
Low, S.M. & Altman, I. (1992), "Place Attachment: A Conceptual Enquiry", in I. Altman & S.M. Low (eds.), *Place Attachment*, New York: Plenum.
Lawton, M.P. & Nahemov, L. (1973), "Ecology and the Aging Process", in C. Eisdorfer & M.P. Lawton (eds.), *Psychology of Adult Development and Aging*, Washington, DC: American Psychological Association, 619–624.
McMahon, A.W. & Rhudick, P.J. (1964), "Reminiscing: Adaptational Significance in the Aged", *Archives of General Psychiatry*, Vol. 10, 292–298.
Parker, R. (2001), *Healing Wounded History: Reconciling Peoples and Healing Places*, London: Darton, Longman & Todd.
Robinson, E. & Powell, D. (eds) (1996), *John Clare by Himself*, Manchester: Carcanet.
Rodwell, J. (2008a), "Forgetting the Land", *Studies in Christian Ethics*, Vol. 21/2, 269–286
– (2008b), "Remembering the Land", *Crucible*, Oct-Dec 2008, 5–16.
Rodwell, J., Ling, C. & Hey, D. (2005), *Future Landscapes & Biodiversity for the Dearne Valley, Yorkshire*, A Report for Natural England, Pennines & Humber Region.
Rodwell, J. & Hey, D. (2010), "The King's Wood in Lindrick" *Landscapes* Vol. 11(1), 47–66.
Sillars, S. (1991), *British Romantic Art and the Second World War*, London: Macmillan.

Spalding, F. (2009), *John Piper, Myfanwy Piper: Lives in Art*, Oxford: Oxford University Press.

Schwarze-Rodrian, M., Bauer, I., Scheuvens, R., Cuppers, J & Luchterhandt, D. (2005), *Masterplan Emscher Landschaftspark 2010*. Essen: Klartext Verlag.

Sheldrake, P. (1995), *Living Between Worlds: Place and Journey in Celtic Spirituality*, London: Darton Longman & Todd.

Sheldrake, P. (2008), "A Spirituality of Reconciliation: Encouragement for Anglicans from a Roman Catholic perspective", *Journal of Anglican Studies*, Vol. 6.1, 106–126.

Stevenson, A. ed. (2011), *Concise Oxford English Dictionary*, Oxford: Oxford University Press.

Taylor, W. (2001), *South Yorkshire Pits*, Barnsley: Wharncliffe Publishing.

Walker, A. (2001), "Feasting in a South Yorkshire colliery district: Resistance and accommodation to customary change in Wombwell and Darfield, c. 1860–1900", *Family & Community History*, Vol. 4, 5–18.

Watkins, J. (2009), "Orford Ness no longer an 'Awful Mess'", *Daily Telegraph*, 20 August 2009.

Webster, J.D. & Haight, B.K. (1995), "Memory Lane Milestones: Progress in Reminiscence Definition and Classification", in B.K. Haight & J.D. Webster (eds), *The Art and Science of reminiscing: Theory, Research, Methods and Applications*, Washington DC: Taylor & Francis.

Williams, R. (1994), *Open to Judgement*, London: Darton, Longman & Todd.

– (2000), *Lost icons: Reflections on Cultural Bereavement*, Edinburgh: T. & T. Clark.

Woodward, C. (2001), *In Ruins*, New York: Phoenix.

Separation and connectedness

RECONNECTING COMMUNITIES AND NATURAL SYSTEMS IN THE LANDSCAPE

Paul Selman

INTRODUCTION

It is a truism to state that landscape is a complex phenomenon, providing many functions and values, and composed of many physical attributes and human meanings. It is both material and intangible. The landscape is generally fairly forgiving, and it can continue to yield human services and absorb new structures despite heavy usage; it can often be restored after being left derelict and even, after the passage of sufficient time, heal itself in fascinating ways. Many people now argue that landscape is an integrating framework, in which nature, people and past voices merge, and in which different disciplines and policy sectors congeal. Some proponents also claim that the landscape behaves as a social-ecological system, and is resilient and dynamically stable until pressurised beyond its 'tipping point' into an alternative state.[1] Due to its distinctive character, unique stories and intimate corners, it may, allegedly, cause people to have a strong sense of place and local attachment. Landscape, though, is continually in a state of flux and subject to drivers of change, which vary in their origin, nature, strength and direction.[2] Sometimes, depending on the intrinsic resilience and vulnerability of the landscape, these drivers may compromise its functions and values.

This chapter argues that damage to landscape manifests itself as 'disconnection' of physical systems, visual continuity and human attachment. This results in a loss of functionality, ecosystem services, resilience and identity. Some people also suggest that it leads to a spiritual disconnection, consequent upon our commodification and selfish use of landscape. Thus, landscape ceases to be "home". Where this is the case, a goal of restoration might be to reconnect landscapes in ways that are sensitive to the unique potentials of place. The same principle could also be applied to newly emerging landscapes that are created in the course of human activity, for example through development, forestry or floodplain management. Such "spaces" will not turn into "places" – they will not become home for humans or animals – unless they are thoughtfully connected in ways that create possibilities for serendipity and emergence.

The Judaeo-Christian tradition is often criticised for its presumed dominion over land, which some allege has led to ecological and moral impairment. Such a view is highly contestable, and it is equally possible that anthropocentrism can be the solution as much as the problem. However, there is a compelling vein of thought that the treatment of land and water as mere commodity jeopardises complex filigrees of interdependence between and within social and natural systems. This raises some significant issues. Disconnection of critical linkages between physical systems and between people and place, regardless of their true values, can lead to both moral and physical dereliction, necessitating, in turn, restoration. One currently popular spiritual perspective on landscape is the possibility that certain places possess a quality of 'thinness', such that there can be an epiphany connecting secular and sacred space.[3] Such a connection between the ordinary and extraordinary would readily be fractured by noise or contamination. Thin spaces may, to the more sceptical observer, seem fanciful, yet it has been demonstrated that certain landscape types do indeed possess qualities that are conducive to specific 'spiritual' experiences. There are numerous voices in the popular environmental literature and blogosphere suggesting that people should "re-connect" to the earth. I want to suggest that, even though such arguments might at times be weakly substantiated, they resonate with an emerging evidence base, and echo an important principle for our occupation of the landscape.

THE CONNECTEDNESS OF LANDSCAPE

Although the long-established use of the word 'landscape' relates to a painterly framed image, the contemporary discourse emphasises qualities that lie 'beyond the view'.[4] The term's origins lie in the Dutch *landschap* – a predominantly visual term which nonetheless reflected a real and physical territory – and the German *Landschaft* reflecting a more complex amalgam of physical space and culture.[5] Even the visual arts now problematise landscape as something more than seen – a space of performance, renewal and change. It is a nexus of ecological, hydrological, geomorphic, social, cultural and economic systems that often combine in aesthetically pleasing or at least amenable ways. Some have argued that landscape is also connected through nested scales, for example in water catchments, sub-catchments and local tributaries. In contemporary jargon, the land or landscape is both multi-scaled[6] and multifunctional.[7]

The connectedness of physical systems is taken for granted. Hydrological systems connect rivers, lakes, groundwater, soil water and artificial drains through complex mechanisms of overland flow, throughflow and precipitation. Ecosystems connect populations and metapopulations through life-cycle processes, and through the percolation of species across corridors and patchy matrices of land and water. The flux of energy and gases between ground layers and atmosphere results in continuous change of local and global climates. The connectedness of social and ecological systems is more contentious, although at a basic level it is self-evident that human systems use and modify natural systems, and that this relationship is often negotiated by a mix of moral and religious imperatives, secular laws and customary practices. The notion of networks that dissolve the binary between human and nonhuman actors is more controversial, albeit influential.[8] The connectedness of human systems, perhaps by as few as six degrees of separation, is equally apparent.

However, the idea of connection between people and place is more hotly contested.[9] Some have suggested that that people in post-industrial societies have scant attachment to place, whereas others suggest that the idea of an intuitively perceived *genius loci* is distinct and compelling.[10] There is abundant evidence that we occupy a *habitus* – a space of acquired sensibilities and mental frameworks that we 'take for granted', and where we may become habituated to a specific locality.[11] In landscape terms, this manifests itself the ease that 'insiders' have in navigating the spaces and unwritten rules of local territory.[12] There is also reasonable evidence that 'place attachment' is more than mere imagination or, indeed, social construction.[13] Certainly, policy makers assume that people identify with distinctive places, including those which are not necessarily acclaimed by polite culture.[14]

LANDSCAPE DISCONNECTION

Contemporary studies of the cultural landscape, especially those written from a policy perspective, tend to presume a loss of distinctiveness and connectivity. As noted previously, these are caused by various 'change drivers', many of which are global and therefore intractable for policy-makers to influence. Drivers lead to three main types of disconnection.

First, physical systemic disconnection is associated with the fragmentation of habitat and disruption of air/water/land systems. A well-known disruption of the atmospheric system is the urban heat island, resulting from the replacement of natural landscape by built environment.[15] In the past, this has been of some concern due to its tendency to exacerbate the effect of urban pollutants; at present, there are growing concerns about its impact on the liveability of cities in a period of climate change when elevated temperatures could cause significant discomfort indoors and outdoors.[16] Similarly, the sealed surfaces of the built environment have disrupted water flows by reducing infiltration into natural 'regulators' – soils and aquifers – and accelerating runoff via culverts and drains.[17] Such practices have not only reduced the time taken for precipitation to reach rivers, they have also by-passed the purifying role of regulators (i.e. removing harmful pollutants). Perhaps the most widely documented aspect of physical disconnection is that of habitat fragmentation, particularly the reduction of traditional systems of field boundaries.[18] The diffusion of species across the landscape is a complex affair, but there is persuasive evidence that widespread declines in general landscape connectivity have accelerated extinctions. Again, this is of growing concern during a period of climate change, when species depend on networks of non-hostile landscape to adjust their 'range'.[19]

Second, visual disconnection is associated with the displacement of organic, harmonic, unifying features by modern development. Commercially driven change may have little regard, beyond cost and convenience, for its setting, and may cause a landscape to experience 'dysfunction' and 'rupture'. Again, it is risky to generalise about the response of humans to visual alteration, although there is evidence from landscape preference studies of the relative unacceptability of certain types of land use change.[20] Loss of strong connecting features (e.g. hedgerow patterns), loss of distant views, and disturbance of mid-range views by sporadic development, for example, appear to reduce the strength of preference. It is likely that the human eye seeks coherence and landmarks as connective landscape attributes. Indeed, some landscape ecological studies suggest that people and animals seek similar patterns, reflecting aesthetic preference and survival strategies respectively. Landscape, whilst generally thought of as visual, is of course multi-sensory, and disconnection of other senses may occur – for example, the disruptive effect of urban acoustic environments on animal communication systems.[21]

Third, social disconnection occurs when people have scant connection with place. This may occur because their locality has been violated or become unrecognisable, or because they are geographically displaced and fail to develop or even desire a personal identification with their current locality. It has also been suggested that disconnection from naturalistic environments results in an impoverishment of the range of experiences during our formative years.[22] Again, there is plausible evidence that people have been strongly connected to place in the past, whether or not they were conscious explicitly of the extent, character and distinctiveness of their physical landscape. For example, Olwig refers to the ways in which people attach to landscape and develop a sense of belonging through customs, practices and unwritten laws, even to the point of 'hefting' to it via pedestrian movement.[23] Those who have insider status in landscapes are attached to it through stories, symbols and memories, as well as more obvious practices such as ownership and land management. The Welsh term 'bro' captures this well. As landscapes change rapidly, and as people move geographically, so these bonds weaken. More commonly, the landscape is now seen as an object of consumption, regulated by 'natural' rather than customary law, and surveyed by the expert gaze. This reduces the prospects for its intelligent care based on intimacy and moral obligation.[24]

LANDSCAPE RECONNECTION

Healing these disconnections is unlikely to happen purely spontaneously although neither will it, of course, be achieved by top-down mandate. In complex contemporary society, continually exposed to powerful change drivers, the process of

reconnection will at least need to be supported by conscious acts of policy intervention. In this regard, it is useful to note some key ideas underlying current landscape policy, namely:
- humans apprehend landscape as a coherent unity, a place – "an area, as perceived by people... whose character is the result of the action and interaction of natural and/or human factors".[25]
- landscape delivers multiple functions and values, including those which supply direct human benefits (such as production and health) and sustain essential life-support processes (e.g. pollination, water regulation).[26]
- landscape pervades the town and urban fringe, not just the countryside, and there is great potential to re-connect this through a system of green infrastructure.[27]
- the landscape can be divided into tracts possessing visual, ecological and spatial coherence, for example within National Character Areas, and this can be used as a framework for recovering landscape-scale character and functionality.[28]
- collective decisions about the landscape need to be democratic, involving communities and stakeholders in ways that not only seek shared solutions, but also facilitate shared learning for sustainable development.[29]
- urban and rural landscape planning contributes to place-making, notwithstanding the great difficulty of creating new landscapes that have information richness, patina, scars and redundant detail.
- we need to protect the aesthetically finest and most biodiverse landscapes, but also acknowledge that "all landscapes matter"[30] and that complementary spaces are needed for "future nature".[31]

As a consequence of the foregoing, it is inevitable that change will be endemic, and that we need to work and dwell creatively with contemporary change drivers. However, an underlying motif of modern policy is that landscapes are being driven in the direction of monofunctionality and banality so that, left to economic forces alone, they will become less resilient and characterful. Public policy and citizen action (for example, through membership-based organisations) are themselves important drivers which can promote biophysical, social, visual and moral reconnection in ways that stimulate landscape services[32] and the 'intelligent care' of cherished places.[33]

As a planning discourse, biophysical reconnection has enjoyed a meteoric rise to prominence over the past couple of years through policies for green infrastructure and sustainable urban drainage systems, complemented by important but less well articulated schemes for re-integrating airsheds, parts of the atmosphere that behave in a coherent way in relation to the dispersal of emissions. Green infrastructure strategies build on existing national and trans-national ecosystem networks like Natura 2000 to link together green and blue spaces at regional and local levels in town and country.[34] Regionally and sub-regionally, planners and conservationists are trying to steer improvements to 'pinch points' in strategic networks as well as conserve and improve important areas of habitat, giving renewed importance to protected areas as sources of replenishment and recovery.[35] Locally, especially within urban areas, there is a growing trend for greenspace strategies to be based on audits of green infrastructure and to reconnect fragmented urban spaces and corridors via rich and multifunctional links.[36] Simultaneously, there are ambitious rural proposals for re-wilding land and re-creating extensive wetlands to reclaim lost territory for nature in the expectation that the scale of intervention will create sufficient space and opportunity to recover a self-sustaining and self-reinforcing dynamic. Likewise, at the urban level, sustainable urban drainage systems aim to 'unseal' the predominantly sealed urban surfaces in order to reconnect surface and ground water so as to grant slow and purifying passage to storm water and to reduce risks of flooding and pollution.[37] Given the likely increase in temperatures over the next thirty years, there is growing interest in the role of profuse vegetation in moderating the urban microclimates.[38] The physical reconnection process is thus closely associated with the climate change mitigation and adaptation agenda, though it also reflects concerns over several other ecosystem processes.

Social reconnection has a number of material and intangible dimensions. Researchers have explored numerous avenues of people-landscape linkages, ranging from cultural appropriation of landscape materials and the performance of rituals, to economic use of multiple natural resources. In recent years, policy-makers have shown interest in reinforcing people-landscape links. First, there is a strong policy and design interest in the apparent 'sense of place' and 'pride in place' that attaches to local landscape character and identity. Thus, projects have sought to reverse apparently antisocial use of landscape by engaging locals in initiatives to celebrate and rediscover their place, to counter the sense of loss and bitterness where settlements lose their economic raison d'être, and to engage residents in the local planning process.[39] Landscape may also assist the assimilation of migrant communities into their new environment, both because it can be evocative of their native territory and because it provides public realm for positive social and cultural engagement.[40] Second, there is a growing interest in the multiple human values that landscape can deliver, including recreation, physical and mental health, tranquillity, education and increased property prices – not least because these can relatively readily be 'priced' and therefore legitimated as objects for protection and enhancement.[41] Third, there is an interest in embedding stronger links between landscape and economy in various ways – such as promoting 'virtuous circles' or synergistic couplings between landscape qualities and products/services (e.g. premium foodstuffs), and creating attractive settings for investment in order to capture new business.[42] Fourth, landscape is seen as an appropriate setting for certain types of governance – notably, where policy delivery or partnership operation can be based on landscape units.[43] This may be linked to wider opportunities for social and institutional learning about future change.[44]

Visual reconnection is a less clear term because some modern changes may lead to land use simplification and thus open up and 'connect' vistas. However, the term here is intended to refer to landscapes where character (place-distinctive materiality) is diminishing, and condition (care and maintenance of characteristic features) is deteriorating. Collectively, these lead to 'dysfunction', or the visual dis-integration caused by new discordant elements and loss of harmonious elements. Even though simplified landscapes may be more 'connected' visually, there may be a dis-connect between viewer and landscape. Humans appear to seek a requisite degree of complexity and information in their surroundings,[45] as well as remanence of imprints from former times, and may react against bleak and featureless landscapes.[46] At a superficial level, therefore, there is an aesthetic case for retaining and restoring elements that appear to link landscapes (e.g. traditional field boundaries) or which anchor views in time and place (e.g. vernacular buildings).

Visual connections also work at deeper levels, however. First, is the biological argument relating to innate preferences for certain landscape types such as savannah or which contain 'prospect-refuge' affordances, often satisfying our atavistic hunter instincts by providing opportunities to gaze on livestock and other animals. Innate preferences seem reasonably consistent but with some variability according to gender and ethnicity; the key point is that we do intuitively seem to connect with, and derive sense of wellbeing and attachment from, landscapes, especially those which possess particular qualities.[47] Second, is the possibility that a landscape which we sense as possessing harmony and vitality might be one which is also ecologically robust; thus, aesthetically-satisfying cues appear to mirror ecological desiderata such as connectivity and diversity.[48] Third, the visual appreciation of landscape is more than a touristic experience, and it may have restorative or spiritual benefits.[49] Several studies confirm that landscape can assist in reconnecting damaged minds with the real world, recovering after surgery, improving mood, animating play, enhancing general health and well-being, and providing therapeutic experience for those with learning or behavioural problems.[50] Much of the writing about sublime and beautiful landscapes suggests a spiritual dimension, or at least a capacity to lift the spirits. It is likely that the progressive loss of visual cues, especially those which intuitively stimulate positive associations, from landscapes undermines the connectivities between people and place.

Moral reconnection is an even more slippery concept, but possibly the most fundamental of all. Land has increasingly been treated as a purely tradable commodity – indeed, one which is separable into a bundle of exclusive rights such as occupancy, minerals and agricultural production. We have been guilty of treating landscape as a scene on which to gaze, as if it were a painting or photograph, and have distanced ourselves from the ways in which it was forged through travail, occupation, conflict and dispossession. Stephenson has shown how insensitive landscape development can change or obliterate locally distinctive characteristics and cultural meanings, creating a break between communities and their past.[51] She therefore argues strongly for an understanding of the values that communities attach to their landscapes, both through their stories and myths, and through the importance that they attach to local "nature". The properties of these connections are complex but can be interpreted through an awareness of the forms of, and relationships and practices associated with, a landscape.

Carruthers has suggested that moral and ethical reconnection with land can occur through: enabling more frequent encounter with land, nature and farming; developing procedures, for example based on rights and value ethics, which shift us away from utilitarian decision-making; and relationships between people/communities and land/nature.[52] The landscape itself provides us with a powerful arena in which necessary types of social learning and shared discovery, based on real world issues in familiar settings, can occur. The potentials of landscape offer hope for a remoralisation of our relationship to land, water and air.

CONCLUSIONS

All these arguments rest on the plausible supposition that, the more a society and its economy are driven by external global trends, the more its landscape will become fragmented and dystopic. This is not, however, to argue for militant relocalisation, which itself can have a dark side. 'Globalist' scenarios have been posited to result in tolerance and prosperity, whilst 'localist' scenarios allegedly may risk a retreat into defensive suspicion of outsiders.[53] More positively, there are three main areas in which we can make progress in reconnecting landscapes.

First, it is suggested here that policy-makers need to grasp at a much more visceral level the ways in which most people experience landscape. Landscape professionalism has been strongly associated with gazing over the formal beauty, relative value and regional character of a definable unit, with the intention of contributing to a spatial policy or physical design. Without diminishing the importance of this pursuit, the participatory toolkits that are used may lack insight into ways that people connect with landscape subliminally and intuitively. Notwithstanding our obvious capacity to contemplate favourite scenery, landscape for most people is actually walked and talked: it is signified by toil, play and chance conversations rather than by codified physical attributes or historical/artistic associations. Hence, these imbued human experiences turn spaces into places.[54] The Australian aboriginal landscape is a cogent illustration of how legend and myth inhabit material features, and how physical and psychological health is connected to dreaming places and 'country'. Land boundaries may be narrow or diffuse, physical, invented (reinforced through myth and story) or linguistic. The landscape may be communicated through war cries, bloodlines, storytelling, biodiversity, totems, body decorations, dialect, burial and belief systems. There is strong moral and intergenerational connection in such landscapes, and rights are synonymous with responsibilities.[55] I strongly suspect that these and similar traditions find resonance and new expression in contemporary culture. Infusing place-making with such wisdom will be an important step towards creating landscapes rather than picture postcards.

Second, a reconnected and resilient landscape will be one which has found a self-sustaining dynamic – a spontaneous synergy in which economic and social practices enhance desirable landscape functions and *vice versa*. In sophisticated mixed economies, such virtuosity does not arise entirely serendipitously: there is a clear and reproducible role for the state and social entrepreneurship in instigating and possibly maintaining the necessary connectivities. Interventions will hinge on the principle of multifunctionality, and will require facilitation of dynamic links between landscape's regulation, habitat, production, information and carrier functions.

Third, more use needs to be made of the landscape as a critical arena for social learning, where vivid and imaginative encounters in familiar settings can turn amorphous and abstract ideas about global warming or ecosystem services, for example, into comprehensible local realities.[56] For example, cultural landscapes are the platforms for our food and fibre production, and they embody our attitudes and practices towards animals, plants, selective breeding and genetic modification, and soil. It is clear that many critics of modern food practices feel that society disconnects itself from violent reality by concealing volume production within industrial scale buildings. This is not necessarily an argument for small-scale organic and permaculture practices, as many people strongly believe that there is an efficient beauty in intensive production of food for a future world of 9bn people. It does, though, suggest that collective learning about food technologies will be related to their visibility, as well as traceability to specific landscape settings.

In summary, the landscape provides a locus not only for belonging, but also for well-being (in its broadest human and economic sense) and for wise anticipation of the future. Presently, one of the main fractures compromising our ability to live sustainably is the disconnection between human wants and ecological capacity. Not least, this is because we have de-coupled ourselves psychologically, physically and ethically from place. I doubt if the solution is a return to traditional systems, and I am sceptical as to whether small really is beautiful; however, I suggest there is a need for us to rediscover the specificities of place as a basis for living justly and well. I doubt whether a crowded earth can be resilient to future shocks if we allow social capital to dissolve and biophysical systems to fragment, or the connections between them to wither.

Notes

[1] Walker et al.; Walker and Salt; Cumming.
[2] Schneeberger et al.

3 Balzer.
4 Countryside Agency.
5 Wylie.
6 Selman 2006.
7 Willemen et al.
8 Comber et al.
9 Massey.
10 Norberg-Schultz; Jivén and Larkham.
11 Bourdieu and Wacquant.
12 Bender.
13 Stedman.
14 Graham et al.
15 Smith and Levermore.
16 Gill et al.; Lafortezza et al.
17 Bartens; Wheater and Evans.
18 Petit et al.
19 Selman 2009; Hopkins.
20 Fyhri et al.
21 Warren et al.
22 Miller.
23 Olwig.
24 Nassauer; Gobster et al.
25 Council of Europe.
26 Termorshuizen and Opdam.
27 Landscape Institute.
28 Natural England.
29 Muro and Jeffrey.
30 Natural England.
31 Adams; Lawton et al.
32 de Groot et al.
33 Gobster et al.
34 Grieve et al.
35 NWGIU.
36 CABE.
37 Melby and Cathcart.
38 Gill et al.
39 Manzo and Perkins; James and Gittins.
40 Rishbeth and Finney.
41 Trust for Public Land.
42 Selman and Knight.
43 Hamilton and Selman.
44 Selman et al.
45 Kaplan and Kaplan.
46 Le-Dû Blayo.
47 Ruso et al.
48 Palmer.
49 Grinde and Patil.

50 Ward Thompson.
51 Stephenson.
52 Carruthers.
53 Creedy et al.
54 Tuan.
55 Low Choy et al.
56 Petts.

REFERENCES

Adams, W., (2003), *Future Nature*. 2nd edition, London: Earthscan.
Balzer, T. (2007), *Thin Places: an evangelical journey into Celtic Christianity*, Abilene, Tx: Leafwood Publishers.
Bartens, J. (2009), *Green Infrastructure and Hydrology*, Warrington: J Bartens and the Mersey Forest Team, Mersey Forest.
Bender, Barbara (2006), "Place and Landscape", in: C. Tilley, W. Keane, S. Küchler, M. Rowlands, and P. Spyer (eds.), *Handbook of Material Culture*, London: Sage Publications, 303–314.
Bourdieu, P. and Wacquant, L.J.D. (1992), *An Invitation to Reflexive Sociology*. Chicago: The University of Chicago Press.
Carruthers, S.P. (2009), "The land debate – doing the right thing: ethical approaches to land use decision-making", in: M. Winter and M. Lobley (eds.), *What is Land For? The Food, Fuel and Climate Change Debate*, London: Earthscan, 319–330.
Comber, A., Fisher, P. and Wadsworth, R. (2003), "Actor–network theory: a suitable framework to understand how land cover mapping projects develop?", *Land Use Policy*, 20, 299–309.
Commission on Architecture and the Built Environment (CABE) (2009), *The green information gap: mapping the nation's green spaces*, London: CABE.
Council of Europe (CoE) (2000), *The European Landscape Convention*, Strasbourg: CoE.
Countryside Agency (2006), *Landscape: Beyond the View*, Report by Countryscape, Newcastle: Natural England Publications.
Creedy, J.B., Doran, H., Duffield, S.J., George, N.J., and Kass, G.S., (2009). *England's natural environment in 2060 – issues, implications and scenarios.* Natural England Research Reports, Number 031, Peterborough: Natural England.
Cumming, G.S. (2011), "Spatial resilience: integrating landscape ecology, resilience and sustainability", *Landscape Ecology*, 26, 899–909.
de Groot, R., Alkemade, R., Braat, L. Hein,L. and Willemen, L. (2009), "Challenges in integrating the concept of ecosystem services and values in landscape planning, management and decision making", *Ecological Complexity*, http://dx.doi.org/10.1016/j.ecocom, 10 June, 2009.
Fyhri A, Steen Jacobsen J., Tømmervik H. (2009), "Tourists' landscape perceptions and preferences in a Scandinavian coastal region", *Landscape and Urban Planning*, 91, 202–211.
Gill, S., Handley, J., Ennos, A., and Pauleit, S. (2007), "Adapting cities for climate change: the role of the green infrastructure", *Built Environment*, 33, 97–115.
Gobster, P.H., Nassauer, J.I., Daniel, T.C. Fry, G. (2007), "The shared landscape: what does aesthetics have to do with ecology?", *Landscape Ecology*, 22, 959–972.

Graham, H., Mason, R. and Newman, A. (2009), *Literature Review: Historic Environment, Sense of Place and Social Capital*. Report to English Heritage, Newcastle: International Centre for Cultural and Heritage Studies, Newcastle University.

Grinde and Patil, (2009), "Biophilia: Does Visual Contact with Nature Impact on Health and Well-Being?" *International Journal for Environmental Research into Public Health* 6, 2332–2343

Grieve, Y., Sing, L., Ray, D. and Moseley, D. (2006), *Forest Habitat Networks Scotland Broadleaved Woodland Specialist Network for SW Scotland*, Edinburgh: Forestry Commission.

Hamilton, K. and Selman, P. (2005), "The 'landscape scale' in planning: recent experience of bio-geographic planning units in Britain", *Landscape Research*, 30(4), 549–558.

Hopkins, J. (2009), "Adaptation of biodiversity to climate change: an ecological perspective", in: M. Winter and M. Lobley (eds.), *What is Land For? The Food, Fuel and Climate Change Debate*, London: Earthscan, 189–212.

James, P. and Gittins, J. W. (2007), "Local landscape character assessment: An evaluation of community-led schemes in Cheshire" *Landscape Research*, 32, 423–442.

Jivén, G. And Larkham, P.J. (2003), "Sense of place, authenticity and character: a commentary", *Journal of Urban Design*, 8(1), 67–81.

Kaplan, R. And Kaplan, S. (1989) *The Experience of Nature: a psychological perspective*, New York: Cambridge University Press.

Lafortezza, R., Carrus, G.,Sanesi, G., and Davies, C. (2009), "Benefits and well-being perceived by people visiting green spaces in periods of heat stress", *Urban Forestry & Urban Greening*, 8, 97–108.

Landscape Institute (2009), *Green infrastructure: connected and multifunctional landscapes. Landscape Institute Position statement*, London: Landscape Institute.

Lawton, J.H., Brotherton, P.N.M., Brown, V.K., Elphick, C., Fitter, A.H., Forshaw, J., Haddow, R.W., Hilborne, S., Leafe, R.N., Mace, G.M., Southgate, M.P., Sutherland, W.A., Tew, T.E., Varley, J., and Wynne, G.R. (2010), *Making Space for Nature: a review of England's wildlife sites and ecological network*, London: Report to the Department for Environment Food and Rural Affairs.

Le Dû-Blayo L. (2011), "How do we accommodate new land uses in traditional landscapes? Remanence of landscapes, resilience of areas, resistance of people", *Landscape Research*, 36, 417–434.

Low Choy, D., Wadsworth, J. and Burns, D, (2009), *Identifying and incorporating indigenous landscape values into regional planning processes*, Australia: Griffith University, Qld.

Manzo, L. and Perkins, D. (2006), "Finding Common Ground: The Importance of Place Attachment to Community Participation and Planning", *Journal of Planning Literature*, 20, 335–350.

Massey, D.B. (2005), *For Space*, London: Sage.

Melby, P. and Cathcart, T. (2002), *Regenerative Design Techniques: Practical Applications in Landscape Design*, New York, Wiley.

Miller, J. R. (2005), "Biodiversity conservation and the extinction of experience", *Trends in Ecology and Evolution*, 20, 430–434.

Muro, M. and Jeffrey, P. (2008), "A critical review of the theory and application of social learning in participatory natural resource management process", *J. Environmental Planning and Management*, 51, 325–344.

Nassauer, J. Iverson (1997), "Cultural sustainability: aligning aesthetics and ecology".in: J. Iverson Nassauer (ed.), *Placing Nature: Culture and Landscape Ecology*, Washington, DC: Island Press, 65–84.

Natural England, (2010), *Natural England's Position on "All Landscapes Matter"* Sheffield: Natural England.

Natural England (2011), *Natural England's integrated landscape project (LIANE)*, Sheffield: Natural England.

Norberg-Schultz, C. (1980), *Genius Loci, Towards a Phenomenology of Architecture*, New York: Rizzoli.

North West Green Infrastructure Unit (NWGIU) (2009), *Green Infrastructure Solutions to Pinch Point Issues in North West England*, Warrington: NWGIU,

Olwig, K. (2005), "The Landscape of 'Customary' Law versus that of 'Natural' Law" *Landscape Research*, 30: 3, 299–320.

Palmer, F. (2004), "Using spatial metrics to predict scenic perception in a changing landscape, Dennis, Massachusetts" *Landscape and Urban Planning*, 69, 201–218.

Petit, S., Stuart, R.C., Gillespie, M.K. and Barr, C.J. (2003), "Field boundaries in Great Britain: stock and change between 1984, 1990 and 1998" *Journal of Environmental Management* 67, 229–238.

Petts, J. (2007), "Learning about learning: lessons from public engagement and deliberation on urban river restoration" *The Geographical Journal*, 173, 300–311.

Rishbeth, C. and Finney, N. (2006), "Novelty and nostalgia in urban greenspace: refugee perspectives", *Tijdschrift voor Economische en Sociale Geografie*, 97(3), 281–295.

Ruso B., Renninger, L. and Atzwanger, K. (2003), "Human Habitat Preferences: a Generative Territory for Evolutionary Aesthetics Research", in: E. Voland & K Grammer (eds), *Evolutionary Aesthetics*, Berlin/Heidelberg: Springer-Verlag, 279–294.

Schneeberger, N., Bürgi, M., Hersperger, A. & Ewald, K. (2007), "Driving forces and rates of landscape change as a promising combination for landscape change research -An application on the northern fringe of the Swiss Alps", *Land Use Policy*, 24, 349–361.

Selman, P. (2006), *Planning at the Landscape Scale*, London: Routledge.

Selman, P. (2009), "Conservation designations – Are they fit for purpose in the 21st century?", *Land Use Policy*, 26S, S142–S153.

Selman, P.H. and Knight, M. (2006), "On the nature of virtuous change in cultural landscapes: exploring sustainability through qualitative models", *Landscape Research*, 31, 295–308.

Selman, P., Carter, C., Lawrence, A. and Morgan, C. (2010), "Re-connecting with a recovering river through imaginative engagement", *Ecology and Society* 15(3): 18.

Smith, C. and Levermore, G. (2008), "Designing urban spaces and buildings to improve sustainability and quality of life in a warmer world" *Energy Policy*, 36, pp. 4558–4562.

Stedman, R.C. (2003), "Is It Really Just a Social Construction?: The Contribution of the Physical Environment to Sense of Place", *Society & Natural Resources* 16(8), 671–685.

Stephenson, J. (2007), "The cultural values model: an integrated approach to values in landscapes", *Landscape and Urban Planning*, 84: 127–139.

Termorshuizen, J.W., and Opdam, P. (2009), "Landscape services as a bridge between landscape ecology and sustainable development", *Landscape Ecology*, 24, 1037–1052.

Trust for Public Land (2008), *How Much Value Does the City of Philadelphia Receive from its Park and Recreation System?*, A Report by The Trust for Public Land's Center for City Park Excellence for the Philadelphia Parks Alliance.

Tuan, Y.F. (2001), *Space and Place: The Perspective of Experience*, Minneapolis, MN: University of Minnesota Press.

Walker, B., Holling, C., Carpenter, S. and Kinzig, A. (2004), "Resilience, adaptability and transformability in social-ecological systems", *Ecology and Society* 9(2), 5.

Walker, B. and Salt, D. (2006), *Resilience Thinking: sustaining ecosystems and people in a changing world*, Washington DC: Island Press.

Ward Thompson, C. (2011), "Linking landscape and health: the recurring theme", *Landscape and Urban Planning*, 99(3), 187–195.

Warren, P., Katti, M., Ermann, M. & Braze, A. (2006), "Urban bioacoustics: it's not just noise", *Animal Behaviour*, 2006, 71, 491–502.

Wheater,H. & Evans, E. (2009), "Land use, water management and future flood risk", *Land Use Policy*, 26S, S251-S264.

Willemen, L., Hein, L. b, van Mensvoort, M and Verburg, P. (2010), "Space for people, plants, and livestock? Quantifying interactions among multiple landscape functions in a Dutch rural region", *Ecological Indicators*, 10, 62–73.

Wylie, J.W. (2007), *Landscape*, Abingdon: Routledge.

Belonging in the Peri-Urban Landscape: Do New Landscapes Require New Conceptions of "Home"?

Vera Vicenzotti

The Problematic of Belonging and *Heimat* in Peri-Urban Landscapes

This contribution explores one aspect of the discourse on peri-urban landscapes, those zones that are neither town nor countryside, those places we all travel through but generally fail to acknowledge. It deals with the ongoing debate in architecture and planning, urban design and landscape architecture on whether these fragmented and hybrid landscapes are and can be considered a place of home, a place of belonging, a place of *Heimat*.

To some readers it might seem an absurd idea to consider peri-urban landscapes a place of home, since these landscapes are often mentioned in the same breath as urban sprawl which usually has negative connotations. Apart from negative effects such as the destruction of biotopes, the fragmentation of ecosystems, the increase in the level of private car use or social segregation,[1] it is also often stated that sprawled landscapes lack any kind of identity[2] and are labelled as being "placeless"[3] or "non-places".[4] Indeed, peri-urban landscapes are characterised by high land use and population dynamics. This has fostered the widespread view of these zones as unstable zones in transition, as "wastelands" awaiting better times,[5] as traditional cultural landscapes which have lost their character or as areas that are seemingly without any recognisable signs.[6] Boris Sieverts[7] notices that if "signs are seen at all, then they are interchangeable – meaning the place as such remains anonymous".[8] So for quite some time now, the prevailing opinion has been that peri-urban landscapes cannot be home to their inhabitants. If anything, it is said that sprawl destroys the environments, both urban and rural, that are capable of evoking a sense of belonging.

However, more recently, the planning discourse has emphasised the specific character and qualities of peri-urban zones. It has been highlighted that these landscapes are a persistent feature of city regions and may even offer the potential of establishing new and beneficial relationships between urban and rural functions. Realising their potential and addressing their deficits, however, requires recognition of the specific character of peri-urban areas and the development of specific policies for their sustainable development. One of the approaches that try to do justice to this specific hybrid character is the concept of the "*Zwischenstadt*", i.e. an in-between city or a city in transition. The term was coined by German urban designer Thomas Sieverts in 1997.[9] Drawing largely on Sieverts' ideas, efforts have been made to conceptualise these new landscapes as *Heimat*.[10] For example, German architect and urban designer Lars Bölling maintains that peri-urban areas satisfy the majority of their inhabitants' needs. Increasingly, he states, "these needs are not merely functional, but are overlaid with a need for spatial quality, localisation [*Verortung*] and potential for identification, ultimately for attributes of home – even if at times only temporary".[11]

In this text, it is asked why landscape architects and urban designers see the peri-urban landscape in such very different ways. It is suggested that these different evaluations (of whether peri-urban areas can be considered as *Heimat* or not) are primarily due to different notions of home. I will therefore analyse different conceptions of *Heimat* in the current discourse on peri-urban landscapes being conducted by landscape architects and urban designers. The focus is on peri-urban landscapes because their specific nature means these areas can be considered focal points or model areas for the study of the problematic of *Heimat*. Since they are areas of rapid change economically, socially, culturally and environmentally, the discourse around them involves all the rationales concerning loss of identity and home on the one hand and the longing and need for identity and home on the other.

Apart from the focus on peri-urban landscapes, a second issue has influenced and informed the approach taken in this contribution: the discourse on the concept of *Heimat* in Germany.[12] Given the National Socialist past and the crucial role the notion of *Heimat* played in Nazi ideology, this concept is highly contested in Germany, including nature conservation, landscape planning and environmental history. The debate is centred on the problem that the concept of *Heimat* in National Socialism was an ideological part of racist politics.[13] So it is simply not possible to adopt this concept. On the other hand, there is a yearning for *Heimat*, especially at a time when globalisation means our environment is changing rapidly and profoundly.[14] Therefore some authors have attempted to conceptualise a progressive notion of *Heimat* that can be democratically legitimised.[15] This text therefore also contributes to an analysis of some of these attempts.

The question posed in the title of this text – whether new landscapes require new concepts of "home" – includes these two research foci. First, it is concerned with the discourse on peri-urban landscapes and the controversy of whether these landscapes can be considered as places that evoke a sense of belonging and based on which concept of *Heimat*. Second, it aims to analyse the search within nature conservation, environmental history and landscape architecture for a progressive concept of *Heimat* that is suitable for a modern democratic society.

The text will initially distinguish two ideal and typical conceptions of *Heimat*

– a conservative one and a progressive one – using two sets of criteria: origin versus future and appropriation versus fitting in (section 2). With this conceptual framework, it will analyse the ideological content of two concepts of home that occur in the discourse on peri-urban landscapes and that conceptualise these areas as places of belonging (section 3). The first concept of home focuses on the one hand on the progressive aspect of appropriation, but also stresses the significance of continuity – in this case it argues that peri-urban landscapes have been home for their inhabitants for several years already. The second concept universalises the notion of *Heimat*, removing any conservative element from it. The text will end with some concluding remarks contemplating, among other things, the implications of this purely progressive notion of *Heimat* (section 4).

TWO ANTITHETIC CONCEPTS OF *Heimat*

The thesis put forward here is that the differing attitudes on whether peri-urban areas can be *Heimat* to their inhabitants depend on the respective conception of *Heimat*. Therefore in order to analyse the conflict, I will distinguish between two notions of *Heimat*, formulating them as ideal types.[16] Even if, by definition, none of these *ideal* types can be found in *reality*, they help to order the discourse by spanning a spectrum of possible positions.

German cultural theorist Susanne Hauser distinguishes between "conservative dreams of belonging [*Beheimatung*]" and the "wish for a development of self-determination undermining the capitalistic production of space".[17] She acts on the assumption that a contrast can be made between a "conservative" concept of *Heimat* and a "leftist", progressive one. Drawing on this distinction, two concepts of *Heimat* at the opposite ends of the spectrum of interpretations of *Heimat* will be explored. To this end, I use different criteria or pairs of criteria that constitute the notion of *Heimat*: the first criterion is whether *origin* or *future* is relevant; secondly, consideration is given as to whether *Heimat* is thought to result from *appropriation* or *fitting in*. I will refer to philosophical and sociological texts because the differences between the two concepts of *Heimat* are often explained in greater clarity there than in texts written by planners and architects.

Origin versus future

Within a conservative mindset, *Heimat* is constituted by the idea of origin. Therefore *Heimat* as the place of origin has both a spatial and a temporal dimension.[18] On the one hand, it is the place of birth and childhood, the place where you live or used to live, where you work, and where your family and friends have been living. On the other hand, mediated by the notion of tradition, the dimension of time is relevant. "Tradition, as well, pertains to *Heimat* in the full sense. It ensures security of demeanour by providing certain traditional patterns of behaviour".[19]

In progressive thinking, future is the notion that constitutes home. *Heimat* is regarded as something which still has to be made; it is framed as an open societal utopia. Practically any text developing a progressive concept of *Heimat* contains the final passage of Ernst Bloch's *The Principle of Hope*:

True genesis is not at the beginning but at the end, and it starts to begin only when society and existence become radical, i.e. grasp their roots. But the root of history is the working, creating human being who reshapes and overhauls the given facts. Once he has grasped himself and established what is his, without expropriation and alienation, there arises in the world which shines into the childhood of all and in which no one has yet been – homeland.[20]

In the utopian dimension that the concept of *Heimat* adopts here, individual and social perspectives coincide: *Heimat* can only be realised in a liberated society. At the same time, however, we are all familiar with it from our childhood. Childhood designates the place in our individual history where development still seems possible. Adults' memories of their childhood *Heimat* is, however, not the memory of a state of security, but rather of hope for the future. Hence Eduard Führ states: "The time character of *Heimat* is not the past, but the future."[21] It is not just the memory of the happy but now past reality of childhood that turns a place into *Heimat*. Rather, in retrospect, childhood seems so happy because of the memory of longing. Usually the reality of childhood was anything but harmonious and happy. It was, however, accompanied by a feeling of longing that was yet to be deflated and disappointed, by a yearning to do this or that, and to be able to do anything once grown up, i.e. through the longing and hope of mastering the whole world. *Heimat*, it can therefore be argued, is what emerges from loss, nostalgia, and memory – especially the memory of a life sentiment consisting of the belief that hopes and longings will be fulfilled.

Appropriation versus fitting in

Heimat, as stated in progressive positions, results from productive appropriation. The conservative position meanwhile argues that objectively the place of origin is *Heimat*, and that subjectively it turns into your *Heimat* if you fit into the given situation in a patient, accepting and appreciative manner.

"Somewhere in the nowhere, everyday spaces are, by appropriation, becoming *Heimat*": this is how German architect Astrid Schmeing characterises appropriation as one of the emergence conditions of *Heimat*.[22] Appropriation seems to be a genuinely leftist concept. According to Körner *et al.*, the term expresses a fundamental cultural and political re-orientation that has permeated all aspects of life since the 1970s.[23] This re-orientation is combined with a criticism of formal-democratic and technocratic politics. Appropriation is understood to be "acting out your full human individuality and creative productivity when using the material facilities of open spaces. Hence this concept describes everyday practical actions that are related to a purpose, but are not just about the pure benefits [*reine*

Nutzenhandlungen] in which you ultimately want to optimise personal gain in an instrumental rational way".²⁴

In this context, *Heimat* stands for the utopia of a non-alienated existence. It is neither something determined by tradition, nor something into which you have to fit. Rather *Heimat* is something created by active subjects and, as a true *Heimat*, it can only emerge as a product of appropriation. German folklorist and cultural anthropologist Ina-Maria Greverus writes in relation to this:

> I conceive of *Heimat* as the active process of making your home [*Prozeß des Sich-Beheimatens*] a space that provides safety, material and emotional confidence in your behaviour, unfolding action, stimulation and identity. Thus *Heimat* is not a unique and unchangeable space characterised by the parental home, lime trees, the mother tongue or songs of the fatherland, but rather a chance of human becoming.²⁵

The way in which home is constituted in the conservative mindset is completely different. Bollnow writes that you only have *Heimat* "if you have converted the environment to your *Heimat*, if you have embraced it. In accordance with the familiar saying, you have to gain [*erwerben*] it to possess [*besitzen*] it".²⁶ The act of embracing to which he alludes has to be distinguished from the above-mentioned appropriation. Bollnow himself brings out the difference explicitly:

> The human being does not manage to feel at home in the *Heimat* [...] by constructing a *Heimat* and designing it in accordance with his needs because *Heimat* is predetermined (fundamentally at least) and for his part he has to adapt to it, become familiar with it and grow fond of it.²⁷

So you cannot make *Heimat*, you come upon it and experience it "by patiently fitting in to the new surroundings".²⁸ According to Bollnow, the human being becomes fond of his or her given *Heimat* and becomes familiar with it by nurturing relationships with neighbours, walking in the immediate or more distant environment and recognising its beauty. Alexander Mitscherlich also regards subordination to a given wholeness as a necessary precondition of *Heimat*.²⁹ He sees the "wealthy single-family-home-pastures" with their 'horrors of convenience [*Komfortgreuel*]' on the outskirts of cities as a result of an overreaching individualism.³⁰ Without subordination to a given wholeness, to a 'group canon', there could be no *Heimat*.³¹ This subordination, however, is not thought to restrain freedom. On the contrary:

> In the process, conscious subordination would only be a prerequisite for being better off, for a form better suited to the technical age that gives the individual scope. But this canon is missing, and therefore our cities 'provincialise' and urban culture – once the bearer of enlightenment – declines.³²

CONCEPTS OF *Heimat* IN THE DISCOURSE ON PERI-URBAN LANDSCAPES

In the following section, a closer look will be taken at two concepts of *Heimat* as proposed by planners and architects, urban designers and landscape architects in the discourse on peri-urban landscapes. To dissect how *Heimat* is conceptualised, the two ideal typical concepts developed above will be used as a means of analysis. The focus is on positions that conceive of those hybrid zones as home because it seems more likely that these approaches are based on a new and progressive notion of *Heimat*. It will be seen, however, that conservative elements are more persistent than might be thought – and with good reason.

Peri-urban landscapes as places with a history of belonging

The first concept of *Heimat* to be analysed in greater detail has been put forward by a group of architects and urban designers: Oliver Bormann, Michael Koch, Astrid Schmeing, Martin Schröder and Alex Wall. In their book *Zwischen Stadt Entwerfen*,[33] the team of authors develops a distinct notion of *Heimat* conceptualising peri-urban landscapes as places where people feel at home.[34] For Bormann *et al.* the peri-urban area "is part of the normal city seen from the inner perspective of its inhabitants. They have [...] created a home for themselves. It actually seems to appeal to most people, just not to architects and planners".[35] This quotation reveals two relevant aspects: first, it becomes very obvious that the authors believe peri-urban regions can be *Heimat*; second, they accuse architects and planners of being narrow-minded. They quote Mitscherlich who denies undesigned suburban spaces the ability of being home: "The designed city can become '*Heimat*', the simply agglomerated not, because *Heimat* does require the identity of a place to be marked".[36] This thought, according to Bormann *et al.*, reveals "the planners' error in reasoning by regarding spaces not identified by them as unidentified spaces". The authors want to avoid this error in reasoning. They want to do justice to the "change in meaning" of the concept of *Heimat*, i.e. to its change from a conservative to a more progressive notion. This reveals their progressive self-conception.[37]

Analysing their concept of *Heimat*, however, will show that with regard to its *structure* it is not a purely progressive concept. Rather it integrates conservative elements. A brief example of this will be given by showing that the progressive aspect of appropriation ties in with a conservative appraisal of the idea of origin.[38]

The *appropriation* of spaces by their inhabitants is of crucial importance to Bormann *et al.* For them, the idea of appropriation, especially that of peri-urban landscapes, is linked to two aspects. First, it frees inhabitants from an identity imposed on them by others – not infrequently by planners and architects – and it gives a place an authentic and unpretentious identity. Second, through activities of appropriation, peri-urban spaces would acquire the quality of public urban spaces. "Freed from the straightjacket of 'identity', they [the inhabitants] create new forms of the public. They produce something that architects generally deny the peri-urban region: the existence of public space".[39] The authors have taken the term 'straightjacket of identity' from Rem Koolhaas who turns against traditional notions of identity.[40] By referring to this guiding spirit of vanguard architecture and planning and by objecting to long-established notions of identity and an elitist, bourgeois-conservative attitude, Bormann *et al.* identify their position and the conception of *Heimat* embedded in it as progressive.

As an example of the integration of conservative elements into the position of Bormann *et al.*, reference shall be made to the significance of history. According to the authors, the "existence of (hi)story/ies [*Geschichte(n)*]" shows that the peri-urban area is no longer *terra incognita*.[41] Rather, so they argue, it has become a space where people live, reside and work, a place they know and acknowledge as their *Heimat*. They mention that the peri-urban area, meanwhile, offers a place of belonging for a 'third generation of inhabitants'.[42] The pun of "(hi)story/ies" signals that the authors do not want to refer to *the* traditional and monolithic history as the moment constituting *Heimat*. Rather, the reference to multiple "histories" and/or "stories" implies the pluralistic acknowledgement of different histories and/or stories of ordinary people, of their *everyday* incidents and habits, which is apart from official bourgeois culture and taste.

Nevertheless, Bormann *et al.* cannot help but refer to history. Even though they refer to a different history than what might be called the classical one, they still feel the need to state the number of generations living and working in peri-urban areas. This need hints at the fact that continuity and continuance are significant to them. Secondly, this brings into play the notion of origin: mentioning the succession of generations turns peri-urban areas into *Heimat* as the place of origin. Bormann *et al.* therefore argue in a context typical for the conservative worldview.[43] Here too, it is the existence of continuity, tradition and origin that turns a space into a place and bestows identity upon peri-urban areas. It might well be that the (hi)stories of these areas differ from the classical ones, however with regard to structure even Bormann *et al.* cannot establish their concept of *Heimat* without the conservative time reference, i.e. without referring to the notion of origin.

So, we have seen that the *structure* of this concept of *Heimat* is, at least in one of its main aspects, not new: it is still by referring to the idea of origin that a space turns into a place of belonging.[44] What is new, however, is that Bormann *et al.* conceive of peri-urban landscapes as home. The authors leave no doubt that peri-urban areas can also be, and already are, *Heimat* to their inhabitants

Universal Heimat?

Another approach that conceptualises peri-urban landscapes as a place of belonging is offered by Swiss authors Franz Oswald and Peter Baccini in their book *Neztstadt*, best translated as "net city". They integrate the originally conservative notion of *Heimat* into their predominantly liberal worldview. Universalising it in the process, they reframe it as a purely progressive notion: as people are familiar with universal things, they argue that generic places without any local characteristics can turn out to be true *Heimat*.

Pragmatically and all too directly, the face of the landscapes mirrors the laws of daily life, allowing us to see that the new urbanity is a universal phenomenon that has benefits too: thanks to familiar images of contemporary architectural culture such as highways, parking lots, streets with the same billboards, subway stations, hotel lobbies, shops, cinemas and vacation paradises, we are made to feel at home wherever we travel in the world.'[45]

According to the liberal credo, the laws of the free market bring about universal progress. The latter is believed to augment the quality of life – not just because the society of free competition is best for increasing production, but also because progress, and progress alone, can achieve what the old order (or the conservative ideology) perceived as the nature of quality of life: a sense of belonging, of *Heimat*. But this old order could only achieve *Heimat* locally and it excluded the other. Now however, the universality of progress has abolished otherness and foreignness. Home is everywhere – and this is true progress.

This idea of a universal home is constitutive for the notion of "New Urbanity" as conceptualised by Oswald and Baccini.[46] They define it as "the lifestyle of the great majority of people living in developed countries". Among its most important influences, they argue, is the peri-urban reality with its ubiquitous and uniform elements: "The image of an urban carpet eating its way into the country – or seen the other way round, of rural tentacles reaching into the city – has imprinted itself on memory as a principal impression of contemporary urban architectural culture".[47] We are familiar with this seemingly formless pattern, since it "[p]ragmatically and all too directly [...] mirrors the law of daily life".[48] If and because everything follows the same global laws, we recognise what we see wherever we are and this makes us feel at home all over the world.

CONCLUSION

We have seen that the controversy over whether peri-urban landscapes can be considered places that evoke a sense of belonging largely depends on the respective conception of home. Analysing an approach by a team of planners and architects, Bormann *et al.*, who conceive of these zones as a place of belonging, have revealed that the structure of their concept of *Heimat* has – in some aspects at least – conservative features. However, compared with the view that peri-urban landscapes cannot be home to their inhabitants – something that has been prevalent in the planning discourse for a long time – the place of home is a new one. They explicitly state that peri-urban landscapes can be and have been home to their inhabitants. A purely progressive notion of *Heimat* has been put forward by Oswald and Baccini: Cities, the countryside and peri-urban landscapes all over the world would resemble one other and thus seem vaguely familiar to their visitors. However, one objection against their view seems obvious: it can be asked whether by universalising the concept of *Heimat* the idea has not become its opposite, leading to an erosion of the concept of *Heimat*.

A key to understanding these conflicting positions again seems to lie in different concepts of *Heimat*. At the centre of Oswald's and Baccini's notion is not the idea of "origin" or "fitting in" or of "future" or "appropriation". Rather, what is important in their concept of '*Heimat*' is the aspect of familiarity. What turns a place into home is, in their view, whether we recognise what we see from where we come from. Even though their attempt to find beneficial aspects in the universalising effects of globalisation can be appreciated,[49] it seems necessary to ask whether the concept of home is not underdetermined if reduced to the aspect of familiarity. The feeling of being at home, of belonging, of *Heimat* seems to be more than just recognising and feeling at ease with the same patterns of land use development, infrastructures, housing types, retail chains and coffee shops.

The hesitation to embrace Oswald and Baccini's concept of *Heimat* fully may be due to the fact that when using the terms "home", "belonging" or "*Heimat*", we have a *unique* place in mind. Against the backdrop of their notion of home, the constitutive meaning of singularity, of the uniqueness of a place – be it due to "origin" or a hope for the "future" whether brought about by "appropriation" or by "fitting in" – comes to the fore. The idea of "uniqueness", however, is embedded in a conservative worldview.[50] This leads to the initial question of whether it is possible to conceptualise a purely progressive notion of *Heimat*. Have we come full circle then? In conclusion, two final remarks can be made. First, it has been seen that in order to conceptualise peri-urban landscapes as home, you do not need a new concept of home, i.e. the structure of the concept can remain the same, and yet the places that we call "home" can become different and new ones.[51] So the search for a new concept of home has to be distinguished from the search for positions within planning and architecture, urban design and landscape architecture that conceive of peri-urban landscapes as places of belonging. Second, it has been seen that it might be possible to conceptualise purely progressive notions of home, but there is the danger that those concepts do not capture the specific qualities of what 'home' means to many people.

It might be worth recalling that the search for a progressive concept of *Heimat* was motivated by a tenuous situation within nature conservation and landscape architecture: on the one hand, there is a certain yearning for places of belonging, but on the other it is impossible simply to adopt the concept of *Heimat* given the racist interpretation of this concept during National Socialism in Germany. This is why calling for a relaxed way of dealing with *Heimat* is so precarious. However, it is important to take into consideration the fact that there is a considerable difference between conservative and nationalistic, let alone racist ideas of *Heimat*.[52] There is therefore no need to demonise conservative aspects within certain concepts of *Heimat*. However, given the course of history and the possibilities of turning a conservative notion of home into one that excludes the other and that can and has been transformed into a nationalistic and racist concept, it is essential that critical reflection be an integral part of any practice and theory that is explicitly or implicitly dealing with the idea of belonging and *Heimat*.

NOTES

1. Cf. Couch, Leontidou, Petsche-Held; European Environment Agency; Meeus & Gulinck.
2. Cf. Bölling & Christ; Spellerberg & Kühne, 31; Vicenzotti & Trepl.
3. Relph.
4. Augé.
5. Cf. Qviström, who critically analyses this view.
6. E.g. Hauser; Sieverts (2003a), 207.
7. Sieverts (2003a), 207.
8. This passage, like all the texts that are originally written in German and of which no English edition is available, are translated by the author.
9. Sieverts (2003b).
10. E.g. Bölling; Bormann, Koch, Schmeing, Schröder, Wall.
11. Bölling, 107.
12. The publication of what are known as the *Vilm Theses on* 'Heimat' *and Nature Conservation* [*Vilmer Thesen zu "Heimat" und Naturschutz*] by Reinhard Piechocki, Ulrich Eisel, Stefan Körner, Annemarie Nagel and Norbert Wiesbinky in one of the more influential German journals on nature conservation, *Natur und Landschaft*, which was published by the German Federal Agency for Nature Conservation in 2003 (Piechocki, et al., 2003) in particular has attracted a certain amount of attention and fuelled the discussion on the concept of *Heimat* in nature conservation. In 2007, four years after the publication of these theses, the Agency published a book containing critical responses to the Vilm Theses, as well as the authors' responses to these critiques (Bundesamt für Naturschutz, 2007).
13. Cf. e.g. Bensch; contributions in Bundesamt für Naturschutz, 2007; Gröning & Wolschke-Bulmahn; Körner (2001, 2003); Piechocki.
14. E.g. Kropp; Piechocki, Eisel, Körner, Nagel & Wiersbinski, 241; Spellerberg & Kühne.
15. E.g. Körner, Eisel & Nagel; Piechocki, Eisel, Körner, Nagel & Wiersbinski.
16. Max Weber described this method in his study *"Objectivity" in Social Science and Social Policy* (originally published in 1904): 'An ideal type is formed by the one-sided *accentuation* of one or more points of view and by the synthesis of a great many diffuse, discrete, more or less present and occasionally absent *concrete individual* phenomena, which are arranged according to those one-sidedly emphasized viewpoints into a unified *analytical* construct (*Gedankenbild*). In its conceptual purity, this mental construct (*Gedankenbild*) cannot be found empirically anywhere in reality. It is a *utopia*.' (Weber, 1904/1949: 90, italics in original)
17. Hauser & Kamleithner, 173.
18. Cf. Piepmeier; Spellerberg & Kühne, 19 ff.
19. Bollnow, 29.
20. Bloch, 1376.

21 Führ, 24.
22 Schmeing et al. 114.
23 Körner, Eisel & Nagel, 387.
24 Körner, Eisel & Nagel, 387.
25 Greverus, 51.
26 Bollnow, 29.
27 Bollnow, 30.
28 Bollnow, 30.
29 It may cause some irritation to mention Mitscherlich in an illustration of this conservative position because he is usually regarded as a 'leftist', i.e. a progressive thinker. Here, however, the intention is not to describe his theories as a whole; but rather solely look at his concept of *Heimat* which does prove to be paradigmatic for the conservative position.
30 Mitscherlich, 11.
31 Mitscherlich, 21.
32 Mitscherlich, 20f.
33 The title is a pun on the term *Zwischenstadt* as a type of landscape between city centres. Literally translated, it means something like 'Designing in-between cities' and alludes to 'Designing the *Zwischenstadt*'.
34 Bormann et al.
35 Bormann et al., 49.
36 Mitscherlich, 15.
37 Bormann et al., 50.
38 For a more detailed analysis, see Vicenzotti, 2009 and Vicenzotti, 2011.
39 Bormann et al., 59.
40 Koolhaas.
41 Bormann et al., 52.
42 Bormann et al.
43 E.g. Greiffenhagen.
44 More (structural) parallels with the conservative ideal type of *Heimat* could presumably be found. However, proving this would need to be the subject of further research.
45 Oswald & Baccini, 21.
46 Oswald & Baccini, 20.
47 Oswald & Baccini, 21.
48 Ibid.
49 Kropp makes an interesting differentiation in this regard when she writes that '*Heimat* cannot be seen as a counterstrategy to globalisation, but rather to McDonaldisation', meaning that regional movements do not have to be against cosmopolitan movements or without global solidarity, but they can very well be against levelling, standardising movements, especially of the consumers' world (Kropp, 2004: 152).
50 Eisel, 2003; Eisel, 2004.
51 A similar interpretation has been suggested for the concept of 'landscape' where the term is applied to places that were not formerly considered as landscapes, such as brownfield or post-industrial sites. See Dinnebier, 1995; Höfer, 1998.
52 Cf. Franke, 2003; Körner, 2003; Körner, Eisel & Nagel, 2003; Piechocki et al., 2003.

REFERENCES

Augé, M. (1995), *Non-Places: Introduction to an Anthropology of Supermodernity*, London-New York: Verso.
Bensch, M. (1999), "Blut oder Boden – welche Natur bestimmt den Rassismus?" in: S. Körner, T. Heger, A.Nagel & U. Eisel, (eds.), *Naturbilder in Naturschutz und Ökologie*, Berlin:Technische Universität Berlin, 37–47.
Bloch, E. (1995, 2nd edition), *The principle of hope*, Cambridge MA: MIT Press.
Bölling, L. (2004), "Zwischenstadt lesen. Spurensuche zwischen Downtown Eschborn-Sossenheim" & "Airportcity Rhein-Main", in: L. Bölling & T. Sieverts, (eds.), *Mitten am Rand. Auf dem Weg von der Vorstadt über die Zwischenstadt zur regionalen Stadtlandschaft*, Wuppertal: Müller + Busmann, 94–113.
Bölling, L. & Christ, W. (2005), *Bilder einer Zwischenstadt. Ikonographie und Szenographie eines Urbanisierungsprozesses*, Wuppertal: Müller + Busmann.
Bollnow, O. F. (1984), "Der Mensch braucht heimatliche Geborgenheit", in: H.-G.Wehling, (ed.) *Heimat heute*, Stuttgart-Berlin-Köln-Mainz: W. Kohlhammer, 28–33.
Bormann, O., Koch, M., Schmeing, A., Schröder, M. & Wall, A. (2005), *Zwischen Stadt Entwerfen*, Wuppertal: Müller + Busmann.
Couch, C., Leontidou, L. & Petsche-Held, G. (eds.) (2007), *Urban Sprawl in Europe. Landscapes, Land-Use Change & Policy*, Oxford-Malden-Carlton: Blackwell Publishing.
Dinnebier, A. (1995), "Landschaft sehen", *Garten und Landschaft* Vol. 9, 18–22.
Eisel, U. (2003), "Tabu Leitkultur", *Natur und Landschaft*, Vol. 78 (9/10), 409–417.
Eisel, U. (2004), "Politische Schubladen als theoretische Heuristik. Methodische Aspekte politischer Bedeutungsverschiebungen in Naturbildern", in: L. Fischer, (ed.), *Projektionsfläche Natur. Zum Zusammenhang von Naturbildern und gesellschaftlichen Verhältnissen*, Hamburg: Hamburg University Press, 29–43.
European Environment Agency. (2006), *Urban sprawl in Europe. The ignored challenge*, Copenhagen: European Environment Agency.
Franke, N. M. (2003), "Heimat und Nationalismus: Historische Aspekte". *Natur und Landschaft*, Vol. 78 (9/10), 390–393.
Führ, E. (1985), "Wieviel Engel passen auf die Spitze einer Nadel? ", in: E. Führ, (ed.), *Worin noch niemand war: Heimat. Eine Auseinandersetzung mit einem strapazierten Begriff. Historisch- philosophisch-architektonisch. Mit der Fotocollage Heimat-süße Heimat*, Wiesbaden – Berlin: Bauverlag 10–32.
Greiffenhagen, M. (1986), *Das Dilemma des Konservatismus in Deutschland: Mit einem neuen Text: ?Post-histoire?'. Bemerkungen zur Situation des ?Neokonservatismus' aus Anlaß der Taschenbuchausgabe 1986*, Frankfurt am Main: Suhrkamp.
Greverus, I.-M. (1979), *Auf der Suche nach Heimat*, München: C. H. Beck.
Gröning, G. & Wolschke-Bulmahn, J. (1987), *Die Liebe zur Landschaft. Teil 3. Der Drang nach Osten. Zur Entwicklung der Landespflege im Nationalsozialismus und während des Zweiten Weltkrieges in den eingegliederten "Ostgebieten"*, München: Minerva.
Hauser, S. (2004), "Anästhesie und Lesbarkeit. Stichworte", in: L. Bölling, L. & T. Sieverts, (eds.), *Mitten am Rand. Auf dem Weg von der Vorstadt über die Zwischenstadt zur regionalen Stadtlandschaft*, Wuppertal: Müller + Busmann, 206–209.
Hauser, S. & Kamleithner, C. (2006), *Ästhetik der Agglomeration*, Wuppertal: Müller + Busmann.

Höfer, W. (1998), "Post-industrial Landscape", in: J. Breuste, H. Feldmann & O. Uhlmann (eds.), *Urban Ecology*, Berlin-Heidelberg-New York-Barcelona-Hong Kong-London-Milan-Paris-Singapore-Tokyo: Springer, 671–67.
Koolhaas, R. (1994/1995), "The Generic City", in: R. Koolhaas & B. Mau, (eds.), *Small, Medium, Large, Extra-Large*, Rotterdam: 010 Publishers, 1239–1264.
Körner, S. (2001), *Theorie und Methodologie der Landschaftsplanung, Landschaftsarchitektur und Sozialwissenschaftlichen Freiraumplanung vom Nationalsozialismus bis zur Gegenwart*, Berlin: Technische Universität Berlin.
Körner, S. (2003), "Naturschutz und Heimat im Dritten Reich". *Natur und Landschaft*, Vol. 78 (9/10), 394–400.
Körner, S.; Eisel, U. & Nagel, A. (2003), "Heimat als Thema des Naturschutzes: Anregungen für eine sozio-kulturelle Erweiterung". *Natur und Landschaft*, Vol. 78 (9/10), 382–389.
Kropp, C. (2004), "Heimat im globalen Zeitalter", in: A. Berger & M. Hohenhorst (eds.), *Heimat. Die Wiederentdeckung einer Utopie*, Blieskastel: Gollenstein, 141–155.
Meeus, S. J. & Gulinck, H. (2008), "Semi-Urban Areas in Landscape Research: A Review". *Living Reviews in Landscape Research*, 2(3), 1–45 [online article].
Mitscherlich, A. (1996, 2nd edition), *Die Unwirtlichkeit unserer Städte. Anstiftung zum Unfrieden*, Frankfurt am Main: Suhrkamp.
Oswald, F. & Baccini, P. (2003), *Netzstadt: designing the urban*, Basel-Berlin-Boston: Birkhäuser.
Piechocki, R. (2006), "Heimat: Begriffsentstehung und Begriffswandel", in: *Bund Heimat und Umwelt in Deutschland & Bundesverband für Natur- und Denkmalschutz, Landschaft- und Brauchtumspflege e.V., Erhaltung der Natur- und Kulturlandschaft und regionale Identität*, 11–30.
Piechocki, R., Eisel, U., Körner, S., Nagel, A. & Wiersbinski, N. (2003), "Vilmer Thesen zu 'Heimat' und Naturschutz" *Natur und Landschaft*, Vol. 78 (6), 241–244.
Piechocki, R, & Wuersbinski, M. (eds.) (2007), "Heimat und Naturschutz. Die Vilmer Thesen und ihre Kritiker", *Naturschutz und Biologische Vielfelt*, Vol. 47, Bundesamt für Naturschutz: Bonn-Bad Godesberg.
Piepmeier, R. (1990), "Philosophische Aspekte des Heimatbegriffs", in: Bundeszentrale für politische Bildung (ed.), *Heimat. Analysen, Themen, Perspektiven*, Bielefeld: Westfalen-Verlag, 91–108.
Qviström, M. (2008), "A waste of time? On spatial planning and 'wastelands' at the city edge of Malmö (Sweden)" *Urban Forestry & Urban Greening*, Vol. 7(3), 157–169.
Relph, E. (1976), *Place and Placelessness*, London: Pion Limited.
Schmeing, A. Bormann, O. & Schröder, M. (2004), "News from nowhere. Entwurfsstrategien für den repräsentationslosen Raum", in L. Bölling & T. Sieverts, (eds.), *Mitten am Rand. Auf dem Weg von der Vorstadt über die Zwischenstadt zur regionalen Stadtlandschaft*, Wuppertal: Müller + Busmann, 114–123.
Sieverts, B. (2003a), "Stadt als Wildnis", in: D.D. Genske & S. Hauser (eds.), *Die Brache als Chance. Ein transdisziplinärer Dialog über verbrauchte Flächen*, Berlin-Heidelberg-New York-Hongkong-London-Milan-Paris-Tokio: Springer, 205–231.
Sieverts, T. (2003b), *Cities Without Cities. An interpretation of the Zwischenstadt*, London-New York: Spon Press.
Spellerberg, A. & Kühne, O. (2010), *Heimat und Heimatbewusstsein in Zeiten erhöhter Flexibilitätsanforderungen: Empirische Studien im Saarland*, Wiesbaden: VS Verlag.

Vicenzotti, V. (2009), "Zwischenstadt als Heimat", in: T. Kirchhoff & L. Trepl (eds.), *Vieldeutige Natur. Landschaft, Wildnis und Ökosystem als kulturgeschichtliche Phänomene*, Bielefeld: transcript, 239–251.

Vicenzotti, V. & Trepl, L. (2009), "City as Wilderness: The Wilderness Metaphor from Wilhelm Heinrich Riehl to Contemporary Urban Designers" *Landscape Research*, Vol. 34(4), 379–396.

Vicenzotti, V. (2011), *Der "Zwischenstadt"-Diskurs. Eine Analyse zwischen Wildnis, Kulturlandschaft und Stadt*, Bielefeld: transcript.

Weber, M. (1949, 2nd edition), "Objectivity in Social Science and Social Policy", in: E.A. Shils & H.A. Finch (eds.), *The Methodology of the Social Sciences. Max Weber*, New York: The Free Press, 50–112.

PLACES AS UNGIVEN, MEMORIES AS COMPETITIVE?

AMBIGUITIES OF BELONGING IN THEOLOGICAL PERSPECTIVE

Peter Manley Scott

For the distance is measured, and that is what matters.
By measuring the distance, we come home.
Raymond Williams

I

In a late interview, Harold Pinter declared that part of his sense of Englishness, of belonging 'here', included a love of the English countryside.[1] On this, I was recently surprised by my older brother Adrian's opinion that he wishes his ashes to be interred in the same grave as Jonathan, our oldest brother. Jonathan, who died at eight weeks old, was buried in 1958 beneath a line of lovely lime trees in the pretty 'old cemetery' at Shrewsbury, Shropshire. In this same grave our father's ashes are also now interred and when the time comes our mother wishes her ashes to be interred there as well. Shrewsbury, in my recollection from the 60s and 70s, was a sleepy, semi-rural and deeply parochial market town in the Welsh marches where my brother and I spent our first 18 years. At one point in our childhood, the town did not even boast a cinema. Why would my older brother, Adrian, who has not lived in Shrewsbury for 30 years, wish his ashes interred there? And my 18 year old son, who also has the name Jonathan, where should he wish to rest his bones?[2] It is this sense of belonging that I wish to explore in this paper: the sense of loyalty to 'home', where your ashes will lie.

Should we be suspicious of this desire to belong? Should we be sceptical of this desire for a post-mortem home? Is such a loyalty in competition with other, better, loyalties? In religious terms, is the desire for belonging an interference with the religious person's love of God? A person divided against themselves cannot stand and thereby should then refuse this loyalty to place? Or is this desire for place a rebuke to theological views in which a sense of locality as place is not granted a high priority?[3]

We should note two matters immediately. First, there is no doubt that such a loyalty to place is open to distortion and manipulation. The end of this particular road may be the revolutionary political romanticism of fascism but there are many intermediate stopping places before that terminus.[4] Additionally, Christian theology has unintentionally offered its own intermediate stopping places: mandates, created grace, natural law and orders of creation. That is, theology has explored the gift of God's blessing in creation by reference to creaturely structures. It has proposed these structures as universal and yet it has not finally always been able to resist their ideological manipulation. Theology offers no pure orientations, resourced from some magical 'elsewhere', as infallible guides.

If such loyalty is open to distortion and manipulation and theological resistance to such distortion and manipulation has at best been partial, which theological protocols shall we lean on to clarify, test and correct that loyalty? If we cannot not desire to belong, how shall we assess that desire so as to affirm what is true in the desire and expose the idolatrous tendencies in that desire? In such a purgative theological phase, it will be important to try to establish some distance from the desire to belong. The aim here, by way of a theological critique, will be to explore such desire to belong so that it finally breaks down and receives its truth, so to speak, by reference to that which exceeds and surpasses that loyalty. Does, finally, the desire to belong 'fail' and by that failure open up a way to radical transcendence?

Second, we should note that, theologically speaking, we could only affirm such loyalty to place if we may also affirm that God encounters the creature in and through this loyalty to place. In other words, I am expanding the following quotation from German Lutheran theologian Dietrich Bonhoeffer: "Without God, without their brothers and sisters, human beings lose the earth... For those who have once lost the earth, however, for us human beings in the middle, there is no way back to the earth except via God and our brothers and sisters".[5] Recovering our situatedness on the earth, our loyalty to place is best established by reference to God and other people. A little later, I shall explore whether 'other people' should be expanded to 'other creatures', but first I wish to explore this encounter, this theological interference of desire, by reference to the ungivenness of place and the competition between memories.[6] In this way, I shall be exploring the relation between connection to place and separation from place.

What do I mean by place as ungiven and memory as competitive? To understand our situatedness in a place is also to acknowledge that the desire for place is a universal desire and thus places evoke the loyalty of others as well as me, of other groups as well as mine. In addition, the evocation of multiple loyalties is partly due to the competition between memories that are constitutive of that place. That is, of one location many places are evoked through memory, through the telling and re-telling of stories about that place. Sometimes these memories are recounted in that place and sometimes from another place, including places of exile. Loyalty to place is thereby never given and there may be other memories in competition with that place. An important moral issue now surfaces: should we work to make places less ungiven and, in the competition between memories, should there be a victor?

So far, I have argued that there is a theological need to establish distance in and through our loyalty to place. That is, we need both to create distance, and we need a way of measuring it. We can create that distance by exploring the metaphor of closeness to and distance from place. And we can measure that distance through the exploration of the ungivenness of place and the competition between memories. The two strategies presented here are related: desire is rendered increasingly abstract in the first strategy and thereby expands to include other creatures than the human. In turn, the second strategy supports a consideration of other inhabitants of places and the investment by memory of other agents in those same places. To see in more detail how this is so, I turn to the first strategy.

II

To begin the exploration of the first strategy, I want to suggest that humanity does not need to be rescued from or suppress such a sense of belonging. The desire to belong is not part of the natural condition of humankind that is to be separated from and contrasted with the redeemed condition of humanity therefore. It is wrong to suggest that the desire to belong has no impact on the graced human being or that the human needs to be rescued from this desire to belong. A sense of belonging is neither before grace nor opposed to grace; to seek to belong is neither a function of *natura pura* [pure nature] nor an outcome of the fall.

What then is the theological status of belonging? In suggesting that a sense of belonging is part of a graced nature I point to the view that to belong is a condition of human living. That is, humans act and know from a particular location and it is this sense of acting and knowing from a particular location that informs a sense of belonging to a place. "To be at all—to exist in any way—is to be somewhere, and to be somewhere is to be in some kind of place".[7]

Of course, humanity also has ways of transcending a particular location, through movement, memory and imagination. Yet, such situatedness and such transcending are a feature of human nature. As such, it is not particular situations and specific attempts to transcend through action, memory and imagination that are to be understood as graced. Instead, the situatedness of the human, as created and as fallen, is to be understood as graced. What is graced—this is the vital point—is an *abstract* concept of human nature: the situated, embodied and transcending human.

To argue that such a conception is abstract is emphatically *not* to argue that such a conception of the human posits the human-as-individual. On the contrary, place cannot be explored satisfactorily by reference to the human as individual. The human inhabiting of places is the inhabitation of spaces that are the sources of and are traversed by collective memories. Yet we should note a further feature of this theological effort at abstraction: in the move from places to situatedness to embodiment, we arrive at a barrier. Moreover, we must make a decision as to whether we wish to cross this barrier. The barrier identifies the difference between the human and the non-human. In this drive towards abstraction, what happens to this barrier?

A further, abstractive effort would recommend equality beyond this divide. In other words, we are able to posit a difference between the human and the non-human because of a wider equality. To notice a difference is to travel in thought beyond that difference, to step past the boundary. To step past the boundary to what, however? An equality held in common! And what is the source of that equality? A theological reply is: a conception of regard maintained by an Agent who exceeds the creatures. Through this process of abstraction, we arrive at a highly abstract conception of God whose being as the creator of the world may be posited but whose character is obscure.

In this theological argument, a distance in our sense of belonging is created. However, it is not created by setting aside that sense of belonging or by undermining our desire to belong. The distance is different: it presses our commitment to place by abstracting from place in such fashion that the equality of places is established abstractly and finally points to that equality of places before God. Places are affirmed but abstractly by reference to equality secured by the regard of the creator God.

In concluding this section, it is important to note that this abstractive argument is not a matter of moving towards a stripped-down account of the human. The process of abstraction is the affirmation of places, and bodies in places. What is affirmed is that this place measures our embodiment, and because we cannot escape our embodiment we cannot escape this place. Nor does my position support the easy abandonment of place: the loyalties that this place calls forth may be worth defending. However, whether a place should be defended *at any cost* is less clear and probably cannot be settled by such an abstractive mode of argumentation.[8] This sort of abstractive argument is less suited to an evaluation of the merits of *particular* loyalties. Instead, it offers a theological critique—both affirmative and critical—of the universal desire to belong by placing that desire to belong in the human, and beyond the human.

III

I turn now to the second strategy in which the distance established above is measured. In this strategy, I have suggested two measures of the distance: place as ungiven and memory as competitive. To argue that place is ungiven is to affirm that places are not best understood as empty until occupied by the group of which I am a member. Places are not given in their fullness only by reference to one inhabitation. A sense of belonging is not a zero/sum game. Different groups may occupy a place with different senses of belonging derived from different constitutions of a community and from different memories. Obviously, a sense of basic equality transferred from the first strategy reinforces such a view. Moreover, the first strategy, pressing as it does the matter of a basic equality, raises the question as to whether it is wise to identify any location as empty. Just because a location has no human inhabitants is it empty—of life, of significance?

Although it does receive support from it, this second strategy is not derived from the first strategy. Instead, to refine this understanding of place as ungiven, I make a distinction between loyalty to a place and identification with a place. I wish to affirm the first and refute the second.

To begin with identification with a place, much attention is paid to the ways in which places are constructed and that with these places people then identify. A sense of belonging or a sense of place is then deduced from the place. That is, identities are deduced from place and thereafter loyalties can be deduced from identities. For example: "I live here and therefore my identity is such-and-such-and so my loyalties are so-and-so—I was born in rural England and my identity is white English and so my loyalty is to Churchillian Englishness, including the freedom of the English to be, well, English."

We may identify two problems with this approach. A theological difficulty is that such an argument fits poorly with the first strategy I have set out: a process of theological abstraction that concludes immanently in a basic equality and transcendentally in the levelling regard of the creator God. An anthropological or political difficulty lies in the logic of the deduction: the process of the construction of place is obscured by beginning from a sense of occupation of a place; the core logic is one of engrossment: the 'I' of the group or community expands through its identity to leave itself unchallenged in its place. Of course, the claimed loyalty that results may then be reified and thereby interpreted as given and so as unrevisable. Yet it must be noted that such loyalty is not in fact received but projected: place is not received as a gift but asserted as an act of violence. The logic that haunts this position is authoritarian. Its success—and this position will often be successful—resides in its ability to defend its occupation of a place.[9]

With this identification with a place, I have contrasted loyalty to a place. This latter is my preferred option. First, it is consonant with the first strategy in that it permits the inhabitation of a place by others. Instead of loyalty being deduced from identity and place rather the construal of place occurs as the *expression* of loyalty. From the facticity of place, loyalty cannot be deduced. Instead, we must pose the question: how does place *express* loyalty?

The answer to this question cannot be ascertained by reference to the facticity of place itself but rather to the inhabitation of a place as a process that calls forth loyalty. Loyalty is here a permissive notion: a place can call forth many different sorts of loyalty thereby creating a competition of attachments. Place is here ungiven in that it is associated with my loyalties that are reactive responses rather than originary deductions. The logic is different here: place as the expression of loyalty may be understood as a human act rather than the tribal, ethnic, cultic or national deduction of loyalty from identity. "For all nations have ancestors, land and history", Kenneth Cragg reminds us. "Who we are, where we dwell and whence we came are universal denominators of humanity. All cherish histories, live by generational sequence and know where they belong territorially".[10] As the expression of loyalty, place humanises.[11]

Moreover, it may be correct to conclude that: "History, land and society are thereby a transcendental condition of human life. Such a condition is enacted in particular, contingent ways that we may then name as 'place'".[12] Place is summative of community, land and memory.

IV

If my argument gives an outline of what it means to understand place as ungiven, what does it mean to say that a sense of belonging is also to be understood by reference to memory as competitive? The answer is not far to seek: if loyalty is expressive of place and a place can be inhabited by many groups, there will be a competition between many memories over the significance of that place. Moreover, some memories of that place may well include memory of other places.[13] Finally, some memories may include actual or imagined efforts to obliterate the memories of others or those people themselves or those markers that are prompts to remembering by these others.

At this point, we encounter the matter that place is always a *normative* concept.[14] That is, the place of a people, and thereby their identity, offers an account of how that people considers that its life should be ordered. The ways in which it owns and disowns, remembers and forgets, shapes and reshapes its past; the ways in which it uses its land, and corrects misuses, and whether and how it opens its land to others; the ways in which a community understands how its common life should be governed—all these indicate normative elements.

The normative principles that are operative are not necessarily just in practice. This question of justice leads us into a discussion of memory as competitive. The interaction between community, land and memory can support many memories; there are as many memories as communities. If a world is revealed to us through our memories, what is disclosed about this world through memories?

Memories of place are community-constituting memories and are thereby collective: we share this place with others, whom we care for /love, and who we know and by whom we are known. My brother's desire to have his ashes interred in a particular grave is fully understandable only by reference to a family's shared memory. A mining community's desire to affirm its place in a coalfield draws on a shared memory of working and living in a particular location, even if that memory includes memories of perceived betrayal. Through memory, we may conclude, there is inter-subjective affirmation.

Additionally, by memory we imagine a future. That is, we appreciate that this sharing of our location as an inter-subjective phenomenon, does not end with our individual death. Thus, a future is posited: to 'memorise' is to expect that the memory will be borne by other members of the group.[15] Finally, if what this place represents is carried by memories we should also expect to find the transmitters of memory; that is, we should expect to find institutions. On account of institutions provided by different groups as transmitters of memories, there is strife in places. Such transmission, as performed by institutions with particular needs and perspectives, is necessarily selective. We do not need to establish a comprehensive list but among the 'ideological memory apparatuses' are patriotism, family, love of security and desire for nature.

The distance from home can be measured a second time by noting memory as competitive. One place may be the location for different and competing memories and acknowledging this competition requires attention to those institutions that are the bearers of those memories. Just as memories compete, it is likely that institutional carriers of memory will also be in competition.[16]

V

So far, I have argued that the theological task is to explore a sense of belonging as graced. Thus such desires for home are not to be immediately set aside as fallen or replaced by revelation. Yet, we do need to establish distance between ourselves and our longing for home. By attention to a strategy of theological abstraction, I argued for a distance-creating 'moment' in a theological hermeneutics of place. That is, an interruption in our sense of belonging may be secured by abstracting from the sense of place to recognise that no places are empty and that a basic equality is to be affirmed by reference to the regard of the creator God. Such an experiment in philosophical or natural theology affirms human dignity and leaves the door open to an affirmation of the flourishing of other creatures by attention to differences and a basic equality.

Moreover, I have been arguing that to affirm the relation of place to a creator God is one way of affirming such determinations. What is required is a proper grounding of belonging in the doctrine of creation in which the realm of human creatures is understood to be a shared realm, alive with other, non-human, creatures. Moreover, these differentiations are real rather than illusory or temporary.

Once such a distance is established, how is it to be measured? I suggested two measures: the ungivenness of place and the competition between memories. Each measure points to the same conclusion: the acknowledgement of others in places. The roots of our desiring of place cannot, if my analysis is right, be dug up and cast away: we cannot desire not to belong. Therefore, there is no merit in attempting to strip the human individual of their cultural attachments. The direction I recommend is one that *avoids* the stripping away of the human until all that is left is the individual and their relation to God.

Instead, to explore the measures of place as ungiven and memory as competitive is to explore a shared realm: a coalition of humans and others, and the relating of places to their many inhabitants and other places. Humanising the future is by way of identifying place as ungiven: the self-development of the human with others through the construal of places, actively and passively. A competition of memories functions to contrast our present sense of place with a sense of place held by others and thereby resists a drift towards nostalgia.

What emerges is a complex account of belonging in which ambiguities are inescapable. Part of the reason for such complexity resides in my two-fold approach. I have resisted a temptation to set aside such desires to belong and have instead sought to place belonging in contexts of immanence and by reference to transcendent regard. Here resides a theological effort of creating distance, of affirming a type of separation yet also and at the same time the desire for connection. Moreover, it is only from the perspective of separation that connectedness may be affirmed. Such connectedness is a creaturely connectedness, I contend, and not only a human connectedness. Additionally, after this transcendental positioning, I have sought through the strategies of places-as-ungiven and memories-as-competitive to explore the concrete ways in which places are ambiguous sites of belonging. The tension between separation and connectedness persists here also.

The double orientation of my argument suggests that separation and connectedness cannot be overcome; they should persist in our efforts to understand the loyalties of belonging and we should be suspicious of analyses that seek to exclude or marginalise one in favour of the other. For example, places of belonging should never be understood *only* immanently, and when they are understood immanently this field (!) of immanence includes non-human creatures and inorganic processes. Such immanence will only be grasped correctly by reference to the transcendent: the regard of the creator God that levels. The desire to belong cannot be judged as either good or bad at this level but can only be understood in relation to the affirmation of distance, of disconnection, that in turn permits a view of a shared realm of connectedness.

Yet even this complexity must be complexified. It is not enough to offer an abstract determination of places as occupied by many creatures and secured as such by the regard of God. For after such consideration comes the discussion of places as ungiven and memories as competitive; places are multiply occupied and the subjects and objects of competing memories. The relation between separation and connection is evident here: by efforts to secure ethnic-only connections, a group may insist on occupation of a place by its separation from other places and the exclusion of other groups from this place. In arguing that neither places nor memories can be regarded as settled and settling, I have resisted such a conclusion. The claimed dis-ambiguity of place is always threatened by the ambiguities generated by the ungivenness and competitive memories of places.

At this point in the argument, it is evident that my position relates well to what we might call political realities: the competition over land, for example, and the efforts at spatial exclusion and any attempted victory of one memory over others. Nonetheless, is not the vital test case in these discussions the actuality of landscapes? Is it not specific landscapes that trigger memories or offer markers of memory and is it not access to landscape over which groups dispute? Moreover, are not these political concerns combined with aesthetic considerations so senses of belonging are available to be mobilised in defence of a specific aesthetic, and thereafter in a defence of a certain presentation of a landscape? In this volume, Paul Selman argues that landscape refers in part to "a painterly framed image". This has been developed in the perspective of contemporary management of landscapes to include "a nexus of ecological, hydrological, geomorphic, social, cultural and economic systems that often combine in aesthetically pleasing or at least amenable ways". Moreover, he suggests that the visual arts have now moved beyond the consideration of the painterly image to interpret landscape as more than the visual, the aesthetic, in favour of "a space of performance, renewal and change".[17]

What is at stake here is what David Lowenthal calls "relics", which "survive in the form of natural features and human artifacts".[18] For in the consideration of place we should consider not only the recollection of the past by history and memory but also that there are items in a landscape—given/natural and constructed/artificial—that trigger or are associated with particular memories and are understood by a particular group to be constitutive of that place. Lowenthal calls this "the tangible past", which is subject both to the attrition of meaning as well as the attrition of substance. In other words, artefacts in a landscape are subject at the very least to erosion as well as destruction and may also be regarded differently by later generations and so have rather less significance to them. It is regarding landscape as anachronistic that is perhaps the greatest temptation for the religious imagination: "relics feel like emanations of a previous age" and thereby suggest a kind of stability, an openness to God. This is what Selman, after Belzer, refers to as "'thinness' between temporal and eternal space, yet where connections between the ordinary and the extraordinary can readily be fractured by noise or contamination".[19] They function in this way, I think, because relics—whether natural or artificial—are a curious combination of past and present. Whereas written and oral histories may clearly distinguish between the past and the present, things, as Lowenthal notes, "differ from thoughts and words in their temporal nature... artifacts are simultaneously past and present".[20]

A theological response to this temptation of the religious imagination to regard things in a landscape anachronistically requires the theologian to reconsider how these things might be understood in a more dynamic doctrine of creation.

By these hermeneutical considerations, we move theologically from landscape to land*inscape*. In other words, understanding places as ungiven and memories associated with those places as competitive suggests that these relics in a landscape acquire no significance in themselves but instead are constructed by groups and their memories. In turn, the relics acquire a certain numinous density. By the neologism, land*inscape*—a development of Gerard Manley Hopkins' term 'inscape'[21]—I am arguing that the identity of a landscape is partly given by its things, the objects that populate it. Yet this identity is dynamic and is not simply received but must be apprehended in its distinctiveness. The presentness of the things in a landscape is not to be referred only to the past but also to the future. Nostalgia is not permitted at this point: the place of a landscape is also part of the ground where bodies wait for the final resurrection of the dead. Hence we may note the importance of marking the places where the dead are buried or cremated. In the concrete counterpart to my abstractive theology, the ground is pregnant with the future: the openness of the ground, the openness of places, the openness of artefacts, to the future of God.

VI

I end where I began: a sense of belonging understood as the place where you wish your ashes to be interred; a wish for a place to be at rest. Such a desire may be understood as rooted in a sense of sharing in a place by memory. This is not the only memory to be related to that place but it refers to a family and its past as well as its future. Death divests control from the individual and yet in that divestment you can relocate yourself in past and future; that the most intimate human community in which you participate endures. This is not to deny others access to that place nor to deny that there may be other ways of remembering that place. However, it is not nostalgic: it makes no claim to that place. Instead, in a theological reckoning, it expresses a loyalty to a place by inhabiting ground where bodies wait for the final resurrection of the dead.

Here is to be found a theological response to the concern that this desire to belong is conservative, and only such. That such conservatism may be virulent is one of the objections to working with the concept of *Heimat*—and such virulence might be thought to be an outworking of conservatism? Part of the response here may be to distinguish between meanings of 'conservative' at this point. If 'conservative' means a defence of the present order, then the critical perspective that I have been developing in this chapter objects to such a defence. However, if 'conservative' has a more 'preservative' sense, then a Coleridgean response might be offered. Recall that in his comparison of Coleridge and Jeremy Bentham, John Stuart Mill makes a distinction between progressive and conservative. According to Mill, "... to Bentham it was given to discern more particularly those truths with which existing doctrines and institutions were at variance; to Coleridge, the neglected truths which lay *in* them".²² To attend to the desire to belong, and its allied sense of home, is to explore the truth of the situatedness of the humanity always by reference to the movement of separation and connectedness. The truth of belonging in place is dynamic, temporal, and so futural.

There is no way to the future except by place; all must pass that way. Yet, although not redeemed, the place is ungiven—inhabited by many creatures—and troubled by many memories as competitive. The temptation to occupy rather than inhabit place is always present; to render *our* place as singular and *our* memory as triumphant; to exclude in defence of space. Nonetheless, we are many, and we belong as many. We desire to belong yet we do not desire on our own. The test of our desiring lies in how to understand 'we': as a desiring before the equalising regard of God or a desiring before the god of 'our' place.

NOTES

1. "I love the English countryside. I love it quite positively. I'm in love with it. I also love cricket, as you know, which is a wonderful tradition. It's not, of course, simply this country that follows it. But we started it, I suppose. And I find there is a, how can I say?, a fundamental decency in the country itself." Interview with Harold Pinter by Jeremy Paxman for BBC 2's Newsnight programme (25 October 2002). http://news.bbc.co.uk/1/hi/programmes/newsnight/archive/2360959.stm, 19 April 2010.

2. In making this connection between belonging and countryside I am not stipulating that burial and interment in an urban setting does not count in the consideration of belonging. To the contrary, I would argue that careful consideration would need to be given to the construal of place in an urban cemetery: presumably the association with family, worshipping and other communities—Manchester has at least one Catholic cemetery—civic traditions, work, allotments, and dwelling place would all need careful consideration. Indeed, it may well be that love of country is also associated with such civic traditions and pride in city and region. Yet I would also wish to note that the cemetery is, like a municipal park, a curious borderland area, neither private nor public and yet open to the skies. Once more, the connection between post-mortem resting place, belonging and the ground is evident. See further, Scott (2010a), 186–202.

3. See a Christological over-determination to be found in parts of Protestantism, especially Reformed Christianity. The Christological over-determination denies to all places any soteriological value, except the place of Christ. See Lincoln, 29–49; and my critique in Bartholomew and Hughes (2004), 151–69.

4. The phrase 'revolutionary political romanticism' is from Paul Tillich; see Scott (1995), 34–44.

5. Dietrich Bonhoeffer, *Creation and Fall*, cited in Scott (2010a), 20–21.

6. Cf. Evans (1992), who, in chapter 3 uses the phrase, 'The ungiven God', to explore the ways in which God is not given in African-American religious experience; my use of 'ungiven' is clearly somewhat different; Sinclair (2006 [2005]), 60: "Memory is competitive, siblings play back the same events in different ways".

7. Casey, ix.

8. I well recall Neil Kinnock, then the leader of the Labour Party and so leader of Her Majesty's loyal opposition, in an interview during the British General Election cam-

paign of 1987 defending the Labour Party's then policy of unilateral nuclear disarmament. What, he was asked, would Britain do to defend itself when the Soviets attacked and Britain had no nuclear deterrent? He answered something like: retreat to the hills and conduct a guerrilla campaign thereby rendering 'totally untenable' any Soviet occupation. For this reply, he was ridiculed mercilessly in the press for his naiveté and lack of patriotism. Yet even now there is, it seems to me, wisdom in the reply: no place is worth defending *at any cost*. And after using nuclear weapons the cost in life—human and otherkind—would have been enormous. Then and now, it remains difficult to make the case that there are conditions under which the launch of nuclear missiles can be justified because the consequence of any launch is the destruction of civilisations. In addition, what then is freedom if there are few left to be free?
http://news.bbc.co.uk/1/hi/uk_politics/vote_2005/basics/election4/past_elections/4393315.stm, 19 April 2010.

[9] Harvey, 324.

[10] Cragg, 1–14 (here p. 3). Given this, it would be interesting to explore whether the two-state solution to the status of Jerusalem will ever be possible and whether a one-state or no-state way forward might be preferable.

[11] Place and embodiment, place and the control of place, see Scott (2010a), "The city's grace", pp. 186–202.

[12] Scott (2004), 151–169 (p. 158).

[13] As, arguably, British Pakistanis understand themselves as the carriers of two 'national' memories.

[14] Scott (2004), 151–169 (this section draws directly on pp. 158–59).

[15] Although the memory does not need to be projected very far: my mother is of the opinion that the current headstone at my brother's grave need only last another 50 years—after that, she reasons, who will be visiting the grave?

[16] Also, see my discussion of past, present and future in 'The future as God's amnesty? A public theology for a changing climate', *International Journal of Public Theology*, special issue on climate change (2010b). What, then, is the relation between place and our sense of time?

[17] Selman, this volume.

[18] Lowenthal, 238–259, here p. 238.

[19] Selman, this volume.

[20] Lowenthal, 248.

[21] '[Hopkins] felt that everything in the universe was characterized by what he called *inscape*, the distinctive design that constitutes individual identity. This identity is not static but dynamic. Each being in the universe 'selves,' that is, enacts its identity. And the human being, the most highly selved, the most individually distinctive being in the universe, recognizes the inscape of other beings in an act that Hopkins calls *instress*, the apprehension of an object in an intense thrust of energy toward it that enables one to realize specific distinctiveness. Ultimately, the instress of inscape leads one to Christ, for the individual identity of any object is the stamp of divine creation on it.' Greenblatt et al, 1513–16.

[22] Mill, 133.

REFERENCES

Casey, Edward S. (1998), *The Fate of Place: A Philosophical History*, Berkeley, Los Angeles & London: University of California Press.

Cragg, Kenneth (2004), "Jesus, Jerusalem and Pilgrimage Today", in: C. Bartholemew and F. Hughes (eds.), *Explorations in a Christian Theology of Pilgrimage*, Aldershot: Ashgate, 1–14.

Evans, James H. (1992), *We Have Been Believers: An African-American Systematic Theology*, Minneapolis: Fortress Press.

Greenblatt, Stephen et al. (eds.) (2006), "Gerard Manley Hopkins", *The Norton Anthology of English Literature*, 8th Ed. Vol. 2, New York & London: W. W. Norton & Company, 1513–1516.

Harvey, David (1996), *Justice, Nature and the Geography of Difference*, Oxford: Blackwell.

Lincoln, Andrew T. (2004), "Pilgrimage and the New Testament", in: Bartholemew and Hughes, 29–49.

Lowenthal, David (1985), *The Past is a Foreign Country*, Cambridge: Cambridge University Press.

Mill, John S. (2004), "Bentham", in: John S. Mill and Jeremy Bentham (eds.), *Utilitarianism and Other Essays*, London: Penguin, 132–176.

Scott, Peter M. (1995), "Prophetic Expectation", *Theology*, Vol. XCIX, No. 787, 34–44.

– (2004), "A Theology of Eucharistic Place", in: Bartholemew and Hughes, 151–169.

– (2010a), *Anti-Human Theology: Nature, Technology and the Postnatural*, London: SCM Press.

– (2010b), "The Future as God's Amnesty? A Public Theology of Resistance for a Changing Climate", *International Journal of Public Theology*, Vol. 4, No. 3, 314–331.

Selman, Paul, "Reconnecting Communities and Natural Systems in the Landscape" (this volume).

Sinclair, Iain (2006 [2005]), *Edge of the Orison: In the Traces of John Clare's 'Journey out of Essex'*, London: Penguin.

THE REFORMATION OF PLACE: RELIGION, SPACE AND POWER

Bronislaw Szerszynski

LOSING ONE'S PLACE

In a remarkable analysis of religious life in sixteenth century Lyon, Natalie Zemon Davis analysed Protestantism and Catholicism as two different spatial languages through which the territory of the city was interpreted and performed.[1] Catholic ceremonial, organised around the liturgical year but also in the build-up to the four fortnight-long fairs held in the town every year, was sensitive to the natural features of Lyon, especially the hill of Fourvière that dominated the town, and the two rivers: the "feminine", slow-moving Saône, and the "masculine", forceful, and often dangerous Rhône. These features were the continuous focus of festivals and ceremonies throughout the liturgical year. For example, at Pentecost, processions would pass the Chapel of the Holy Ghost at the end of the bridge over the Rhône, marking the importance of that river to the life of the city, and asking for protection from its unruliness. Nearby, young men would dress up as horses – *chevaux fous* – and dance through the streets that led from the end of the peninsula where the two very different rivers "embraced". On holy days such as Corpus Christi, processions with banners, bells, candles and torches would also move between different key sacred sites in the city, symbolically overcoming the division between different communities represented by the Saône, and thus giving the city identity and protection.

The Calvinist Huguenots had a very different orientation to urban space. As Davis puts it, "[t]he streets through which the dark-clad Calvinists marched singing their Psalms were not sacred routes, but avenues for the expression of the believer's faith, a message of communion to other Christians and of reproof to the canon-counts. That the sacred could be enclosed in a thing—in a host, in a bone, in a building, in a piece of land—was a notion smacking of idolatry." The Calvinist crowds thus performed the city in a very different way: they "purged the Catholic holy places... opening urban space and making it more uniform and available for exchange, traffic and human communication." They smashed crosses at crossroads, built public squares on top of old cemeteries, and set up shops in old chapels. The Calvinists recognised that places were not all the same: for example, places could be consecrated to prayer or other holy usage, or they could be polluted by licentiousness. Yet such characteristics were seen as accidental rather than essential features of the places in which they were encountered, and their sacral landscape did not exhibit the dramatic highs and lows of spiritual intensity of that of the Catholics. Instead, the environment was "held together by a middling tension, by listening and by watchfulness".[2]

This dramatic contrast lends credence to the idea that the Reformation may have played a key role in the constitution of the modern experience of space: in the displacement of what Henri Lefebvre called *absolute space* in favour of *abstract space*.[3] Absolute space is complex and discontinuous; it is made up of different kinds of "place" with radically different qualitative properties: enclosures and openings, interiors and exteriors, public and intimate places, places of joy and of desolation.[4] Furthermore, incommensurable bonds between people, places, symbols, supernatural realities, memory and custom serve to fragment absolute space into sites that have to be known through practices of naming and storytelling rather than those of surveying and measuring. By contrast, abstract space is merely a container for objects and activities; it is a space made suitable for practices of comparison, exchange and movement; it is the space of modern science, of bureaucratic rationalism, of market relations. Abstract space is a kind of space in which "place" – *topos* – is no longer primary and fundamental, but is at best a ghostly, secondary epiphenomenon caused by the arrangement of objects in space. The Reformation, Davis's account suggests, helped to lay the ground for the modern experience of abstract space, by breaking with what I will call the "archaic" experience of certain places and objects as having intrinsic connections to sacral power. And, as capitalism and modern technology spread around the world from their origins on the North Atlantic rim, it could be argued that they took with them not just a Protestant ethic of work, but a Protestant experience of space.

The link between abstract space and the erosion of a sense of place has become particularly apparent in the most recent phase of modernity, commencing in the late twentieth century, dominated as it has been by the globalisation of capitalism and increasing mobility of people and commodities. Manuel Castells[5] argues that in this "network society" there is clash between two spatial logics, between the subordinated *space of place*, of historically rooted human experiences,[6] and the dominant *space of flows*, a space made suitable for and constituted by the mobility of people, things and information.[7] This mobility (both real and virtual) is conditioned by, and in turn reproduces, a logic of abstract space: each given locality is tending to become not a unique place, with its own associations and meanings for those dwelling or even visiting there, but a particular combination of abstract characteristics that mark it out as similar or different to other places. The multiple mobilities of "liquid modernity" have thus produced a mindset for which places are collections of abstract characteristics in a mobile world, ever easier to be visited, appreciated and compared, but not known from within.[8] People are increasingly seeing and experiencing the world from afar, "at home" only in movement and in comparison.[9]

Even Europe, with its dense mosaic of languages and cultures, has been increasingly subjected to the logic of abstract space; Jensen and Richardson argue that the contemporary neoliberal approach to European integration is now one that tries to construct European space as a *monotopia* – "an organised, ordered and totalised space of zero-friction and seamless logistic flows" of goods, services, capital, labour and technologies across the Union.[10] This has given rise to a proliferation of what Marc Augé calls 'non-places', which, while taking up quantitative space, lack the kind of qualities we think of as making places.[11] Thus it could be argued that the Reformation helped to create the cultural conditions not only for capitalism (Weber) and modern science (Merton), but also for lay-bys, lorry parks, shopping malls and airport terminals.[12]

In this paper I want to reflect on the role of the Reformation in the transformation of our experience of place. Firstly I want to broaden this initial claim that the Reformation helped to effect a shift from absolute to abstract space, or from place to space, by situating this development within the *longue durée* of western religious history. In doing this I draw on the analysis that I developed in *Nature, Technology and the Sacred*, which explored how our modern ideas of nature and technology are shaped by western religious history.[13] In this book, I drew on the work of Max Weber, Robert Bellah, Jürgen Habermas and Marcel Gauchet to develop an account of how the western experience of the world has passed along a highly distinctive and contingent historical trajectory through the last two millennia – a succession of "orderings of the sacred" which together I term the "long arc of monotheism". In the next section I will draw on this analysis to help understand the transformation of the experience of place.

But secondly, I suggest that it is too simplistic to decry the Reformation in this regard and lament the loss of absolute space. As Davis herself argues, the Calvinists of sixteenth century Lyon were engaged not in a disenchantment of the world, but in a redefinition of its relationship to the holy. I will suggest that the reshaping of the experience of place in Western history is part of a cultural struggle between monotheism and what I call "archaic religion", in which spiritual power is seen as attached to specific people, things and objects. I will argue that the Reformation promised a final overcoming of archaic religion, and the possibility of a new experience of space and place. The hypermodern dissolution of space into shopping malls, gated communities and global flows of commodities may have been facilitated by the Protestant spatial logic, but it was not necessitated by it. Thirdly, I will thus argue for the possibility of a distinctive (post)Christian mode of placing, one which offers liberation from a bondage to place without thereby condemning the world and its inhabitants to placelessness.

PLACE IN WESTERN RELIGION

The branching path that Western religion has taken over the last two or three millennia is extraordinary complex and resists schematic analysis – especially by any schema that attempts to present it as an almost inevitable teleological unfolding, as evolutionary social theorists such as Habermas might claim. However, it is possible to discern a broad pattern. In tracing this path, we will pass through the unified sacro-natural cosmos of the primal and archaic sacred, the transcendental dualism of the monotheistic and Protestant sacred, and the immanent sacred of the modern and postmodern sacred (see Figure 1). The transition between these stages are generally not abrupt, but gradual and often highly conflictual; at any one place and time different orderings of the sacred might be clashing with one another. Nevertheless, overall, the West underwent a passage into and out of monotheism, with a momentous effect on western thought in general, and on the experience of place in particular, because of the way that the divine was separated from nature and place, purified, and then recombined with it. In one sense, the decline of monotheism in the West returns us to the unified cosmos of the primal sacred; but in another it leaves us in a very different landscape from the one in which we started.

PRIMAL	ARCHAIC	MONOTHEISTIC	PROTESTANT	MODERN	POSTMODERN
monistic		dualistic			immanent
multiple space	absolute space		abstract space		multiple space

Figure 1.

The story of the long arc of monotheism starts with what I call the ***primal sacred***, typical of hunter-gatherer societies, in which there is no clear distinction between the natural and the supernatural. The world is not understood as the unified creation of a transcendent and unique creator God, but as the ongoing interplay of multiple, this-worldly agencies. In this sacral ordering, mythical narrative is not seen as referring to a separate, heavenly realm but is woven into the empirical details of the physical world. Particular features of the landscape might be seen as having particular spiritual significance, but every natural feature is experienced as related to the actions of mythical beings. However, these beings are not seen as controlling the world, nor are they worshipped as "gods"; instead, they are approached through identification and the "acting out" of primal myths, or through mundane forms of social interaction. The purpose of such rituals is to secure the reproduction of life within this world, rather than to escape it or to live according to laws originating from outside it.[14]

However, as the rise of agriculture brings a relative distancing from the natural world and new forms of social organisation based on the concentration of power, a rather different, ***archaic sacred*** emerges, for example in the "pagan" cultures that preceded the emergence and spread of Judaism, Christianity and Islam in the Middle East and Europe Like primal religion, archaic religion is similarly monistic in its experience of the world as a unified "natural-divine cosmos", and is similarly concerned with securing existence in this world rather than with other-worldly salvation.[15] But with the development of priests and other intermediaries between humans and spiritual power there is a relative shift from magic – the *ad hoc*, circumstantial meeting of needs and crises – to religion "proper" – a systematic regulation of relations with gods and other supernatural beings.[16] Importantly for present purposes, sacred, natural and worldly hierarchies are seen as continuous – resulting, for example, in African ideas of divine kingship, where an individual is seen as encapsulating sacred order and power. A common characteristic of the archaic sacred is thus the marking out of certain places, people or objects as having a privileged relationship with the sacred, and other things as relatively profane. The *genius loci* of Roman religion belongs properly in this ordering of the sacred, in which specific parts of nature are protected by tutelary spirits that have to be propitiated.[17]

With the birth of "axial" or "world" religions such as Judaism and Christianity, the supernatural powers of ancient divinities are gathered together into the idea of the numinous, monotheistic God, and expelled from the empirical world into a supernal reality. Western religion thereby progressively leaves the monistic cosmos of the primal and archaic orderings of the sacred for a dualistic **monotheistic sacred**. In this ordering of the sacred – that inhabited by the Catholics of Lyon described by Davis – religion continues to operate through the material and the bodily in ways that echo primal and archaic religion, but the sacred is ordered around a new dualism of the natural and the supernatural. The individual starts to undergo a process of becoming more clearly separated from his or her environment, as experience is increasingly organised around vertical relations of dependency on and obligation to priest, saint and God, rather than around horizontal relations with the natural, social and supernatural worlds.[18] Yet, in medieval Christianity, as in archaic religion, supernatural realities are still mapped on to physical features. Relics and places of worship are scattered everywhere – in chapels, springs, fountains, woods, as well as great urban centres – a sacred topography which organises worship, pilgrimage and site-specific rituals.[19] However, the meanings of these features are apprehended in a different way than they would be in primal and archaic religion – as pointing to external, higher realities.[20] Natural objects, and not just words, are seen as *referring* – to other objects and events in nature and history, but finally to moral and spiritual truths as laid out in scripture. This semiotic subordination of the natural to the supernatural world – the reading of nature and place as "about" spiritual truths – both reinforces and expresses the move away from the monism of the primal and archaic sacred: the highest values are those associated not with the cyclic, homeostatic maintenance of *this* world but with the anticipation of the *next*.

The emergence of the **Protestant sacred** sees a radicalisation of this division between the natural and supernatural, as the Reformation strips away the institutional and supernatural hierarchies that both constituted and spanned the gulf between the transcendent divine and the world. The divine is thus removed from this world in a more absolute sense – becomes more infinite, unconditioned and unknowable – and with seemingly paradoxical consequences. The gulf between creator and creation is made at once infinite and infinitesimal, absolute and vanishingly small; at the same time as the Reformation amplifies the gulf between the empirical and transcendent worlds, the latter is also brought close to each individual and to the natural world. As Weber argued, the very idea of what it is to serve God is transformed: no longer is it conceived primarily in terms of devotional or ascetic acts to be carried out at specific places and times of heightened spiritual significance, or as the responsibility solely of the cloistered few.[21] Instead, the duty to God is experienced as an inner orientation, one towards a divine command that has to be acted out in all areas of profane life. This formulation allows the centred self of the monotheistic sacred to operate *outside* world-denying practices and sacred spaces, amidst the complexities of social life. The unmediated relation with the divine meant that religious action is now "conceived to be identical with the whole of life", and the world to be an arena in which to work out the divine command.[22] As we saw with the Huguenots of Davis's Lyon, the spatial correlate of this is a shift from a complex, discontinuous "absolute" space to a unified, homogeneous "abstract" space. The conception of the natural world, too, is transformed by this shift, in ways that favour the rise of modern science; matter comes to be seen as wholly passive, and space as continuous and homogenous, so that the laws that God has impressed on matter can operate identically at all points in the universe.[23]

With the emergence of what I call the ***modern sacred***, the transcendent axis is pulled into the very empirical world that was constituted by its ejection, producing a new immanentist ordering of the sacred, grasped through Enlightenment reason or Romantic sensibility. Being and order, instead of being seen as deriving from a supernatural source external to empirical reality, are increasingly seen as *properties of that reality itself*. The world thereby comes to be seen as profane in a newly radical sense – not just as being less sacred than its divine source and reference point, but as having no relation to the sacred at all. The transcendent axis, now introjected into the material world as an immanent ordering principle, still operates in a hidden way to maintain the idea of a single truth and abstract space. But with the emergence of the modern sacred, we see the demise of that crucial world-relation that emerged with the axial religions and the monotheistic sacred: the sense that this world points towards the next one either by symbolising transcendent truths or preparing the faithful for eternal life. Instead, there is a focus on the endless reproduction of immanent life-processes within *this* world.

Finally, in the ***postmodern sacred*** – which does not supplant but in various ways coexists with the modern experience of space – we see a more thoroughgoing collapse of the organizing dualism of the monotheistic and Protestant sacred, and the emergence of a multiple reality, one filled with and constituted by different cosmologies, worldviews and experiences of place grounded not in organised religion but in subjective experience.[24] With the dropping of the doctrinal certainties and Puritan character ideals of early-modern religion, religious action thus becomes in a sense even more demanding than it was within the Protestant sacred, with a growing imperative for each individual to work out their own spiritual meanings, whether inside or outside the structures of organized religion.[25] Under these conditions it is the "aesthetic community" that is the paradigm form of sociality – a community that "has no other foundation to rest on but widely shared agreement, explicit or tacit (that is) woven entirely from the friable threads of subjective judgements".[26] Space is experienced in multiple ways that are contingent on the membership of these elective, affectual tribes.[27] This ordering of the sacred is encountered in the contemporary, heterotopic city with its multiple, overlain spatial orders of meaning – its numerous competing spirits of space kept alive by the city's varied inhabitants and visitors.

In what kind of place does this journey leave us? The rise and fall of "absolute" space seems to have deposited us in a postmodern experience of space that shares features with the monistic cosmos of the primal sacred in which our story started – the world, once again, is experienced as neither dependent on an external sacred reality, nor organised according to a single logic of sacrality and power. Yet the journey through the long arc of monotheism also transforms human experience. This passage initially abstracts space, making it possible to experience the world as a unified domain whose operation is capable of being grasped as a whole rather than a collection of independent agencies and sources of power, and as a homogenous space without centres of sacral power. But then, with the rise of a postmodern register a further dimension is added to the experience of space: this abstraction *itself* is abstracted, so that even the experience of existing in the shared, abstract space of modernity is dimmed, and instead people increasingly feel themselves as inhabiting private worlds of meaning. So, while contemporary experience is "*after* monotheism", in that is no longer characterised by a belief in the radical, ongoing dependency of the being and becoming of the world on a transcendent creator God, it is also "after *monotheism*" – transformed by the passage through monotheism into something quite different. And a crucial element of that difference is the abstraction of space and loss of the intense sense of place typically experienced by members of pre-modern societies.

PLACE AND POWER

There are many reasons one might lament this loss of place. One reason is *cultural and spiritual*: that the dilution of place represents an impoverishing of human experience. If there were no places, how – and where – could *Dasein*, being-in-the-world, "take place"?[28] This, I take it, is one of the key insights of Tim Ingold's work on space and dwelling, in which the modern experience of space is contrasted with the perception of the environment characteristic of indigenous peoples and found wanting.[29] According to this view, the dweller in abstract space is in a state of privation, alienated from their environment, no longer capable of the participatory relationship with the world that is seen as a primary dimension of authentic human being-in-the-world. But another reason to lament the abstraction of space is *political*. Historically, the abstraction of space has been a key element in the strengthening of the power of the centralised state and of disembedded market relations. The modern state requires and reinforces the abstraction of space across its territory, unifying it through a single system of relationships and duties, and a single logic of representation which makes the territory and what happens in it "legible" to disciplinary state power. Markets, too, operate dependent on space being abstracted and "striated" through mechanisms of reification, standardisation, quantification and motility.[30], This move from absolute to abstract space generally has the effect of tipping the balance of power away from the local and the situational and towards more distant, abstract and often unforgiving forms of power.[31] Even the postmodern individual can serve to strengthen the disembedding power of markets, by taking the form of the consumer whose subjective experience and preferences cannot be gainsaid.[32]

However, I want to argue that it is not so clear that the contrast between absolute and abstract space is a simple one between good "place" and bad "space". The geographer Doreen Massey[33] argues that that overly stark contrasts between space and place, such as those made by Tuan[34] and Castells,[35] makes place too rooted, and thereby too resistant to reflexivity and to progressive social dynamics. According to this view, an element of abstraction in the experience of space is to be welcomed, ethically and politically. In terms of the language that I am using in this chapter, one might say that a strong sense of place is linked to the archaic sacred, and that the tension between absolute and abstract space in Western history is thus implicated in a wider spiritual struggle over the nature of social, natural and divine power.

From a Protestant point of view, the Reformation is a more systematic working-through of a key move made by the arrival of Christianity. Marcel Gauchet's analysis of the development of Western religion can help us to think through this argument, if we extend his analysis from the domain of social relations to that of space and power.[36] Gauchet suggests that in the West the notion of political rule had been initially constituted in the context of what we are calling the archaic sacred, by the making of explicit connections between specific empirical people, objects and places and divine power. In many ways, the incarnational logic of Christianity seems to continue that particular disposition of the sacred; God was born in a particular man, at a particular place, at a particular time. However, as Gauchet argues, Christianity brings about a radical departure from the "organic interlocking of the Natural and the Supernatural" that is characteristic of the archaic sacred.[37] Unlike the warrior Messiahs predicted by many Jewish cults, Jesus is an "inverted Messiah", in whom divine power is identified not with the highest – the sovereign – but with the lowest – the weak and excluded. In contrast to the divine kingship of the archaic sacred, this performed not a continuity but a *radical gulf* between heaven and Earth.[38] After Christ, Gauchet suggests, no one person – and, we can add, no one place – could claim uniquely to inhabit the fulcrum between the natural and the supernatural.

Whereas a traditional messiah would have preached war, and thus reaffirmed the primacy of the collective, Christ preaches love and peace, constituting an interiority to human experience which permitted individuals a new distance from the social bond. Similarly, the infinite distance of the Christian God and the refusal of the demonstrations of magical power that were characteristic of the archaic sacred led to new forms of collective being, where distanced individuals were gathered together into a salvation community distinct from political power, paradigmatically represented by the notion of "Church". Because the Incarnation had taken a form which broke with the sacral continuities of archaic religion, a yawning gap had opened up between divine and earthly truth. This separation of sacred and earthly authority meant that individuals were thrown back on themselves to make sense of sacral truths in terms of their own inner understanding. The Church at once symbolized and promised to fill that gap, but in a way such that "what legitimated the Church's existence – the human understanding's uncertainty about revealed truth – simultaneously justifies challenging its authority".[39] Thus the breaking of the connection between divine and earthly rule gave the individual the right to withdraw assent from worldly power, helping constitute the individual as a centre of consciousness and judgement in their own right, developments which lead up to concepts of individual conscience central to modern democracy. The spatial correlate of this social transformation – of the shift from an understanding of "virtue" as an external and objective power to that of an internal and subjective conscience – is the displacement of absolute by abstract space: the separation of power and significance from particular locations, and the rise of a new experience of space in which the moral individual is centre-stage.

Yet, even in the modern world, spatial politics is still partly shaped by the archaic sacred. There are many examples of space being organised materially and semiotically in a way that privileges certain sites over others, and subordinates the individual to a prescribed spatial ordering of value. For example, it is not only imperial cities like Beijing and Paris that are laid out to concentrate symbolic power. Even the apparent placelessness of contemporary global finance is organised in ways that favour centres such as Wall Street and the City of London; by contrast, the transport infrastructures of developing world spaces such as Africa and Latin America are laid out as "open veins", designed for extraction.[40] Aesthetic representations of nature and landscape are frequently used to invoke ideas of nation in a revival of modes of sacralisation characteristic of the archaic sacred.[41] The collective awestruck moments experienced by Americans in the face of "their" nature and technology seem to mark out the American nation as having a privileged connection to the universal destiny of humankind.[42]

And even environmental thought, so often critical of existing structures of social power, can draw on archaic modes of spatial ordering. The ideology of conservation in the nineteenth and twentieth centuries was conditioned by a colonialism which itself had roots in the archaic sacred's notions of continuity between earthly hierarchies and divine power, as evidenced in its singling out of particular landscapes, wildlife habitats and species for concern and protection. Even the contemporary concern for global nature can be understood as a reinstatement of the archaic sacred at the level of the world itself: where once tutelary spirits watched over particular forests or particular species, now it is nature as a whole which is sacralised. For the critics of the technological domination of nature, nature is guided and guarded by its own immanent teleology, sometimes personified as Gaia.[43] For the proponents of global environmental management, by contrast, the environment is under the protection of the abstract ruler of democratic society, who shapes and optimizes it for his own interests, interests rendered sublime and universal through the language of technical reason.[44] In both, the sacrality of nature brooks no argument; the ritual demands of the tutelary god of nature are absolute and non-negotiable.

Ultimately, even the placelessness of modern experience can be seen as an archaic sacralisation of abstract space itself, one which produces either a blasé indifference to place – a modern version of Stoic apathy – or a subordination to a global imperative that represents a recapture of human freedom. It appears that the emancipatory potential of monotheism to break the archaic equation between sacred and profane power and thereby opening up a new space of freedom for human being-in-the-world has been far from fully realised. Without the transcendent axis, without the idea of a divinity beyond the empirical world, nature would likely have remained conceived as a cyclical realm of violence seen as symbolically underwriting a conservative social order, rather than as capable of peaceable coexistence with a human social order constituted though relations of gift and speech – what Klaus Eder calls the "bloodless" tradition within Western culture, a tradition which refuses the symbols of earthly social power that are grounded in the totemism of the archaic sacred.[45] Yet in the modern experience of place we can see that even the abstraction of space itself has become subordinated to the logic of the archaic sacred, thereby frustrating the emancipatory power of this move. What we need in order to prevent this thwarting, I want to suggest, is to reform reformed space.

THE REFORMATION OF THE REFORMATION OF PLACE

How can we escape archaic relations between space and power without being recaptured by the sacralisation of abstract space and consigned to the placelessness of much modern experience? I have recently suggested that clues to such an escape can be found in the work of Søren Kierkegaard, who, while not directly talking about space, shows us how reformed space can *itself* be reformed.[46] In *The Concept of Irony*, Kierkegaard uses the life of Socrates to illustrate the idea that the life of "immediacy", simply living within the moral horizon of one's own culture is inconsistent with the genuinely ethical life.[47] For Kierkegaard, Socrates' ironic self-distancing from the culture into which he had happened to be born, and indeed from the concrete details of his own life, was the awakening of subjectivity itself, without which there can be no genuine moral responsibility. This applies to the archaic sacred and place: to be able to distance oneself from a place, to understand its contingency, to be able to compare and contrast it with other places, is the awakening of a spatial subjectivity which is also necessary for justice and responsibility.

However, as Andrew Collins points out, a simple negation of concrete existence, a severing of private meaning from the shared, emplaced world of culture, can by itself only offer a *negative* freedom, not a positive form of life.[48] Kierkegaard himself recognised this; in *Either/Or* he carries out a caustically perceptive critique of the blasé Romantic aesthete in his depiction of the character "A" – egotistical, bored and incapable of engagement.[49] He argues that the very inadequacy of A's existence is connected to the fact that the ironic attitude is not fully carried through. Similarly, with the liberation of the modern individual from absolute space, the archaic sacred is reinstated at the level of abstract space itself, and rendered immune from critique. The Romantic aesthete is not free but captured by his or her own alienation from the public world, by an ironic attitude that becomes a new immediacy, a new and equally constraining horizon of thought. Similarly, the dweller in abstract modern placelessness is not free from the intertwining of worldly and supernatural power, but is recaptured at a higher level by the sacralisation of abstract space itself.

In his later *Concluding Unscientific Postscript*, Kierkegaard, writing under the pseudonym Climacus, suggested a way out of this trap.[50] For Climacus' ironist, the ironic distancing from immediacy is only a transitional stage to the fully ethical life of responsible choice. Climacus' ironist identifies *neither* with the finite, empirical self of his immediate, conditioned existence, *nor* with the infinite, unconditioned ironic self of pure choice, but with the contradiction between the two. From the vantage point of his unconditioned, ironic distance, he thus regards his conditioned, finite existence not as a set of constraints to be rejected, but as "a home in which he chooses to dwell".[51] The ironist does not abandon, but *returns* to his finite, worldly existence, and takes *responsibility* for it. As John Evan Seery rather similarly puts it, the spirit of irony requires one "to return to the finite world of politics, to act in and for such a world, even in the face of knowledge that puts the world and that activity into perspective".[52]

As we have seen above, the reformation of spatial relations involves a self-distancing from the shared world of place, one which can seem to lead inexorably to the placeless experience of modern life – of space as a mere objective container, or as a mere subjective phantasm. Yet if the modern distancing from place is followed by the return gesture of re-entering the world with a new sense of reflexivity towards and responsibility for the attachment one feels for one's place, the meaning and significance of the shared living space of human existence does not have to be eroded. On the contrary, it is only through the ironic negation of received meanings that space and place can be re-formed as a fit dwelling place for ethical freedom and responsibility. If we can learn to experience space as consisting of places that are neither unique nor equivalent, that neither define us nor leave us indifferent; if we can recognise that the post-Reformation distancing from place should make it possible to relate to places not less but *more* fully; then we will know a spirit of place that is at once grounded and open to the wider spaces of justice – a spirit of place that is our own.

NOTES

[1] Davis.
[2] Davis, 58–59.
[3] Lefebvre.
[4] Bachelard.
[5] Castells.
[6] Tuan.
[7] Urry.
[8] Bauman.
[9] Szerszynski and Urry.
[10] Jensen and Richardson, 3.
[11] Augé.
[12] Weber, 1985; Merton.
[13] Szerszynski, 2005.
[14] Bellah.
[15] Bellah.
[16] Weber, 1965.
[17] Hughes.
[18] Brown.
[19] Muchembled.
[20] Harrison.
[21] Weber, 1930.
[22] Bellah, 36–39.
[23] Funkenstein; Harrison.
[24] Cf. Heelas; Roof.

25 Bellah.
26 Bauman.
27 Hetherington; Maffesoli.
28 Heidegger.
29 Ingold.
30 Deleuze and Guattari.
31 Porter; Scott.
32 Keat et al.
33 Massey.
34 Tuan.
35 Castells.
36 Gauchet.
37 Gauchet, 143.
38 Gauchet, 118–124.
39 Gauchet, 137.
40 Galeano.
41 Hays; Lowerson.
42 Nye.
43 Lovelock.
44 Arendt.
45 Eder; Cf. Hamilton.
46 Szerszynski, 2007.
47 Kierkegaard, 1989.
48 Collins.
49 Kierkegaard, 1992b.
50 Kierkegaard, 1992a.
51 Collins.
52 Seery, 139.

REFERENCES

Arendt, Hannah (1958), *The Human Condition*, Chicago: University of Chicago Press.
Augé, Marc (1995), *Non-Places: Introduction to an Anthropology of Supermodernity*, London: Verso.
Bachelard, Gaston (1958), *The Poetics of Space*, Boston, MA: Beacon Press.
Bauman, Zygmunt (2000), *Liquid Modernity*, Cambridge: Polity Press.
Bellah, Robert N. (1970), "Religious Evolution", in, *Beyond Belief: Essays on Religion in a Post-Traditional World*, New York: Harper & Row, 20–50.
Castells, Manuel (2000), *The Rise of the Network Society*, Oxford: Blackwell.
Collins, Andrew (1998), "The Perils of Reflexive Irony" in: A. Hannay and G.D. Marino (eds), *The Cambridge Companion to Kierkegaard*, Cambridge: Cambridge University Press, 125–153.
Davis, Natalie Zemon (1981), "The Sacred and the Body Social in Sixteenth Century Lyon", *Past and Present*, Vol. 90, 40–70.
Deleuze, Gilles, and Félix Guattari (1988), *A Thousand Plateaus: Capitalism and Schizophrenia*, London: Athlone Press.

Eder, Klaus (1996), *The Social Construction of Nature: A Sociology of Ecological Enlightenment*, London: Sage.
Funkenstein, Amos (1986), *Theology and the Scientific Imagination from the Middle Ages to the Seventeenth Century*, Princeton, New Jersey: Princeton University Press.
Galeano, Eduardo H. (1973), *Open Veins of Latin America: Five Centuries of the Pillage of a Continent*, New York: Monthly Review Press.
Gauchet, Marcel (1997), *The Disenchantment of the World: A Political History of Religion*, Princeton, NJ: Princeton University Press.
Hamilton, Malcolm (2000), "Eating Ethically: 'Spiritual' and 'Quasi-Religious' Aspects of Vegetarianism", *Journal of Contemporary Religion*, Vol. 15, 1, 65–83.
Harrison, Peter (1998), *The Bible, Protestantism, and the Rise of Natural Science*, Cambridge: Cambridge University Press.
Hays, Samuel P. (1987), *Beauty, Health and Permanence: Environmental Politics in the United States*, Cambridge: Cambridge University Press.
Heidegger, Martin (1962), *Being and Time*, Malden, MA: Blackwell.
Hetherington, Kevin (1998), *Expressions of Identity: Space, Performance and the Politics of Identity*, London: Sage.
Hughes, J. Donald (1986), "Pan: Environmental Ethics in Classical Polytheism" in: E.C. Hargrove (ed.), *Religion and Environmental Crisis*, Athens, GA: University of Georgia Press, 7–24.
Ingold, Tim (2000), *The Perception of the Environment: Essays in Livelihood, Dwelling and Skill*, London: Routledge.
Keat, Russell, Nigel Whiteley, and Nicholas Abercrombie (Editors), (1994), *The Authority of the Consumer*, London: Routledge.
Kierkegaard, Søren (1989), *The Concept of Irony, with Continual Reference to Socrates: Together with Notes of Schelling's Berlin Lectures*, Princeton, NJ: Princeton University Press.
Kierkegaard, Søren (1992a), *Concluding Unscientific Postscript to Philosophical Fragments*, Princeton: Princeton University Press.
Kierkegaard, Søren (1992b), *Either/Or: A Fragment of Life*, Harmonsworth: Penguin.
Lefebvre, Henri (1991), *The Production of Space*, Oxford: Blackwell.
Lovelock, James E. (1987), *Gaia: A New Look at Life on Earth*, Oxford: Oxford University Press.
Lowerson, John (1980), "Battles for the Countryside" in: F. Gloversmith (ed.), *Class, Culture and Social Change: A New View of the 1930s*, Brighton: Harvester Press, 258–80.
Maffesoli, Michel (1996), *The Time of the Tribes: The Decline of Individualism in Mass Society*, London: Sage.
Massey, Doreen B. (2005), *For Space*, London: Sage.
Merton, Robert K. (1970), *Science, Technology and Society in Seventeenth Century England*, London: Harper.
Muchembled, Robert (1985), *Popular Culture and Elite Culture in France, 1400–1750*, Baton Rouge: Louisiana State University.
Nye, David E. (1994), *American Technological Sublime*, Cambridge, MA: MIP Press.
Porter, Theodore M. (1995), *Trust in Numbers: The Pursuit of Objectivity in Science and Public Life*, Princeton: Princeton University Press.

Scott, James C. (1998), *Seeing Like a State: How Certain Schemes to Improve the Human Condition Have Failed*, New Haven, CT: Yale University Press.

Seery, John Evan (1990), *Political Returns: Irony in Politics and Theory from Plato to the Antinuclear Movement*, Boulder, CO: Westview Press.

Szerszynski, Bronislaw (2005), *Nature, Technology and the Sacred*, Oxford: Blackwell.

Szerszynski, Bronislaw (2007), "The Post-Ecologist Condition: Irony as Symptom and Cure", *Environmental Politics*, Vol. 16, 2, 337–355.

Szerszynski, Bronislaw, and John Urry (2006), "Visuality, Mobility and the Cosmopolitan: Inhabiting the World from Afar", *British Journal of Sociology*, Vol. 57, 1, 113–131.

Tuan, Yi-Fu (1974), *Topophilia: A Study of Environmental Perception, Attitudes, and Values*, Englewood Cliffs, NJ: Prentice-Hall.

Urry, John (2007), *Mobilities*, Cambridge: Polity.

Weber, Max (1930), *The Protestant Ethic and the Spirit of Capitalism*, London: George Allen & Unwin.

Weber, Max (1965), *The Sociology of Religion*, London: Methuen.

Weber, Max (1985), *The Protestant Ethic and the Spirit of Capitalism*, London: Unwin Paperbacks.

POSTSCRIPT

John Rodwell and Peter Manley Scott

The post-war settlement in Western Europe and the rediscovery of democracy in the East with the collapse of the Soviet empire have now been challenged by a resurgence of older loyalties to identity and place and a flux of migrations by those in search of a more secure future elsewhere. How and where to feel at home and among whom, these are questions pressed upon us once again. Here we consider whether our own deliberations have advanced an understanding of belonging together and having a place in a future which looks newly insecure and, in particular, how a theological perspective might enrich an interpretation of *Heimat* that could be put at the service of us all.

NEGOTIATING A HOME

In our exchanges, Stefan Körner provided a clear rationale for the way in which notions of *Heimat* could be used to legitimise tyrannical claims to identity and territory and effect definitive solutions to exclude those defined as being too 'other' to share our own traditional homeland. In the post-war atmosphere of taboo about the word *Heimat* itself in Germany, more dynamic interpretations of belonging, such as those articulated by Greverus,[1] Bausinger[2] and Mecklenburg[3] have helped rehabilitate and safeguard the idea of *Heimat* for our own challenging times. On this view, it involves a dialectical relationship, a negotiable reciprocity, a constant re-appropriation, that can redeem attachment to place from dangerous exclusivity.

Among our own contributors, Vera Vicenzotti has shown how such flexibility might give the peri-urban, frequently seen as a fleeting in-between world, neither one thing nor the other, its own creative opportunities whereby we might come to feel at home even there. Paul Selman, speaking of restored landscapes, often characterised as repetitive stretches of nowhere, makes a plea for open textured infrastructure, where such connectedness of different functions might leave room for intuitive individual response and social learning, such that there might be a negotiated and serendipitous emergence of place. Understandings of *Heimat* must also do justice to Ian Thompson's concerns that the *genius loci* or 'spirit of the place' might retain its meaning in a world of complex interweaving of flows, particularly those involving the migrations of peoples, some of whom move willingly, maybe transporting their sense of belonging with them on the move, as well as traumatic economic change such as de-industrialisation.

Among our number, it is Bergmann and Scott who explore the theological import of these particular challenges to our relationship to place. For the former, our own *Beheimatung* in turbulent times and shifting situations should be a reflection of God's own willingness to 'make himself at home' in our flesh and blood in Jesus Christ and through the indwelling of the Holy Spirit in the Church. For Scott, such divine generosity shows that all places are essentially gift, quite independent for their significance on our own particular occupation of them in any one time.

At this point, we find Bergmann's insistence on the importance of negotiated encounters across boundaries to be important. Although there remains a fear of contamination across boundaries, we consider that in such encounters new boundaries may be formed. The issue is not the simple levelling of boundaries but also the creation of new boundaries. Such boundaries mark events and sites of welcome and hospitality. Such new boundaries may function as a challenge to older boundaries. And they always raise the question of at whose cost the new sense of belonging within the bounds has been negotiated? Do we sit comfortably within our home at the expense of others? We shall return to this point at the end of this section in our discussion of the Church as placed community and the rite of Eucharist.

If Scott is correct that all places are divine gift, then all are strangers. How should strangers behave towards one another? For us, this raises the matter of balance between the risk of welcome and our *security* in the process of negotiating a shared home. For there to be the work of making oneself at home, then all must enjoy a basic level of security. Security operates at a number of levels: personal, economic and cultural. The encounters with strangers will only be successful—that is, contribute to a situation in which people find ways of making themselves at home together —if levels of security are maintained. Among the countries of Europe to which all our contributors belong, there is a specific challenge in the sense that the guarantor of security is often held to be the State. Whether the State contributes positively to home making requires further discussion. In contrast to top-down, State-based, approaches, we would also propose that attention be paid to bottom-up approaches to security for, as Eidson and others suggest, it is through communities and neighbourhoods that *Heimat* is negotiated

A further contextual issue arises as to how we think about boundaries themselves. As we talked though this issue, we realized these essays offer the reader accounts of different sorts of boundaries. Bergmann refers us to the boundary of the Indonesian slum; Vicenzotti identifies the less distinctive boundaries of the peri-urban. We also considered the boundaries of the ghetto, of contested spaces, and of the altogether new settlement. It was clear to us, too, that the places we belong may be nested within larger bounds – like the separate states of the European Union – such that our loyalties have to be negotiated at various scales and with subsidiarity. All these commitments to place require and create boundaries.

In what ways are these boundaries different, and what impact does this have on negotiating a home?

We have already said that we shall return to the matter of the Church as place and the rite of the Eucharist. The practice of hospitality is addressed to all who are strangers—and that is everyone. Dwelling in Christ, we suggest that God assumes place, and by the operation of the Holy Spirit, grace exceeds places. In Christ, we have a glimpse of another place in this place, and by the Holy Spirit anticipations of that other place as a future for these places. This delicate balance needs to be maintained: a defence of unsurpassibility of places and also the moving beyond of these places; that present loyalties are penultimate loyalties and thereby receive their affirmation and their criticism. By this means, place is assumed theologically – given its proper status in theological enquiry and also affirmed – and some resources are offered for affirming the need for negotiation, and hopes for good outcomes. Yet, the situated church does not seek to defend place at any cost but notes the transcending of places and the consequent qualification of situated loyalties. In its priestly role, the Church seeks to affirm and connect places; in its prophetic role, the Church rebukes the injustices and exclusions related to claims to belong in the name of a greater belonging.

A church as community practises such hospitality in response to God's hospitality enacted and proclaimed in the Eucharist. God takes place in the Eucharist, in two senses: God happens, and God commands place. In this sense, we have the redrawing of boundaries: the distinction between the sacred built environment of the church and the wider community is not the boundary. Instead, boundaries are tested in the perspective of the welcome of the Eucharist. It is important to note that this testing takes place independently of participation in the Eucharist. Through the logic of the Eucharist, all are made welcome, and the church as community is invited to practice or model that welcome. Such modelling may take many forms, and is not restricted to participation in the life of the church as community.

RECONCILING RIVAL CLAIMS

John Eidson's case study of a small home town in Germany shows that, even a century ago, it was more dynamic local processes of settling contradictory claims on shared space that enabled rival groups to establish their own sense of belonging, rather than their jostling to situate themselves in some unitary frame of the national imagination. Contested claims to antiquity, tradition and continuity in Boppard had an explicitly religious flavour but Eidson sees them at play more widely among quite different social groups in Germany, negotiating alternative relationships to place through resource management, text production and performance. And, for him, where *Heimat* gains a wider simplicity or force is where the failure of some over-arching order in civil society, in legal or political protection, allows particular understandings of belonging to privilege themselves over others.

For Bron Szerszynski, the resolution of such rival claims to place should be seen in a long perspective of Western cultural development where clusters of significance, performed through custom, ritual and story-telling, such as were characteristic of an absolute sacral world, have been swept away in a reformation in which each given locality gains its own particular combination of characteristics independent of inherited frames of reference. In our postmodern era on this trajectory, what should rescue us from a surrender to placelessness is not a temptation to make such abstract space our own with modes of ordering that are anachronistically sacral, but rather a Kierkegaardian ironic negation of received meanings and a return gesture which leaves us neither indifferent to nor wholly defined by just where we happen to find ourselves.

From another perspective in these postmodern times, Philip Sheldrake considers that sense can still be made of the particular here and now within what Christians perceive as the universal frame of the presence and activity of God. The rehearsal of his sacrificial love in the central act of Christian worship, the eucharist, is more than a sacral rite. In the light of God's own occupancy of our flesh and blood in Jesus Christ, this ceremony challenges placelessness by asserting the holiness of wherever it is celebrated, yet disputes our own rival claims there and the stories each of us want to tell about our own occupancy and ownership. Where God thus makes Himself at home, He challenges our reluctance to reconcile and He demands repentance and restitution for our own failure to accept who or what is not familiar to us, those we wish to 'colonise, demonise, generalise, trivialise, homogenise, ignore'.[4] Rather, in a sacrificial way, power may be redistributed in ways that are not theoretical or cheap.

We might then expect that the Church has a distinctive role to play in articulating how we might exist appropriately in the world in more than a general sense; and to show what ethical purchase we should have on the planning and ordering of the particular places where we live, just who else they might be home to and how together we could foster and celebrate a sense of belonging in the reconciliation of rival understandings and claims. In their contributions here, Paul Selman and John Rodwell have both demonstrated how disconnectedness with place in damaged landscapes also reflects a shortfall in negotiating moral reconnection, social learning and the generation of a wisdom that links people with one another and with land. Theologians such as Walter Brueggeman[5] see such a relationship with land lying at the heart of who we are and how we should behave.

For William Cavanaugh,[6] the catholicity of the eucharist collapses spatial divisions by a gathering into local assemblies that allow things to take place and permit stories to be told. Among Ian Thompson's conceptions of 'spirit of place', such a welcome for alternative stories may give his 'narrative' a more potent role in renegotiating 'spirit of place' in dramatic scenarios of change than at first seems likely. Such exchanges also resist the imposition of global topographies and unitary narratives that are effectively a single dominant notion of *Heimat*, whether these are the product of political despots, globalised interests or regional planners. As such, this Christian rite might be expected to provide a model of engagement, discourse and resolution that could critique the tendency to over-coding and exclusion of itineraries, *sensu* de Certeau,[7] that can so readily mark the practice of landscape design, planning and regeneration.

The eucharist is one key identifier of Dietrich Bonhoeffer's idea of the Church's gathered presence. In the 1930s, as Hitler promulgated the export of the idealised Nazi *Heimat* beyond the bounds of Germany itself, Bonhoeffer's reading of *Lebensraum* was diametrically opposed to such territorialisation of new land.[8] For him, the Church itself occupied a visible living space that was characterised by people living *miteinander* und *füreinander*, with and for one another. The eventual fate of Bonhoeffer demonstrates how sacrificial such a stance can be *in extremis*. And the history of the Church through the ages, locally and globally, shows how readily it might not only connive with persuasive national ideas of belonging but itself impose a centralised frame that effectively denies the glorious liberty of the children of God it is meant to proclaim (Romans 8, 21).

A FORGIVEN PAST, A TRANSFORMED FUTURE

Rival claims to contested space may leave a painful inheritance of loss. How best these might be performed in traumatized battle grounds is the interest of Paul Gough, for whom military cemeteries provide a startling illustration of how landscape might be 'memory's most serviceable reminder'; and just what care is thought necessary to tenderly safeguard the sacrificial cost of past events. There, neat greensward and carefully ordered gravestones remain, for many people, communities of survivors and their descendants, and for nations, the fitting mark of respect that the fallen will not be forgotten. Yet this can be seen as a sanitised surface of peace that keeps shattered bodies safe from view. And individuals, feeling their own personal loss untouched, may be moved to subvert the institutional remembering with commemorations of their own private grief.

Right remembering has generally been a luxury in the kinds of post-industrial landscapes out of which John Rodwell writes and thoughtful reflection on the cost of this has been missing from both the planning processes there and also the response of the Church which finds itself still standing in places from which most reminders of past lives and livelihoods have been swept away in what passes for 'regeneration'. Yet, for Rodwell and Philip Sheldrake, it is the *anamnesis* of the eucharist, that denial of forgetting of our own shared past as redeemed people, that provides the definitive performance of the reconciliation of memories. For the gathered Christian community, this rite rehearses the healing of the broken body of Jesus and offers a re-membering of the believers into a shared new life. In the performance of its own narrative of past sacrifice and recovery, it makes room for memories of competing claims that might otherwise go unheard. Without such a proper memorialisation, we cannot hope for healing of past belittlement and denial, we of others and they of us, and we cannot hope to live with memories that are often contested, ambiguous, dangerous. We want to suggest that this applies to how we negotiate a home in the world in relation to the past which we and places inherit.

Where communities lament some past loss, such as may occur in damaged landscapes denied any memorials of what has happened in that place before, there can be what Williams[9] has called 'cultural bereavement' when whole areas of discourse become inaccessible, thus endangering the shared sense-making and just social order that are marks of true belonging. This is precisely what Selman and Rodwell recognise as characteristic of so many post-industrial landscapes and what needs serious attention from planners, landscape architects and designers. Only rarely are there the kinds of imaginative prompts to memory, its celebration and its healing, such as are seen in the Emscher Landschaftspark. Over the abandoned colliery, coke ovens and blast furnaces in that landscape, we see a progress to ruination softened by the unplanned colonisation of greenery accommodating to the passage of time and healing of loss. Guarded against romanticism by a recall of sacrifice, we consider that such landscapes could be deeply therapeutic for those whose memories have otherwise been made homeless by the reconstruction around them. It is a landscape of memorialisation very different from the neatness of the military cemetery but both proclaim that we will not allow others to forget on our behalf and impose their own territorial hegemony.

Avoiding an "ontological over-determination of the primacy of the present",[10] the resolution of past discord can enable a future to begin. Indeed, as Rodwell suggests in his comparison of the forgetfulness of landscapes with the pathology of dementia, our ability to conceive of our shared future in a particular place might be hard-wired into an acceptance of a past. It is this which will guarantee a common sense of belonging, a 'making ourselves at home' in the tomorrow of that place. In this sense, the kind of *anamnesis* performed in the eucharist is truly "the memory of the future"[11] inaugurating what was previously just a distant hope. Thus we would avoid the two extremes of tension which Vicenzotti explicates in her analysis of *Heimat* the conservative and the utopian, and find ourselves truly at home in a *Zwischenstadt*, "for here we have no abiding city" (Hebrews 13,14). The eucharist establishes what Christians would call the Kingdom here and now and the challenge for the Church is to ensure that Kingdom values inform and enrich how we make ourselves at home in the world. In changing times, the future can only lie ahead and our place in it found by welcome and sacrifice.

AT HOME IN THE FUTURE

Our closing reflections here have been theological in character, not because of any desire to co-opt the ideas and conclusions of those contributors who willingly participated in our exchanges from the realms of planning, landscape architecture, art history, social anthropology, culture and public policy; still less to suggest that some other deeper level of meaning might be discerned in their own reflections. Rather we have gratefully listened to the richness of meaning they have themselves found in notions of belonging and place convinced that sacramental approaches to religious belief, and the academic exploration of such commitments, can only benefit from an openness to how the world we share is found to be, and how others respond to where they find themselves. Only by means of such conversations can we hope, in societies with complex histories and uncertain futures, to move forward to a shared understanding of what it will mean to live together in contested places with one another and all that is.

NOTES

1. Greverus.
2. Bausinger.
3. Mecklenburg.
4. Sheldrake, 109.
5. Brueggemann.
6. Cavanaugh (1999).
7. de Certeau.
8. Fergus.
9. Williams.
10. Marion, 101.
11. Zuzoulas, 180.

REFERENCES

Bausinger, W. (1980), *Heimat und Identitüt*, Neuminster: Wachholtz;

Brueggemann, W. (2002, 2nd edition), *The Land: Place as Gift, Promise and Challenge in Biblical Faith*, Minneapolis: Fortress Press

Cavanaugh, W.T (1999), "The World in a Wafer: A Geography of the Eucharist as a Resistance to Globalisation", *Modern Theology* 15(2), 181–196.

de Certeau, M. (1984). *The Practice of Everyday Life*. Berkley, CA: University of California Press.

Fergus, D. (2014), "Lebensraum – just what is this 'habitat' or 'living space' that Dietrich Bonhoeffer claimed for the Church?" *Scottish Journal of Theology* 67(1), 70–84.

Greverus, I-M. (1987), "The '*Heimat*' problem", in H. Seliger, (ed.). *Der Begriff 'Heimat' in der deutschen Gegewartsliteratur*, Munchen: iudicum Verlag.

Marion, J-L., 2nd edition, trs. T.A. Carlson (2012), *God Without Being: Hors-Texte*, Chicago: University of Chicago Press.

Mecklenberg, N. (1986), *Erzählte Provinz: Regionalismus und Moderne in Roman*, Konigstein/TS: Athenäum.
Sheldrake, P. (2008), "A Spirituality of reconciliation: Encouragement for Anglicans from a Roman Catholic perspective". *Journal of Anglican Studies*, 6, 106–126.
Williams, R. (2000), *Lost Icons: Reflections on Cultural Bereavement*, Edinburgh: T & T Clark.
Zizioulas, J. (1985), *Being as Communion*, Crestwood, NY: St Vladimir's Seminary Press.

Contributors

Sigurd Bergmann

Sigurd Bergmann works as Professor in Religious Studies at the Department of Philosophy and Religious Studies at the Norwegian University of Science and Technology in Trondheim. His previous studies have investigated the relationship between the image of God and the view of nature in late antiquity, the methodology of contextual theology, visual arts in the indigenous Arctic and Australia, as well as visual arts, architecture and religion. He has initiated and chaired the "European Forum on the Study of Religion and Environment", and ongoing projects investigate the relation of space/place and religion and "religion in climatic change". His main publications are *Geist, der Natur befreit* (Mainz 1995, Russian ed. Arkhangelsk 1999, rev. ed. *Creation Set Free*, Grand Rapids 2005), *Geist, der lebendig macht* (Frankfurt/M. 1997), *God in Context* (Aldershot 2003), *In the Beginning is the Icon* (London 2009), *Så främmande det lika* ("So Strange, so Similar", on Sámi visual arts, globalisation and religion, Trondheim 2009), *Raum und Geist: Zur Erdung und Beheimatung der Religion* (Göttingen 2010), and *Religion, Space & the Environment* (New Brunswick and London 2014). Among his edited and co-edited books are *Architecture, Aesth/Ethics and Religion* (Frankfurt/M. and London 2005), *The Ethics of Mobilities* (Aldershot 2008), *Theology in Built Environments* (New Brunswick and London 2009), *Nature, Space & the Sacred* (Farnham 2009), *Religion in Environmental and Climate Change: Sufferings, Values, Lifestyles* (London and New York 2011), and *Christian Faith and the Earth: Current Paths and Emerging Horizons in Ecotheology* (New York and London 2014).

Sigurd Bergmann, prof. dr.theol.,Department of Philosophy and Religious Studies, Norwegian University of Science and Technology, NO – 7491 Trondheim, Norway. Telephone: +47-73 59 65 87, e-mail: sigurd.bergmann@ntnu.no.

John R. Eidson

John R. Eidson is Senior Research Fellow in the Department "Integration and Conflict" of the Max Planck Institute for Social Anthropology in Halle an der Saale, Germany. Since receiving his B.A. in anthropology from Duke University in 1976 and his PhD in social anthropology from Cornell University in 1983, he has taught in the anthropology departments of the University of Maryland and the University of New Hampshire and in the Institut für Kulturwissenschaften of the Universität Leipzig. He has done ethnographic and archival research in two field sites in Germany: in Boppard, a small town in the Upper Middle Rhine Valley, and in a group of neighboring villages in the agricultural and industrial region south of Leipzig. Research topics in these two sites have included local politics, voluntary associations, local festivals, local traditions of amateur historical research, property relations, tourism, agriculture, and coal mining and related industries. More generally, his interests include social theory, the history of anthropology, and the development of anthropological approaches to Germany in the modern era. He is the editor of *Das anthropologische Projekt: Perspektiven aus der Forschungslandschaft Halle/Leipzig* (Leipziger Universitätsverlag 2008) and the author of numerous articles and chapters, including, most recently (in 2013), "Between Groitzsch and Deutzen: The Rise and Transformation of an Area of 'Cooperation' in East Germany, 1945-2004," in *Acta Ethnographica Hungarica* 58 (1):123-147.

Dr. John R. Eidson, Max Planck Institute for Social Anthropology, Advokatenweg 36, 06114 Halle (Saale), Germany. Telephone: +49 345 2927 119, email: eidson@eth.mpg.de.

Paul Gough

A painter, broadcaster and writer, Paul Gough has exhibited widely in the UK and overseas, most recently in Canada, New Zealand and Australia, and is represented in several permanent art collections – including Imperial War Museum, London; Canadian War Museum, and the National War Memorial, New Zealand. His research interests lie in the iconography of commemoration, the cultural geographies of battlefields, and the representation of peace and conflict. Amongst his recent publications is a monograph on the British artist Stanley Spencer (2006), *A Terrible Beauty*, an extensive study of British art of the Great War (2010), and the edited correspondence between Desmond Chute and Stanley Spencer, published in 2011. A book on the street artist Banksy – *Banksy: A Bristol Legacy* – was published in April, 2012. His book – 'Brothers in Arms' – about the post-war work of Paul and John Nash was published in summer 2014. As part of a broad portfolio of activity linked to the centenary of the Great War, he is curating five funded exhibitions – in London and Bristol – in 2014, and has been advising the Royal Mint in the UK on the design principles, iconography and potential artists for their commemorative coinage linked to the centenary of the war, 2014-2019. During ten years work as a television presenter, researcher and associate producer he worked for ITV, BBC and C4 on a range of creative arts programmes from dance to drama, poetry to painting, including the award-winning documentary Redundant Warrior, about the photographer Don McCullin, and 'Drawing Fire' a documentary on military sketching and panorama drawing.

Professor Paul Gough, Pro Vice-Chancellor, College of Design and Social Context Vice-President, RMIT University, Melbourne, Australia. Telephone: +61 3 9925 2234, email: paul.gough@rmit.edu.au.

STEFAN KÖRNER

Following a gardening apprenticeship, Stefan Körner studied landscape planning at Technical University of Berlin and then worked as a landscape architect in Berlin. From 1994 to 2001 he served as a research assistant to the chair of Landscape Ecology at the Technical University of Munich. From 2001 to 2005, he was a research associate at the Institute of Urban Ecology at the TU Berlin while also serving as assistant professor in the Department of Cultural History of Nature in the Landscape Planning Program. Since 2005 he is the head of the Chair of Landscape Construction, Landscape and Vegetation Management at the University of Kassel. His research focuses on a cultural and not only ecological and technical approach to landscape theory, theory of nature conversation, monument conservation, urban plant use, planting design and the management of tree care. See for example in English language: Körner, S. (2005): 'Nature Conservation, Forestry, Landscape Architecture and Historic Preservation: Perspectives for a Conceptual Alliance' in Kowarik, I. & Körner, S. (eds.), *Wild Urban Woodlands. New Perspectives for Urban Forestry* Heidelberg/New York. 193-220; Körner, S. & Bellin-Harder, F. (2009), 'The 7000 Eichen of Joseph Beuys – experiences after twenty-five years', *Journal of Landscape Architecture*. Autumn 09. 6-19; Körner, S. (2013), 'Landscape and Modernity' in Girot, G.; Freytag, A.; Kirchengast, A. & Richter, D. (eds.), Topology. Landscript 3. Berlin. 117-136.

Prof. Dr.-Ing. Stefan Körner, Universität Kassel, FB 06 Architektur, Stadtplanung, Landschaftsplanung, FG Landschaftsbau/Landschaftsmanagement/ Vegetationsentwicklung, Gottschalkstraße 26, 34127 Kassel, Germany. Telephone: 0561/804-1820/21, Fax 0561/804-1822.

JOHN RODWELL

John Rodwell has worked as an ecologist and Anglican priest for over 40 years. After a research career which earned him the President's Medal from the Institute of Environ-mental and Ecological Management and Life Membership of the International Association for Vegetation Science, he resigned his post as Professor of Ecology at Lancaster University to work as an independent consultant. He now provides research and expert advice for environmental agencies and NGOs in the UK and elsewhere in Europe including for the European Commission Environment Directorate. Increasingly in recent years, he has worked at the interface between ecology and theology, researching place and memory in post-industrial landscapes for the M B Reckitt Trust, leading the 'Belonging & Heimat project' based in the Lincoln Theological Institute at Manchester University and exploring inspiration and wonder as ecosystem services for the UK Department for Environment, Food & Rural Affairs and Natural England. He continues thinking about spiritual aspects of scientific enquiry (as in *Faith in Science*, Routledge, 2001 & *Knowing the Unknowable*, I.B. Tauris 2009), on ruination in the landscape and human experience (in *Objects of Curious Virtue*, Ruskin Library, 2010) and the relationship between human well-being and environmental condition (in *The Practices of Happiness,* Routledge, 2011). With faith communities and those exploring the spiritual and nature, he regularly speaks at conferences and leads retreats.

John Rodwell, 7 Derwent Road, Lancaster LA1 3ES, United Kingdom. Telephone: +44-07908-420058, email: johnrodwell@tiscali.co.uk.

Peter Manley Scott

Peter Scott is Samuel Ferguson Professor of Applied Theology and the Director of the Lincoln Theological Institute at the University of Manchester. Previously, he was lecturer in theology at the University of Gloucestershire. He is the author of *Theology, Ideology and Liberation* (Cambridge University Press, 1994), *A Political Theology of Nature* (Cambridge University Press, 2003), *Anti-human Theology: Nature, Technology and the Postnatural* (SCM Press, 2010), and numerous articles; and co-editor of the *Blackwell Companion to Political Theology* (2004)—translated into Arabic and Korean, *Future Perfect* (2006), *Re-moralising Britain?* (2009), *Nature, Space and the Sacred* (2009), and *Systematic Theology and Climate Change* (2014). He is a member of the Center of Theological Inquiry (Princeton, USA). His research is to be found at the intersection between theology and studies of nature, technology and society, politics and salvation, and he is widely published on these topics. His current research is towards a monograph, *A theology of postnatural right*; he also writing a book on *Marx and Theology* (Bloomsbury).

Peter Scott, Religions & Theology, School of Arts, Languages and Cultures, Samuel Alexander Building, The University of Manchester, Oxford Road, Manchester M13 9PL, UK   Tel: +44 (0)161 275 3064 Fax: +44(0)161 306 1241 peter.scott@manchester.ac.uk

Paul Selman

Paul Selman was Professor of Landscape at the University of Sheffield, and is now an Emeritus Professor, having retired to Ayrshire in 2011. Previously he was Professor of Environmental Planning at the University of Gloucestershire. His key interests have been in rural land use, especially the ways that economy and landscape can work to mutual benefit. Latterly, his interests extended towards the regeneration of industrialised landscapes and the promotion of urban green infrastructure. His books included *Environmental Planning* (Sage, 2000), *Planning at the Landscape Scale* (Routledge, 2006) and *Sustainable Landscape Planning* (Routledge, 2012), and he has authored around sixty research papers on aspects of landscape, environment and sustainable development. He also edited *Landscape Research* for a ten year period. He has undertaken research for a range of government agencies and has received numerous grants from Research Councils and other organisations. He continues to advise on landscape matters as well as pursue interests in hill walking, music and creative writing.

Professor Paul Selman, Department of Landscape, University of Sheffield, Arts Tower, Sheffield S10 2TN, United Kingdom. Email: paulhselman@gmail.com.

PHILIP SHELDRAKE

Philip Sheldrake is currently Senior Research Fellow at Westcott House in the Cambridge Theological Federation and Director of the Institute for the Study of Contemporary Spirituality at the graduate Oblate School of Theology, San Antonio Texas. Previously he was The Veale Visiting Professor of Spirituality at the Milltown Institute, Dublin (2010-11), The Joseph Visiting Professor of Catholic Theology at Boston College, Chestnut Hill, MA (2008-9), William Leech Professorial Fellow in Applied Theology at Durham University (2003-8), Vice-Principal & Academic Director of Sarum College (1998-2003), Honorary Professor of Theology & Postgraduate Research Supervisor at the University of Wales (1998-2013), Director of Pastoral Studies, Westcott House Cambridge & Affiliated Lecturer in Church History, Faculty of Divinity (1992-97) and Director, Institute of Spirituality, Heythrop College University of London (1984-92). He has taught and written extensively in the field of Christian spirituality, on spirituality more generally, and on the nature of space and place in religion. His 1999-2000 Hulsean Lectures at the University of Cambridge were published as *Spaces for the Sacred: Place, Memory, Identity,* London: SCM Press/Baltimore: The Johns Hopkins University Press, 2001. His most recent book is *The Spiritual City: Theology, Spirituality and the Urban,* Oxford: Wiley-Blackwell, 2014. Philip Sheldrake is also involved internationally in interreligious, particularly Christian-Muslim, dialogue. He is a Past President of the international Society for the Study of Christian Spirituality which is related to the American Academy of Religion.

Professor Philip Sheldrake, Senior Research Fellow, Westcott House, Jesus Lane, Cambridge CB5 8BP, United Kingdom. Telephone: +44 (0)1223 741000, email: ps220@cam.ac.uk.

BRONISLAW SZERSZYNSKI

Bronislaw Szerszynski is Senior Lecturer at the Department of Sociology, Lancaster University, UK, where he also works at the Centre for the Study of Environmental Change (CSEC). Previous research projects explored topics such as the perception of distinctiveness and change in the landscape, global citizenship and the environment, conflicts over the use of genetically modified crops in agriculture, urban ethical foodscapes, and the changing nature and role of religion in advanced capitalist societies. For the last, he was co-investigator in the Kendal Project, which resulted in the multi-authored book *The Spiritual Revolution* (2004). His book *Nature, Technology and the Sacred* (2005) argued that contemporary ideas and practices concerning nature and technology remain profoundly shaped by the religious history of the West. He also co-edited of *Risk, Environment and Modernity* (1996) *Re-Ordering Nature: Theology, Society and the New Genetics* (2003), *Nature Performed: Environment, Culture and Performance* (2003) and special double issues of *Ecotheology* on 'Ecotheology and Postmodernity' (2004), and *Theory Culture and Society* on 'Changing Climates' (2010). His more recent work, including both academic publications and multi-media performance pieces, places contemporary changes in the relationship between humans, environment and technology in the longer perspective of human and planetary history, exploring themes such as the Anthropocene, climate geoengineering and the interplanetary. A collaboration with Bruno Latour, Olivier Michelon and thirty artists resulted in an exhibition and colloquium on the Anthropocene Monument at Les Abattoirs Museum of Contemporary Art, Toulouse, in 2014.

Dr Bronislaw Szerszynski, Senior Lecturer in Sociology, Department of Sociology, Bowland North, Lancaster University, Lancaster LA1 4YT, United Kingdom. Telephone: +44 (0) 1524 592659, email: b.szerszynski@lancaster.ac.uk

Ian Thompson

Ian Thompson is Reader in Landscape Architecture in the School of Architecture, Planning and Landscape, Newcastle University. He studied philosophy before becoming a landscape architect. Prior to before becoming an academic, he worked as a landscape architect, both in Glasgow and on Tyneside, where he was involved in the reclamation of derelict land. His book *Ecology, Community and Delight*, based on PhD research and published by Spon in 1999, investigates the beliefs and value systems of practising landscape architects. He is also the author of *The Sun King's Garden* (Bloomsbury, 2006), *The English Lakes. A History* (Bloomsbury, 2010) and *Landscape Architecture, A Very Short Introduction* (Oxford University Press, 2014). In recent years he has begun to question aspects of the land reclamation programme, which he believes has contributed to the erasure of cultural heritage and the erosion of identity in the former Great Northern Coalfield. He is currently undertaking an MA in Photography at the University of Sunderland, where his main project is to investigate the present condition of former colliery sites.

Dr Ian Thompson, Reader in Landscape Architecture, School of Architecture, Planning and Landscape, Newcastle University, Newcastle upon Tyne NE1 7RU, United Kingdom. Telephone: +44 (0)191 8812, email: i.h.thompson@ncl.ac.uk.

Vera Vicenzotti

Vera Vicenzotti is currently Marie-Curie Research Fellow and Senior Lecturer in landscape architecture, with specialisation in design theory and architecture criticism, at the Swedish University of Agricultural Sciences in Alnarp. She studied landscape architecture and planning at the Technische Universität München (Germany) and urban design at the Politectico di Milano (Italy). In 2010, after a research stay at the University of California *in* Berkeley (USA), she obtained her doctoral degree from the Technische Universität München.She then spent two years at the School of Architecture, Planning and Landscape at Newcastle University with a Feodor Lynen Research Fellowship for Postdoctoral Researchers from the Alexander von Humboldt Foundation. Her research interests are, broadly speaking, landscape architectural theory, history and methodology. In particular, she is interested in how cultural ideas and ideals of nature, landscape, and city inform the current practice of landscape and urban design and planning. She has explored this connection by analysing the German discourse on the so-called *Zwischenstadt*, i.e. fragmented, hybrid, peri-urban landscapes, and by focusing on the idea of wilderness. Vera is continuously intrigued by the complexity of 'landscape' and her recent and current research has allowed her to explore this idea: she has been studying the movement of Landscape Urbanism and, in her current research project, is comparing the discourses of urban sprawl in Sweden and Germany.

Vera Vicenzotti, Swedish University of Agricultural Sciences, Department of Landscape Architecture, Planning and Management, PO Box 58, 230 53 Alnarp, Sweden. Telephone: +46 40-41 54 30, email: vera.vicenzotti@slu.se.

INDEX OF NAMES

Abercrombie, N. 184
Adam, T. 49
Adams, W. 136, 137
Alkemade, R. 139
Altman, I. 124, 125
Appadurai, A. 73, 76, 77, 78
Applegate, C. 46, 47
Arendt, H. 181
Ashworth, G. 98
Atzwanger, K. 139
Augé, M. 150, 125, 171, 180, 181

Baccini, P. 147, 148, 149, 151, 153
Bachelard, G. 101, 180, 181
Baker, C. 72, 73, 77, 78
Balla, G. 78
Ballantyne, A. 61, 63
Balzer, T. 136, 137
Banning, J. 91, 93, 95, 98
Barnes, J. 97, 98
Bartens, J. 136, 137
Basu, P. 84, 98
Bate, J. 122
Bauer, I. 121, 124
Bauman, Z. 76, 78, 180, 181
Bausinger, H. 9, 185, 191
Bausinger, W. 30, 45, 46, 47
Bellah, R.N. 171, 180, 181
Bender, B. 84, 98, 99, 136, 137
Benner, F. 46, 47
Bennett, A. 89, 90, 97, 98
Bensch, M. 30, 150, 152
Bergmann, S. 2, 5, 9, 67-79, 186, 193
Bergmann, K. 46, 47
Berleant, A. 110
Beumelberg, W. 9
Bimmer, A.C. 47, 50
Blackbourn, D. 30, 46, 47
Blair, S. 83, 97, 98
Bloch, E. 3, 9, 10, 144, 150, 152
Boa, E. 9, 10
Boccioni, U. 71, 72, 77, 78
Bölling, L. 140, 148, 150, 152, 153

Bollnow, O. 73-78, 145, 150, 151, 152
Bormann, O. 146-48, 150, 151, 152, 153
Bourdieu, P. 136, 137
Braat, L. 137
Bramke, W. 47
Braubach, M. 50
Braze, A. 140
Brook, I. 52, 54, 57, 59, 62, 63, 87
Brown, D. 111, 116, 120, 124
Brueggemann, W. 2, 9, 10, 101, 110, 118, 121, 122, 191
Buell, L. 66, 76, 77, 78
Bürgi, M. 139
Burkard, K.J. 46, 48
Burns, D. 138
Butler, R.N. 122
Buttimer, A. 110, 111

Carpenter, S. 140
Carrà, C. 78
Carrus, G. 138
Carruthers, M.J. 122
Carruthers, S.P. 134, 137
Casey, E.S. 101, 165, 167
Castells, M. 170, 176, 180, 181
Cathcart, T. 136, 138
Cavanaugh, W. 122, 188, 191
Chaudury, H. 119, 122
Christ, W. 150, 152
Christiansen, J. 46, 48
Clare, J. 114, 118, 121, 122, 123
Clarke, K. 121, 123
Clemen, P. 46, 48
Codina, V. 108, 110, 111
Collins, A. 179, 181
Comber, A. 136, 137
Confino, A. 35, 46, 48
Coombes, R. 98
Couch, C. 150, 152
Cox, H. 2, 9, 10
Cragg, K. 160, 166, 167
Creedy, J.B. 137
Cumming, G.S. 135, 137

Cuppers, J. 121, 124

Daniel, T.C. 137
Dann, O. 46
Danto, A. 97, 98
Davies, C. 138
Davis, N.Z. 169, 170, 171, 173, 174, 180, 181
de Botton, A. 88, 98
de Certeau, M. 119, 122, 123, 189, 191
de Groot, R. 136, 137
de Nora, A. 67, 76, 79
Deakin, R. 121, 123
Deleuze, G. 61, 181, 183
Dinnebier, A. 151, 152
Ditt, K. 46, 48
Doran, H. 137
Dovey, K. 62, 63
Duffield, S.J. 137
Dulles, A. 110, 111

Eder, K. 178, 181, 182
Eidson, J.R. 33-50, 186, 187, 193, 194
Eisel, U. 15, 16, 29, 30, 31, 150, 151, 152, 153
Eley, G. 46, 47
Elliott, B. 121, 123
Ennos, A. 137
Ermann, M. 140
Evans, E. 136, 140
Evans, J.H. 166, 167
Ewald, K. 139

Fergus, D. 191
Finney, N. 136, 139
Fisher, P. 137
Ford, D. 110, 111
Fort, T. 94, 98
Franke, N.M. 151, 152
Freeman, L. 9, 10
Fry, G. 137
Führ, E. 151, 152
Funkenstein, A. 180, 182
Fyhri, A. 136, 137

Galeano, E.H. 181, 182
Garrett, L. 53, 62, 63
Gauchet, M. 171, 176, 177, 181, 182
Geertz, C. 110, 111
George, N.J. 137
Gill, S. 136,137
Gillis, J.R. 83, 98
Girouard, M. 117, 121, 123
Gittins, J.W. 136, 138

Gittoes, J. 122, 123
Gobster, P.H. 136, 137
Goethe, J.W.v. 65, 76, 77, 78
Gorringe, T.J. 2, 9, 10
Gough, P. 6, 83-100, 115, 121, 123
Graham, B. 98
Graham, H. 136, 138
Gray, L. 95, 98
Greenblatt, S. 166, 167
Gregg, D. 122, 123
Greiffenhagen, M. 151, 152
Greverus, I.M. 9, 10, 26, 30, 145, 150, 152, 185, 191
Grieve, Y. 136, 138
Grinde, B. 136, 138
Grisbrooke, W.J. 122, 123
Gröning, G. 31, 150, 152
Guattari, F. 61, 63, 181
Gulinck, H. 150, 153
Gurevich, A. J. 110,111

Haber, W. 9, 10
Haight, B.K. 124
Haindl, E. 30
Hamilton, K. 136, 138
Hamilton, M. 181, 182
Handley, J. 2, 9, 10, 114, 121, 123, 137
Hannerz, U. 77, 78
Harding, S. 54, 62, 63
Harrison, P. 180, 182
Hartung, W. 46, 48
Harvey, D. 166, 167
Hauser, S. 143, 150, 152, 153
Hays, S.P. 181, 182
Heffernan, M. 85, 98, 100
Hegel, E. 47, 48
Heidegger, M. 101, 110, 111, 119, 122, 123
Hein, L. 137, 140
Heller, H. 9, 10
Helphand, K. 85, 86, 97, 98
Hersperger, A. 139
Hetherington, K. 181, 182
Hey, D. 123
Heyen, F.J. 46, 48
Hill, A. 86, 88, 98
Höfer, W. 151, 153
Holling, C. 140
Holmes, R. 121, 123
Hopkins, J. 136, 138
Hughes, D. 180, 182
Hurst, S. 98

Index of Names

Iles, J. 97, 98
Inge, J. 2, 9, 10
Ingold, T. 70, 77, 78, 176, 181, 182
Irvine, C. 122, 123
Ish, L. 97, 99

Jackson, J. B. 30
Jaggi, M. 58, 63
James, P. 136, 138
Jeffrey, P. 136, 138
Jivén, G. 136, 138
Johler, R. 46, 48

Kamleithner, C. 150, 152
Kaplan, R. 136, 138
Kaplan, S. 136, 138
Kass, G.S. 137
Katti, M. 140
Keat, R. 181, 182
Kerr, A. 62, 63
Kierkegaard, S. 8, 179, 181, 182, 188
Kinzig, A. 140
Klein, J. 46, 48
Klueting, E. 46, 48
Koch, M. 146, 150, 152
Konold, W. 9, 10
Koolhaas, R. 147, 151, 153
Körner, S. 4, 15-32, 144, 150, 151, 152, 153, 185
Koshar, R. 46, 48
Kramer, D. 46, 48
Kreuzberg, B.J. 38, 41-44, 46, 47, 49
Kropp, C. 150, 151, 153
Kühne, O. 150, 153
Kurtén, T. 77, 78

Lafortezza, R. 136, 138
Larkham, P.J. 136, 138
Lawton, J.H. 136, 140
Le Dû-Blayo, L. 138
Lefebvre, H. 172, 180, 182
Leontidou, L. 150, 152
Leopold, A. 2, 3, 9, 11
Lepsius, M.R. 47, 49
Levermore, G. 137, 139
Lewis, C. 10, 123
Lincoln, A.T. 164, 167
Lindner, W. 19, 30, 31
Ling, C. 123
Lively, P. 102, 110, 111
Loades, A. 10, 111, 120, 122
Longworth, P. 85, 97
Lovelock, J.E. 54, 181, 182

Low Choy, D. 137, 138
Low, S.M. 123
Lowenthal, D. 84, 97, 99, 163, 165, 167
Lowerson, J. 181, 182
Luchterhandt, D. 121, 124

Mäding, E. 24, 31
Maffesoli, M. 181, 182
Maier, F. 46, 47, 49
Maisel, O. 49
Manzo, L. 136, 138
Marinetti, F.T. 71, 77, 79
Marion, J.L. 191
Mason, R. 138
Massey, D.B. 136, 138, 176, 181, 182
McKay, G. 84, 86, 96, 99
McMahon, A.W. 122, 123
Mecklenberg, N. 9, 10, 192
Meeus, S. J. 150, 153
Melby, P. 136, 138
Merton, R.K. 180, 182
Mill, J.S. 164, 166, 167
Miller, J. R. 136, 138
Mißling, H.E. 46, 47, 49
Mitscherlich, A. 145, 146, 151, 153
Morley, D. 60, 62, 63
Morris, M.S. 84, 90, 97, 99
Moseley, D. 138
Mosse, G.L. 84, 89, 97, 99
Muchembled, R. 180
Murdock, C.E. 46, 49
Muro, M. 136, 138
Nagel, A. 30, 31, 52, 150, 151, 152, 153

Nahemov, L. 122, 123
Nassauer, J.I. 136, 137, 139
Newman, A. 138
Nikitsch, H. 46, 48
Norberg-Schultz, C. 136, 139
Nye, D.E. 181, 182

O'Donovan, O. 2, 9, 10
Olwig, K. 130, 136, 139
Opdam, P. 136, 139
Oswald, F. 147, 149, 151, 153
Ott, K. 27, 30, 31

Palfreyman, R. 9, 10
Pallasmaa, J. 66, 68, 75, 76, 79
Palmer, F. 136, 139
Parker, R. 122, 123
Patil, G. 136, 138

Pauleit, S. 137
Pauly, F. 46, 47, 49
Perkins, D. 136, 138
Peters, R.H. 55, 62, 63
Petit, S. 136, 137
Petri, F. 48, 50
Petsche-Held, G. 150, 152
Petts, J. 137, 139
Piechocki, R. 30, 31, 150, 151, 153
Piepmeier, R. 150, 153
Pirschel, I. 31
Pollan, M. 88, 97, 99
Pope, A. 51, 59, 62, 63
Porter, T.M. 181, 182
Pott, H.-G. 9, 10
Powell, D. 121, 123

Qviström, M. 150, 153

Radkau, J. 30, 31
Ray, D. 138
Relph, E. 150, 153
Renninger, L. 139
Retallack, J. 47, 49
Rhudick, P.J. 122, 123
Riehl, W.H. 30, 31, 17, 154
Rilke, R.M. 67, 68, 70, 71, 73-75, 76, 77, 79
Rishbeth, C. 136, 139
Robinson, E. 121, 123
Robinson, P. 9, 10
Rodwell, J. 1-13, 96, 97, 99, 113-124, 187-192, 194
Rollins, W. 46, 49
Rottmann, R. 9, 11
Rowland, C. 2, 9, 10, 110, 111
Rowlands, M. 97, 98, 99, 137
Rudorff, E. 18, 19, 30, 31
Ruland, J. 46, 49
Ruso B. 136, 139
Russolo, L. 78

Sager, T. 76, 78, 79
Saliers, D. 110, 111
Salt, D. 135, 140
Samuel, R. 88, 99
Sanesi, G. 138
Saunders, N. 85, 99
Scheuvens, R. 121, 124
Schmeing, A. 144, 146, 150, 151, 152, 183
Schmidt von Lübeck, G.P. 65, 76, 79
Schneeberger, N. 135, 139
Schoenichen, W. 23, 30, 31

Schramm, M. 46, 49
Schröder, M. 146, 150, 150, 152, 153
Schüller, A. 46, 49
Schwarze-Rodrian, M. 121, 124
Scott, J.C. 181, 183
Scott, P.M. 1-13, 78, 155-168, 185-192, 195
Seery, J.E. 179, 181, 183
Selman, P. 7, 127-140, 163, 165, 167, 185, 188, 190, 195
Severini, G. 78
Sheldrake, P. 2, 7, 9, 10, 101-112, 122, 124, 188, 189, 191, 192, 196
Shepheard, P. 89, 99
Sieverts, B. 141, 153
Sieverts, T. 142, 151, 152, 153
Sillars, S. 117, 121, 123
Sinclair, I. 165, 167
Sing, L. 138
Smith, C. 136, 139
Spalding, F. 121, 124
Speitkamp, W. 46, 49
Spellerberg, A. 150, 153
Sperber, J. 47, 49
Spohn, W. 110, 111
Spranger, E. 9, 10
Stammer, F. 41, 47, 49
Stavenhagen, K. 9, 10
Stedman, R.C. 136, 139
Steen Jacobsen J. 137
Steensen, T. 46, 49
Stephenson, J. 133, 137, 139
Stevenson, A. 121, 124
Stollenwerk, A. 46, 50
Szerszynski, B. 10, 171-183, 188

Taylor, W. 121, 124
Termorshuizen, J.W. 136, 139
Thill, H.H. 46, 48
Thompson, I. 5, 51-63, 185, 188, 196
Tømmervik, H. 137
Trepl, L. 150, 154
Tschofen, B. 46, 48
Tuan, Y. 137, 140, 176, 181, 183
Türcke, Ch. 27, 31
Turner, T. 51, 62, 63

Uekötter, F. 30, 31
Urry, J. 180, 181, 183

Vesting, Th. 31
Vicenzotti, V. 7, 141-154, 185, 186, 190
Von Bredow, W. 10

von Ledebur, A. 49
Von Moltke, J. 9, 11
Vorstand der Untermärkter, N. 47, 50

Wacquant, L.J.D. 136, 137
Wadsworth, J. 137
Wadsworth, R. 138
Waldenfels, B. 69, 77, 79
Walker, A. 121, 124
Walker, B. 135, 140
Wall, A. 146, 150, 152
Walter, T. 84, 99
Ward Thompson, C. 140
Ware, F. 85, 97, 99
Warren, P. 136, 140
Watkins, J. 9, 121, 124
Weber, M. 150, 154, 171, 172, 180, 183
Weber-Kellermann, I. 47, 50
Webster, J.D. 122, 124
Wehler, H.U. 46, 47, 50
Weisgerber, L. 50
Welsch, W. 77, 79
Wheater, H. 136, 140
White, S. 2, 9, 10
Whiteley, N. 182
Wickham, C.J. 9, 11
Wiersbinski, N. 31, 150, 153
Willemen, L. 136, 137, 140
Williams, R. 110, 111, 120, 122, 124, 190, 191, 192
Winer, M. 98, 99
Winter, J. 89, 99
Wolschke-Bulmahn, J. 150
Woodward, C. 116, 121, 122, 124
Woudstra, J. 60, 62, 63
Wurzel, A. 9, 11
Wylie, J.W. 136, 140

Zender, M. 46, 50
Zizioulas, J. 192

INDEX OF SUBJECTS

Archaic religion 8, 171, 173, 177
Amnesia 9, 78, 118
Anamnesis 120, 123, 189, 190
Animism 51
Architecture 7, 19, 20, 22, 24, 38, 51, 55, 56, 57, 63, 66, 74, 75, 84, 141, 142, 147, 149, 191, 193, 197
Authenticity 2, 40, 56, 57, 61, 63, 85, 138

Battlefields 6, 84, 85, 92, 194
Beautification Society (*Verschönerungsverein*) 5, 35, 37-39, 47, 50
Beheimatung (making ones-self at home) 4, 5, 6, 65-79, 143, 193
Belonging 1-13, 101, 102, 11, 119, 130, 135, 141-154, 155-168, 185-191, 195
Boppard (town) 5, 33-50, 187, 193
Boundaries 4, 7, 106, 107-109, 117, 118, 129, 133, 134, 186, 187
Bourgeoisie 17, 34-40, 45, 46

Catholicism/Catholics 103, 104, 106, 107, 109, 111, 122, 124, 165, 169, 170, 173, 188, 192
Cemeteries 6, 83-99, 169, 189
Christian humanism 4, 16, 17, 19, 21, 23, 27
Christianity 101, 165, 171, 173, 176, 177
Church 2, 7, 21, 33, 36, 40, 72, 73, 78, 88, 92, 103, 104, 106, 108, 110, 115, 177, 178, 186-190
Climate Change 4, 5, 90, 91, 92, 95, 129, 130, 132
Closure 96, 115, 118, 170
Coal mining 1, 59, 116, 194
Commonwealth War Graves Commission 6, 83-99
Community, communities 1-6, 16, 34-46, 51, 55, 69, 88, 97, 102-110, 115-120, 127-139, 159, 160, 164, 165, 169, 171, 175, 177, 186, 187, 189, 190, 195, 197
Conservation 4, 5, 16-29, 53, 55, 60, 131, 142, 149, 150

Creation 4, 6, 7, 15, 19, 21, 24, 26, 73, 74, 75, 76, 110, 156, 161, 163, 167, 172, 174, 186
Culture, *Kultur* 5, 8, 16-23, 27, 49, 51-59, 66, 72, 78, 79, 87, 88, 101-104, 128, 129, 135, 145-148, 171, 178, 179, 182, 191
Cynefin 9

Dasein 101, 176
Dearne Valley 1, 2, 6, 113-118
Death 39, 83, 85, 86, 89, 96, 104, 107, 110, 161, 164
Dwelling (as noun) 70, 114, 165, 178
Dwelling (as verb) 6, 51, 52, 70-75, 101, 170, 174, 184, 187,

Ecosystem 5, 55, 56, 101, 127, 128, 131, 132, 141, 195, 170, 174, 184, 187,
Ecosystem services 7, 9, 137, 193
Emscher Landschaftspark 118, 190
Englishness 87, 96, 155, 159
Eucharist 7, 101-111, 120, 186-190

Faith communities 1, 195
Fall, the 157

Gardens, gardening 6, 29, 36, 40, 51, 76, 84, 85, 86, 87, 88, 90, 92, 96, 114
Genius loci (Spirit of Place) 5, 51-63, 129, 173, 185
Ghetto 186
Gift 2, 3, 8, 109, 118, 156, 159, 178, 186
Globalisation 51, 69, 142, 149, 151, 170
Grace 8, 89, 105, 156, 157, 161, 187
Green Infrastructure 7, 131, 132, 137, 139, 196
Grief 83, 84, 90, 96, 189

Heft 9, 61, 130
Heimat 15-50, 65-79, 141-191, 164, 185
Heimatschutz, *Heimat* conservation 17, 18, 31, 35, 38, 41, 42
Heritage 6, 35, 38, 44, 56, 57, 61, 114-118

Home 1-11, 17, 21, 27, 28, 33, 35, 38, 44, 46, 53, 55, 58, 60, 65-79, 84, 87, 88, 96, 102, 103, 113, 127, 141-153, 155, 161, 165, 170, 179, 185-191
Holy Spirit 6, 74, 75, 110, 186, 187
Homesickness, *Heimweh* 3
Human Nature 104, 157
Humanism, humanist 4, 14, 16, 17, 19, 21, 23, 27

Individuality 4, 15-32, 87, 117, 114
Irony 8, 56, 179, 180

Jesus Christ 6, 104, 111, 177, 186, 188, 189
Jews, the Jewish people 23, 46, 53, 59
Judaeo-Christian 2, 118, 119, 127

Lake District 55, 57, 59
Landespflege 24
Landschaft 17, 24, 118, 128, 190
Landscape architecture 4, 7, 24, 51, 57, 141, 142, 149, 191
Landscape design 3, 19, 21, 23, 24, 51, 189
Lebensraum, Living space 4, 21, 23, 189
Liberals 16, 37, 44, 45
Lincoln Theological Institute 4, 6, 8, 77, 195
Local distinctiveness 5, 6, 58, 59, 61, 113
Loyalty/Loyalties 4, 8, 155-164, 185, 186, 187

M.B. Reckitt Trust 2, 118
Memorial 84, 90, 97, 115, 117, 120, 190, 194
Memory (see also, Remembrance) 3, 6, 83, 84, 89, 90, 92, 96, 97, 101-111, 114-121, 144, 148, 156-170, 189, 190
Monotheism 8, 171, 172, 175, 178
Migration 5, 51-63, 66, 71, 74, 185
Miners' Strike 113, 115, 120
Modernity 1, 66, 71, 73, 170, 175
Mourning (see also, Grief) 83

Nazis, Nazism, National Socialism 4, 17, 21, 2 24, 29, 60, 142, 149, 189
Neighbourhood association, *Nachbarschaften* 5, 37-44
Netzstadt, Net city 147, 153
Nostalgia 3, 8, 17, 66, 114, 144, 162, 164

Orgelborn-Kirmes 40-47

Panpsychism 5, 54-61
Pantheism 5, 54-61
Parochialism 61

Performance 5, 7, 9, 34, 35, 37, 39, 40, 45, 108, 128, 132, 163, 187, 189, 190
Peri-urban 7, 8, 59, 141, 153, 185, 186
Phenomenology 51, 101
Place, sense of 5, 68, 101, 107, 127, 132, 159, 161, 162, 170, 175
Planning 1-10, 24, 25, 40, 60, 61, 84, 114, 118, 119, 131, 132, 137, 141-149, 188, 191
Post-industrial 1, 6, 58, 113, 114, 116, 117, 119, 129, 189, 190, 195
Protestants, Protestantism 8, 36, 37, 44, 165-176
Public policy 3, 8, 131, 191

Real presence 106, 108, 109
Reconciliation 7, 24, 37, 101-111, 120, 124, 188, 189
Re-enchantment 66
Reformation, the 8, 169-183
Regeneration 1, 7, 59, 86, 113-120
Relics 8, 163, 164, 173
Remembering, Remembrance 6, 7, 24, 58, 69, 81, 84, 92, 96, 97, 102, 106, 113, 160, 164, 189
Restoration 7, 10, 38, 59, 105, 117, 127, 128
Reminiscence (see also, Memory, Remembering) 118, 119
Ruins, ruination 38, 86, 116, 117, 118, 190

Sacrament 104, 108, 191
Sacred, Sacral, Sacralised 2, 7, 8, 52, 102, 104, 128, 169, 170-179, 187-191
Sacrifice 87, 107, 118, 190
Salvation 2, 74, 173, 177
Salvation history, *Heilsgeschichte* 2
Security 3, 17, 45, 118, 143, 144, 161, 186
Somme, Battle of the 115
Slum 67, 186
Sustainability 1, 2, 3, 90

Theology 2, 7, 8, 9, 72-76, 103, 105, 108, 156, 161, 164
Third Reich 21, 65
Trinity, Trinitarian 74, 75
Tourism 5, 33, 35, 83
Turmoil, *Gewoge* 6, 68, 70-75

Ungiveness 8, 155-169
Urban 2, 4, 8, 29, 68, 70-75, 129, 130, 131, 132, 141-149, 165, 169, 173

War Graves 6, 83-99

World War I 113, 117
World War II 4, 21, 24, 60, 102, 117

Zwischenstadt 142, 190